Blowfish's
Oceanopedia

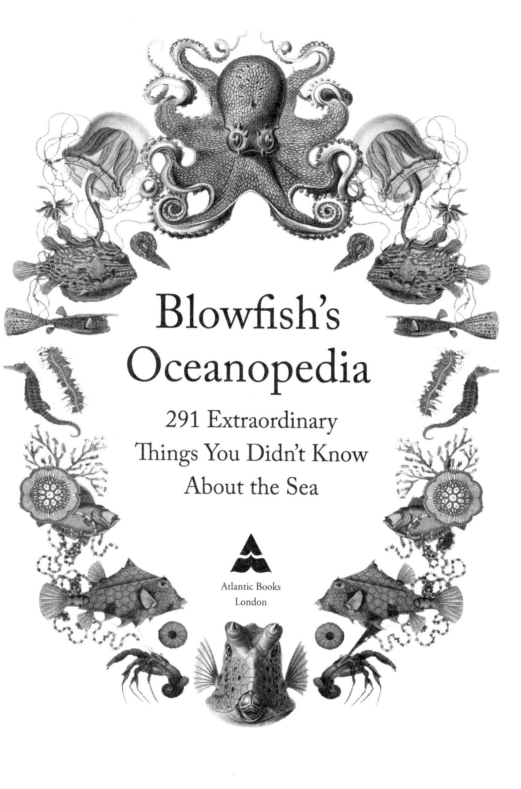

Blowfish's Oceanopedia

291 Extraordinary
Things You Didn't Know
About the Sea

Atlantic Books
London

Published in hardback in Great Britain in 2017 by Atlantic Books,
an imprint of Atlantic Books Ltd.

Image copyright © Shutterstock, pages 43, 44, 45, 67, 71, 91, 93, 103, 108,
115, 118, 132, 144, 158, 167, 171, 179, 181, 192, 208, 228, 234, 238
and plates 1, 2, 3, 4, 5, 6, 7, 9, 10, 11, 13, 16.

Image copyright © Wikimedia Commons, page 106 and plates 8, 12, 14, 15.

Image copyright © Roger Hall, page 193.

10 9 8 7 6 5 4 3 2 1

A CIP catalogue record for this book is available from the British Library.

Hardback ISBN: 978 1 78649 2 401
E-book ISBN: 978 1 78649 2 418

Designed by Carrdesignstudio.com
Printed in Sweden.

Atlantic Books
An imprint of Atlantic Books Ltd
Ormond House
26–27 Boswell Street
London
WC1N 3JZ

www.atlantic-books.co.uk

Contents

Introduction

Welcome to my *Oceanopedia*! A wonderfully made-up name for a book about a wonderfully real world. First, I'd just like to say thanks to all of you who have spent your hard-earned cash on this book: I love you all. To those of you who have received this book as a gift or stocking filler ... tough break. Be happy, at least, that it is heavy enough to be used to smite annoying insects, throw at door-to-door salesmen, or just prop up that wobbly table leg.

I wrote this book because I wanted to give you a glimpse into what the oceans have hidden deep within them. I have been fascinated by the seas for so long now I can't really remember when my passion for *poisson* began. What I do know, though, is that I learn something new every day – and it's not just the ordinary stuff we can often guess about terrestrial creatures, since a lot of them are, basically, pretty much like us. The stuff I'm talking about is truly unique, guaranteed to blow your mind.

My hope is that after reading this book you will love the oceans a little bit more and may start to realize that, even though you might not be wet right now (unless you're reading this in the bath), the oceans and their health are the key to our own long-term survival. Don't worry, this isn't some kind of radical tome on Mother Ocean and how you need to start eating seaweed soup. But it should make you think twice next time a fish finger shows up on your plate.

Some of you may already have noticed that this isn't your standard book on wildlife or the environment. The chapters and 'nuggets' of info are not meant to be a boring reference guide to getting a degree in marine biology, but rather a rough guide to the science that you can use to improve your own knowledge, impress your friends, and bore people at dinner parties.

But who is this handsome, bearded fellow who has so painstakingly written this impressive volume? Well, it's me. Tom 'The Blowfish' Hird. A proud Yorkshire lad with more body hair that the average Wookiee. Growing up, I always loved nature and can't remember a time in my life when I haven't had some sort of animal around me. This is thanks to my mum and dad, who are also keen animal-lovers – though my mum now seems to be obsessed with collecting wire-haired dachshunds, while my dad has a bizarre penchant for various sizes of rubber and metal washers. Either way, my early days were spent travelling with my dad, who is a vet, to see horses, cows and other critters up and down the moors of West Yorkshire. At home, my mum would show me how to care for small animals, taking note of their different ways, meeting their daily needs, and thereby ensuring their long-term happiness within our family.

It goes without saying, then, that I wanted to emulate my parents and follow my dad into the veterinary profession. Sadly for me, I am not blessed with his prodigious intellect (although I am a damn sight better-looking), and after a trip through a famous aquarium at the age of twelve, decided to become a marine biologist. Perhaps this was fated, as I had already developed a terrible fear of sharks due to a particularly well-known film. So scared was I of being eaten by a massive shark that I wouldn't hang my feet over the bed when sleeping, just in case! Yet, as is the way with most childhood fears, I became obsessed with sharks and just couldn't read enough about them. Soon, I knew more about sharks as a thirteen-year-old than most people would ever learn in their whole lives, and one thing I knew for certain was that they needed our help.

Sharks have been persecuted to a truly apocalyptic extent. These incredible creatures are in decline worldwide thanks to a barrage of human influences, none of which show any immediate sign of stopping. I have dedicated my life to changing the way people think about sharks, and the oceans, in the hope that when I finally dance my last tango, there will be a few more sharks swimming around than there were when I came screaming into the world.

So what about The Blowfish then? Well, originally I was going to follow the righteous path of academia, getting a Master's, PhD and more . . . writing papers which would change minds and laws, and defend my beloved sharks and rays. But in 2005, after taking part in a trip to the Adriatic to chum for sharks, and seeing precisely none over a two-week period, I realized I needed to make a more immediate impact. So I decided to use my voice to speak to you, the public, the people with the money who make the decisions at the grass-roots level. If we can change our ways when it comes to the fish we buy, the products we use and the waste we make, we can change the planet without the need for laws or politics. So it was time to stand up and give a voice to the creatures of the blue! However, 'Tom Hird' didn't exactly have the right ring to it, so I settled on a nickname I had received from the surf club at my university and The Blowfish was born.

So, this is from The Blowfish, the world's only heavy metal marine biologist (patent pending) to you, the awesome people of planet Earth! Enjoy this book, read it, share it, gift it, learn from it. But please, even if you only like one small section, think about what you can do to make a change and ensure this world remains a shining blue jewel for all the generations of little blowfishes to come.

Acknowledgements

There are too many people to properly thank for helping towards the completion of this book. Without a doubt, big thanks to Ben for his guidance and graft, to Mark for dealing with my biological terms, and to Andrew for sorting out the devil in the details. Thanks to Atlantic Books for giving me some paper to print the whole thing on and giving me a chance to tell my tales to the world at large. My huge and constant thank-yous to my mum and dad, who have supported me through all this TV and media madness with kind words, beers and roast dinners. And a special thank-you to Nick, who has kept me sane during these long months.

Finally, this book is dedicated to Alice, my beautiful, funny, intelligent and compassionate wife. You are the waves on my ocean, the sand of my beach and the water beneath my fins.

The Ways of the Sea

Water is an extraordinary molecule, vital for life as we know it. It first appeared on our planet around 4.5 billion years ago, and although science still hasn't found a unifying reason for why Earth has so much water, its arrival began the planet's transformation from spherical rock to a thriving Eden. Water allows chemicals to travel, offers electrons for reactions, dissolves salts and gases, stabilizes temperatures and provides buoyancy, giving relief from the harsh effects of gravity. In this highly active environment, the first life appeared – and evolution did the rest.

Although it is theoretically possible for water from all over the planet to mingle, in reality powerful physical forces and physical rules affect and restrict its movement. So, while some water dynamics are on a colossal scale, traversing the entire globe, others are small and predictable; but all have very specific attributes and associations, reflected in the way we designate distinct bodies of water. The oceans, seas and channels identified by humankind over the centuries are, at root, artificial separations – as man-made as the lines we scrawl over maps to divide countries and empires. But this doesn't mean they have no merit. Although the physical, biological and chemical interactions of our blue planet have set the rules for all aquatic life, this doesn't mean that a water molecule in the Bahamas is interchangeable with one in Bournemouth – you can't just hop from one to the other.

Mapping the seas has not been an easy task, and it is true to say that the final frontier is the great oceans, where there is still much to learn. What we do know is that the oceans have many permutations of the basic physical factors, producing amazing environments to which life has adapted itself and then exploited. The Southern Ocean is a roaring mass of waves and wind, ensuring some of the harshest seafaring conditions on the planet; yet here we also find some of the densest concentrations of aquatic life. By contrast, water molecules further north, around the Equator, sit still and stagnant in the barren expanses of the Pacific: the warmness of these waters does not dictate that life will thrive in them. The picture is far more complicated than that, though, and each ocean has its own set of requirements, sometimes extremely testing, with which its denizens must comply in order to prosper.

All in all, living on our wet planet is complicated and difficult. The rules are strict, but can change in a heartbeat; they are fluid in every sense. Only the very strongest lifeforms survive, and even then you never know when the oceans might change the game all over again.

Once upon a time . . .

When the Earth first formed, there were no oceans at all, just a hot ball of rock spinning in space. All the water we now have was in gas form, in what developed into our atmosphere. Only after the Earth had cooled significantly did the water vapour get a chance to condense into clouds and dispense rain into the hollows below – and geologists believe there may have then been a centuries-long downpour (sound like Yorkshire?) as the primal oceans filled.

After this point in the planet's evolution, the oceans' shapes were decided not by water but by land, as continents shifted, and by the changing climate. In fact, 250 million years ago, when all the continents existed as one giant landmass known as Pangaea, there was consequently just the one vast ocean surrounding its coastline. After another 50 million years had passed by and Pangaea had started to break up, individual seas with more distinctive characteristics started to form, most famously the Tethys Sea. Splitting the northerly Laurasia continent from the southern Gondwana, the Tethys provided new ecological niches for life to colonize. Sediments and fossils from the Tethys give us great insight into what this forming world was doing during that geological age. As the continents continued to drift, more seas opened up, and in time the mighty Tethys itself closed, around 65 million years ago.

It is only in relatively recent geological time that today's oceans took shape, when, as the continental drift slowed and the polar ice caps formed, currents started to connect and isolate different bodies of water. Continued movements in landmasses created relatively new seas, such as the Mediterranean, and in the twenty-first century the oceans continue to move, shift and adapt.

A tidal tale

'Time and tide wait for no man …' – a familiar phrase, but one that I have always enjoyed because of its honest simplicity, especially when it comes to the tide. Long before we invented clocks, nature had its own rhythm, the seasons giving colour to the year. And the tide provides the constant beating heart of the planet.

At a basic level, the tide is widely understood, for it flows in to reach high tide, and ebbs away to make low tide. In doing so, it swallows up the largest beaches, completely exposes harbours, and drives water through the smallest channels. But how does so much water move on a global scale?

Well, the first answer usually given is that the tides are controlled by the gravitational pull of the Moon. However, this is only half right. The tides are also controlled by the gravitational pull of the Sun, with both

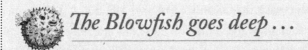

The Blowfish goes deep …

NOT MOVING, BUT WAVING

The ocean is never still. It constantly shifts and swells, ebbs and flows, as waves ripple and roll across its surface. Waves manifest themselves through tides, affected by the pull of the Moon and the Sun, and sometimes as surges, caused by large storms and hurricanes, or even more ferociously as tsunamis, caused by underwater geological disturbances.

Waves form as the wind blows over the surface of the ocean, creating friction and causing water molecules to begin moving in a circular direction. As they do so, they are replaced by molecules underneath, in turn dragging in yet more molecules alongside just as the original surface molecules are pulled around to join the chain. The result is numerous tiny circular motions, all stacked directly on top of one another, but decreasing in size and energy depending on the strength of the original wave-forming force.

Although waves have serious and sometimes catastrophic effects, they don't technically *move* water; they are just energy transferring though water. To demonstrate this point, just get in the bath with your favourite rubber duck and make a wave. You'll see how the wave travels across the whole bath, but the duck merely bobs up and down in the same spot as the wave passes.

When a wave hits a hard substance like a reef, beach or rocks, it breaks and forms surf – the circular motion of the water molecules is interrupted. But when unimpeded, waves are able to travel unchecked around the globe. In the Southern Ocean, where there are no landmasses lying between the inhabited continents and Antarctica, they do just that. The largest natural waves on the planet, reaching 30 metres in height, are found in these deadly, freezing waters.

Sun and Moon exerting a similar control. As beach-goers know, the timing of tides differs each day, usually by around 50 minutes, depending on location. More than that, some shorelines can experience two high and two low tides daily, while others can have just one, and yet other shores vary depending on the time of the month. And then, twice a month respectively, there are spring tides and neap tides. Spring tides occur when the Sun and Moon are in alignment, either on opposite sides of the Earth or complementing each other on the same side. The combined gravitational pull of the celestial bodies brings higher high tides and lower low tides, covering and then exposing more shoreline than normal. But when the Sun and the Moon are 90 degrees apart when viewed from Earth, the opposite occurs. The gravitational pull is compromised and the result is a neap tide, in which little water moves in any direction.

Over thousands of years, humankind has studied the tides, acquiring a pretty good grasp of the whole phenomenon. More remarkable, though, is the way that marine animals are wonderfully in tune with the rhythm of the seas and in synchronicity with the tidal ebb and flow.

Tidal titans

Around the world, there are some extraordinary daily tidal events. The Bay of Fundy in Canada has the highest tide on the planet, exposing more than 26 kilometres of shoreline during the ebb of a high spring tide. Put another way, that's an estimated 160 billion tonnes of seawater flowing in and out of the bay twice a day. Scientists attribute the phenomenon to the topography of the bay itself, which complements the wavelengths of the incoming tides to create an effect called tidal resonance.

Massive movements of water like this do not go unnoticed by man or beast, and areas of large tidal flow often exhibit great biodiversity. For us, the chance to harness the power of the tides is just too tempting, and across the globe tidal barriers are constructed as a method of producing clean, renewable energy.

By contrast, there are points around the planet where the arrangement of the continental shelves, landmasses and local topography result in there being very little tidal movement, and in some places almost nothing at all. These are termed amphidromic points. This is not to say that there are no low or high tides, but these points are like the fulcrum of a seesaw, never changing amid the contrasts on either side.

The current picture

Looking at a map of the ocean currents reveals a really quite incredible and intricate system, like some wonderful clockwork mechanism. You can see exactly where the water goes as it moves around Earth's landmasses.

The major currents work in a reasonably uniform way. This means that in the northern hemisphere the currents move in clockwise whirls – gyres – while in the southern hemisphere they travel anticlockwise. This is due to the 'coriolis effect', a phenomenon produced by the Earth's spinning rotation, pulling at both the water and the driving winds. As the currents move across the oceans, they are heated at the Equator, and then at higher latitudes their heat dissipates – and creates the weather we experience. Think of the Gulf Stream. This current begins in the tropical Gulf of Mexico and then moves across the Atlantic towards the UK; it typically brings with it the mild winters and warm summers a country at our latitude would not otherwise have, thanks to the heat it picked up at its Caribbean origin.

As warm water moves away from the Equator, it pulls in nutrient-rich cold water from the dark depths and/or the polar regions that is often directly responsible for an explosion of life. This phenomenon is evident in South America, where the bloom of plankton and the subsequent population explosion of anchoveta provide the basis for an entire ocean food chain, right up to humans, all of it originating in those cold waters.

There is only one current that seems to break all the rules – and this is known as the Antarctic circumpolar current. Driven by the turning of the Earth and the roaring winds, and without any landmass to stop it circulating, this current rips around the bottom of the planet in one huge loop. It can easily be ranked as the roughest sea on the planet.

Turn, turn, turn: the coriolis effect

Currents around the planet are driven by many factors – the wind, temperature, landmasses – but they're also influenced by the constant spinning of the Earth. It's hard to explain, but it's really important, and it's called the coriolis effect.

In a nutshell, as the Earth spins on its axis, objects near the Equator have to travel faster than objects nearer the poles to complete a single rotation. This is because they have further to travel to complete a single rotation than objects further away from the Equator, where the rotational distance is shorter. Water molecules are being subjected to this force all the time, and those molecules fractionally closer to the Equator move slightly faster than those further away. The effect of these fractional differences is to cause a spiral to form. While this effect is very weak on the Equator, where the large majority of water molecules are all subject to the same forces, as you move further towards the poles the effect increases.

The coriolis effect's greatest impact is on the planet's winds, as seen in weather patterns where large spirals of cloud can cover whole oceans. The winds then drive the oceans into the planet-spanning gyres and currents we rely on for our weather, for sea travel and for food. Without the coriolis effect and the spinning of the Earth, life would be dull indeed: our only major water movement would be the cycle of hot water to cold water in a very boring convection current.

Rip currents: a real drag

Knowing about rip currents could save your life. They are a powerful force to be reckoned with, and while they are found off some beaches all year round, they can appear anywhere under the right conditions.

Strong rip currents form when large waves and strong winds drive in towards the beach. Once a wave of water has broken, it wants to roll back into the sea; but behind it are more and more waves pushing in, trying to force it back towards the beach. So, the mass of water finds the path of least resistance back into the ocean. On long sandy beaches, this path can begin as a very slight depression in the sand and very quickly develop into a trench. Gulleys that form between rocks in the sand allow rip currents to establish themselves.

Although a rip current eventually merges back into the ocean to reappear as more waves, the problem is that their speed and strength can drag a swimmer out behind the breakers and into deep water very quickly indeed. Some rip currents will move at 8 kilometres an hour – faster than anyone trying to swim against it. So, if you do get caught in a rip, you have two options: either let it take you all the way out and then signal for help, or swim parallel to the beach until you get out of the current, before swimming back to shore.

Rip currents can be hard to spot, so local knowledge and looking out for warning signs are important. But if you see a thin strip of darker, calmer water at right-angles to the beach, cutting through white breaking waves, that's a rip current.

Into the vortex: whirlpools

Whirlpools are awesome, be they the little ones in the bath when you pull the plug or the wilder ones in the natural world. I have been lucky enough to see the strongest whirlpools on the planet. In the Saltstraumen strait in Norway, currents of up to 40 kilometres an hour smash 400 million cubic litres of water through a gap only 150 metres across, producing the world's strongest tide and a watery chaos truly living up to its name: the Maelstrom.

The formation of whirlpools is actually quite simple. They are just the meeting of two opposing currents, which, as they pass each other, interact and spiral downwards. The strength of the vortex, or downward pull, will depend on the power of the original currents. Most whirlpools struggle to pull down perhaps a metre or more; but the one at Saltstraumen can be 5 metres deep in just its cone. Getting pulled down into it would mean certain death for any swimmer, but fish don't seem to be bothered by large whirlpools for the most part: any small fish or plankton sucked downwards are likely to resurface unharmed, while larger adult fish can simply skirt around the base of the vortex without concern.

More ingeniously, fish exploit smaller whirlpools for food: they use the eddying currents to minimize the effort needed to swim, while positioning themselves ready to feed rapidly on anything edible that the vortex brings down to them.

Tree-stripping tsunamis

The stuff of disaster movies, tsunamis are one of the most destructive and terrifying natural events that can be witnessed on Earth. Unpredictable and unstoppable, they are a constant reminder that we are guests on this planet and not its masters.

Tsunamis mainly occur through sudden movements in the Earth's tectonic plates. These underwater earthquakes cause a massive shift in the water column above as one plate jerks suddenly beneath another, forcing the other plate to pitch upwards. This sends an enormous jolt of energy into the sea, and water is displaced either upwards or downwards. At the surface, directly above the epicentre of the quake, a single wave forms and radiates out in all directions. At first, this wave may not be very high at all, and the water column may have been displaced by less than a metre. But all the water down to the ocean floor will have been affected, and all that incredible energy means that the wave can travel at 800 kilometres an hour or faster. As the tsunami starts to reach land, its wave height drastically increases as all those energized water molecules start to bunch up on top of each other, reaching extraordinary heights. At the same time, as the wave height grows and the wavelength shortens, speed is lost – the wave might now be travelling at 50 kilometres an hour.

The 2004 Indian Ocean Tsunami formed waves of 30 metres in height, but this is a long way from the largest ever recorded. That honour belongs to a freak mega-tsunami in 1958, in Alaska. An earthquake and rockslide sent a wave across the ocean into the narrow bay of Lituya, reaching a mind-boggling height of 525 metres. In this case, the combination of the bay's shallow water and a narrow channel allowed the tsunami to strip trees and other vegetation from the sides of the valley 500 metres up from the usual shoreline.

The riddle of the sands

What is a beach without the mesmerizing patterns found in the sand at low tide? These sand ripples are an artefact made by waves and currents, and they can tell us much about what is physically happening on the beach.

The ripples are formed when sand particles on the seabed are picked up by the circular movement of water molecules, accompanying the water on its oscillatory wave motion before being deposited back pretty much where they started. However, if the energy of the wave is not consistent – and it is very unlikely that it would be, especially at the coast – the sand does not complete a full circular journey. A sand particle, being naturally heavier than water, requires a given amount of wave energy to get picked up and carried; but if the wave, whether outgoing or incoming, doesn't have the required energy to keep the particle in suspension, it gets dropped. Repeat this process countless times with a beach-worth of sand and the result is that the majority of sand particles are dropped in the same places, creating humps – the ripples in the sand. The distance between ripples reveals the wavelength of the energy at that particular time.

It can get a lot more complicated than this – but I'll leave the rest for the physical oceanographers, as they like maths more than I do.

Delicate dunes

The physics behind sand-dune formation is fearsome! And just one look at the many individual kinds of dunes, not to mention the conditions in which they form, would give anyone an ulcer. But sand dunes are a critical part of coastal ecosystems, providing the land with life-saving protection from the sea.

An onshore breeze blowing onto a beach will pick up sand and take it away from the shoreline. Anything the breeze hits will cause the sand to stop and settle, which in turn will cause more sand to settle on top. Over sufficient time, a bank of sand will form, albeit remaining unstable and liable to shift and move with the wind and local climate. The pile of sand doesn't form into a true dune until plants start to colonize it, providing stability with their deep roots and branching stems. Sand isn't exactly the best home for most plants, for it's not only soft and unstable, but fresh water drains through it very quickly. However, marram grass doesn't seem to mind these conditions, which is why it is often the first pioneer species to colonize a new dune environment. These first settlers have to be hardy, as they also have to deal with salt spray from the nearby ocean. But those same seas bring a useful bounty in the form of organic matter like seaweed deposited by storm surges, which then rots down on the dunes to provide fertilizer for the plants fighting for survival.

Given time, sand dunes become more and more stable, and less hardy plants are able to move in behind the protection now afforded them. An established dune system then reduces the effects of land erosion and can protect coastal land from the ravages of future storm surges.

From pole to pole: the water molecule

Water – as seemingly simple as it is essential. While water has many properties that chemists and physicists might swoon over, for me it is the little molecule's polar nature that equips it with such important biological abilities. How so?

To answer this question means getting technical about H_2O. The oxygen atom, which is situated at the crux of the V-shaped water molecule, pulls so strongly on the molecule's electrons that it ensures the two hydrogen atoms attached do not have a fair share of the electron spread. It's like hogging the duvet in bed. But the extra time spent with negative electrons makes the oxygen atom slightly negatively charged, whereas the hydrogen atoms become slightly positive as their positive, proton-rich nucleus becomes mildly exposed. This leaves the whole water molecule with positive and negative poles.

The reason why this is so critical is that polar substances *love* to dissolve things. Anything with positive or negative ions that water molecules come across will be desperate to interact with them and move away from its original home. Look at salt: a positive sodium ion and a negative chloride ion, happy and bonded together, break apart into a solution when introduced to water. And it is when chemicals are dissolved in solution that they can really start to interact with each other. It is this key stage that allowed life on Earth to begin in the first place.

Put simply, the interaction and movement of chemicals *is* life – and without the polar nature of water shoving things around, it would never have started in the first place.

Oceanic gas-guzzling

Life takes advantage of a basic principle: when oxygen burns with a carbon source, energy is produced for biochemical reactions, and one of the by-products is carbon dioxide. This simple rule started in the oceans, where the role of dissolved gases isn't just important to living and breathing biological life, but also to the planet's climate.

All atmospheric gases are found dissolved in seawater. This mixing occurs at the ocean's surface and is aided through the effects of waves and wind, driven by concentration gradients and controlled through factors such as salinity and temperature. For example, warm salty water cannot hold as much dissolved oxygen as cooler fresher water. Thanks to the movement of currents, gases exchanged at the surface can be transported down into the deep ocean, while upwellings from below can bring deep waters back to the surface for more chemical interaction. But there are also areas in the ocean called oxygen minimum zones, which usually lie between 200 and 1,000 metres in depth, and where restrictive currents and the presence of respiring, organic life mean that the oxygen gets used up and is not replenished via mixing. Life is constrained in these areas, though they are not completely barren, as some creatures have evolved to deal with the low oxygen levels.

In discussions of the watery gases, carbon dioxide currently attracts the most attention. For a start, it dissolves quite rapidly in seawater to form carbonic acids. The increase in greenhouse gases in the atmosphere has meant that more and more CO_2 is dissolving into the seas, making them more acidic and causing great damage to ocean life. But there is also a limit to how far the seas can absorb the Earth's CO_2, and once that limit is reached, and less and less carbon dioxide dissolves in the ocean, there would be a pronounced jump in the amount of CO_2 remaining in the atmosphere. The result of that would be significant climate change for us all.

A salty story

The sea is salty. Everyone knows that. But the seas are not *uniformly* salty – they vary, being affected by global position, currents, tides and landmasses. For example, the Mediterranean has a salinity of around 38 parts per thousand (ppt), essentially meaning a salt content of 3.8 per cent, whereas the waters around the UK have an average of 35 ppt. When you get closer to the poles, where meltwater dilutes the seas and the low temperatures mean less salt gets concentrated through evaporation, the proportion is even lower, at around 33 ppt.

Differing levels of salinity create challenges for fish and other ocean life. Salt attracts water molecules through the process of osmosis, and water can pass happily through most biological barriers. Sea creatures with thin biological barriers such as gills would rapidly lose water from their cells to the surrounding salty sea unless they had a clever way of dealing with the problem. Which, luckily, they do. Fish, for example, have specially designed cells that actively take in salt and move it around the body in an attempt to retain as much water as possible. The effort is biologically expensive, costing the animal a lot of energy; but it means fish can maintain a stable internal salinity, allowing them greater freedom to move around the oceans. By contrast, invertebrates such as shrimp or squid cannot adjust their internal salt levels, so they have to be content with mirroring the salinity of the water around them. While this means that they expend less energy in simply surviving, they are also very susceptible to rapid changes in salinity, which could be life-threatening. If an animal acclimated to the saltiness of one body of water attempts to move too rapidly across the gradients to a different level of salinity, it could easily die. In this way, these invisible salinity barriers play an important role in the diversity of many oceanic ecosystems.

In short, salt is the very first hurdle evolution had to overcome for life to thrive, and the way sea creatures deal with salts affects their reproduction, diets, habitat choices and life cycles.

Going all hot and cold: thermoclines

The temperature of the oceans may seem fairly straightforward: after all, anyone who takes a dip in the sea off Cornwall knows it's not going to be as toasty as the water of Bali (that's why most of us wise folk don a wetsuit before plunging into British waters). But rather more interesting, and certainly more biologically important than the whims of holidaymakers, is the phenomenon of the thermocline.

As the Sun beats down onto the oceans, its heat energy is transferred into the water. Yet the Sun's rays can only penetrate so far, so the surface waters become uniformly warmer than the deeper waters beneath them. This distinct transition barrier between the cooler water and the warmer water is known as the thermocline, and it has a significant impact on the marine world.

As the warm waters on the surface are constantly being hammered by the Sun's rays and mixed by choppy surface waves, they tend to become barren of the essential nutrients for life. In contrast, the cold, calm, deep waters are jam-packed with important compounds. The depth at which the thermocline occurs can vary from year to year, and between distinct regions. Still, regardless of the depth of the thermocline, the laws of physics will not allow the cold, dense water to push up into the warmer, lighter water above it, so thermoclines tend to stay relatively stable. For a thermocline to break down, there needs to be a shift in the amount of sunlight and energy being given to the surface, usually in the form of seasonal storms.

Eras of stagnation: El Niño

Everyone in recent years must have heard about the weather phenomenon called El Niño. Once touted by climate-change deniers as the reason for our changing weather, it is a periodic anomaly whose effects, as a result of man-made climate change, are becoming greater.

In the southern Pacific Ocean, water warmed at the Equator is usually driven by trade winds from the western coast of South America across the Pacific towards Indonesia, South-East Asia and Australia. As a result, rich and deep cold-water upwellings occur off the coast of Peru and Chile, rising to the surface and causing huge blooms of biodiversity, notably in the population explosion of anchoveta. But in El Niño years, the trade winds weaken, and the hot surface water is not blown across the ocean, instead stagnating off the coast and preventing the nutrient-rich cold water from reaching the surface.

Worldwide, a big patch of warm water languishing on the Equator doesn't help the climate. The lack of hot, moist air moving across the Pacific can cause significantly reduced rainfall in places like Australia, and can lead to drought in many parts of South-East Asia. For marine life, there can be huge effects too. When the vital blooms of anchoveta fail to materialize, many seabirds, tuna and other ocean predators have to travel further in an attempt to find pockets of life where some cold water has made it to the surface. Fish stocks are disrupted, and in countries like Peru, where fishing is a key industry, there can be serious economic upheaval.

El Niño events eventually wear out, and the usual pattern of east–west trade winds establishes itself again. The problem today is that the oceans are in such a fragile state that El Niño episodes have the potential to inflict far more damage than they used to, and their frequency may be increasing.

Carbon sinks and climate stresses

I've said it before – but if we burned all the trees on Earth, it wouldn't be the end of everything. Scientists estimate that up to 85 per cent of the world's oxygen comes not from trees, but from the sea. The oceans control our climate, and we would do well to remember how.

First, tiny oxygen-producing phytoplankton cover a far greater surface of the globe than do the forests. Furthermore, although plants may create oxygen during the day, they consume much of that oxygen at night, when they cannot photosynthesize. Phytoplankton *can* photosynthesize at night and so, in some cases, can carry out round-the-clock oxygen production.

Second, the seas also act as a vitally important carbon sink, by sending carbon to the deep ocean floor in the form of the dead bodies of plankton, and through the molecular nature of seawater, which actively absorbs CO_2 and turns it into carbonic acids.

But there are limits, and unfortunately we're putting too much strain on our oceans. More and more greenhouse gases are being produced, and the ocean is reaching saturation point. Should we see yet more melting of the polar ice caps, the consequences will not just be rising sea levels swelling over low-lying islands and swamping coasts; the influx of fresh water could easily disrupt the vitally important currents that bring us our weather.

And there's the rub. Those currents normally move hot water away from the Equator and towards the higher latitudes, where it can warm coastlines or evaporate into life-giving rain. But global warming may actually result in higher-latitude places, such as the UK, becoming colder rather than warmer, as currents break down and warm water stagnates around the Equator.

When reduced salt is bad: haloclines

Just as a thermocline is a barrier between waters of distinctly different temperatures, a halocline is a barrier between bodies of water with two different salinities. Salty water is heavy and tends to sink, whereas fresher water is less dense and so will rise to the surface. This is particularly important for the waters around the poles, where the cold but fresher water from the pole sits atop the warmer, saltier water below. The halocline helps to maintain this division, and it's a good thing too. Fresher, colder water can form sea ice far more easily than it would if mixed with the saltier water from the deep.

Fresher water doesn't always win the battle to be on top. Sometimes, a thermocline and halocline interact, as when surface waters around the tropics get heated by the Sun and experience increased evaporation, become saltier than the water beneath. This process does not tend to last long though. Eventually, small pockets of heated salty water become too salty and too dense; they sink down through the thermocline to be replaced by fresher, cooler water from below.

Haloclines can be particularly difficult barriers for fish to cross, because jumping from one salinity to another represents an extreme physiological process for any marine creature. For one thing, there are the lower levels of dissolved oxygen in saltier water. Unsurprisingly, in areas where haloclines are common – such as in fjords and estuaries – the fish and invertebrates that make them their home are often hardy and specialized. In truth, haloclines can be as varied and unique as the environment around them, leading to some amazing adaptations.

A dying sea

In the Middle East, on the borders of Israel, Palestine and Jordan, lies one of the strangest bodies of water on the planet: the Dead Sea. At 300 metres deep and lying some 430 metres below sea level, it is ten times saltier than the ocean and a lot denser than normal seawater. Swimming in the Dead Sea is a common bucket-list experience, mainly because you don't have to try . . . you just lie back and float instead, held suspended by that super-salty water. Needless to say, such conditions prove almost impossible for life, and there's a complete absence of large multicellular aquatic creatures. However, small bacterial blooms do occur, as do blooms of salt-loving red algae after it rains, when the high salinity drops just a little.

There are many theories about how the Dead Sea formed. Some believe it was once connected to the Red Sea or to the African Rift lakes; others think it's a spillover from the Mediterranean that then became cut off when land levels rose. Either way, from the minute the Dead Sea became isolated, it started to dry up; and although this process had reached an equilibrium, because of an inflow of water from the River Jordan, it now seems that the Dead Sea is slipping away. Since the 1930s, when regular measurements and studies began, its area has dropped by 400 square kilometres. This drying-up is down to the diversion of rivers and the reduction in groundwater upwellings, caused by human development. Alas, the Dead Sea is in real danger of drying out completely.

Estuary life

The boundary between fresh water and salt water is a pretty stark one to cross, and not many fish can live in both worlds. There are, however, quite a few species that exploit the environments where fresh and salt water mix, and a classic case is the estuary.

In the tidal mouth of a river, there is a constant shifting and mixing of fresh and salt water, depending on local conditions and the position of the tide. All this variability requires that the animals, plants and algae that make their homes here be very tolerant of the ever-changing salinity. Even so, distinct biological barriers remain, for few aquatic species truly span the entire gradient of salinities. What makes an estuary so productive is the food supply. The ebb and flow of the tide regularly brings in fresh nutrients and organic material to be consumed, while the fresh water conveys sediments, detritus and chemicals whose properties change on entering seawater, becoming accessible to a whole different range of critters.

Estuaries are often quite sheltered, because their rivers have cut their way through a lot of rock to reach the ocean, and so the animals making their home here are often protected from the rough waves and harsher conditions of the open ocean. Making the best of these waters are often the invertebrates, such as the green shore crab, and different kinds of particulate filter-feeding worms. This abundance attracts predators, both above and below the water. Wading birds like oystercatchers and curlews have perfectly evolved beaks to access the tasty world beneath the sediments, and fish such as plaice and wrasse can access the shallows at high tide to hunt for prey.

Pining for the fjords

There are many truly wonderful and unique environments to be found in the seas of this world, each with its own set of biological rules and regulations that sets it apart. But when it comes to those areas where the ocean meets the land, there's so much more than beaches.

Fjords, for example, are fascinating ecosystems found on certain coastlines around the world. A fjord is a narrow inlet, characterized by high-sided cliffs and formed through glacial erosion. So you will tend to find fjords where there have been, or still are, glaciers, and countries such as Norway, Iceland and New Zealand are famous for these geographical features.

Usually, there will be a river or stream running into the fjord at the landward end, perhaps even from the remnants of the glacier that carved it out. During the winter, the freshwater inflow tends to freeze up and the fjord becomes fully saline; but in the summer, with meltwaters flowing rapidly, a fjord exists in more of an estuarine condition, often with haloclines forming between the bodies of water. At the seaward-most end of a fjord, there is often a narrowing of the inlet and a sill, or deposit of rocks and moraine, left when the glacier could move no further. This is a choke point, leading into what are often extremely deep channels within the fjord proper, and sometimes the tidal current generates quite extreme effects in such specialized conditions, such as whirlpools.

All this shifting of cold, rich waters, not to mention the deep and protected environments typical of fjords, leads to high biodiversity: lots of seaweeds and static filter-feeders like anemones carpeting the rocks, and fish such as cod, pollack and halibut all dominate the fjord's undersea world.

The white cliffs of coccoliths

It can be easy to forget that the rocks we walk over and build our houses on were once, eons ago, under the sea. Stranger still is the concept that the famous White Cliffs of Dover were once not just objects in the sea, but organisms *of* the sea.

The cliffs are white because they are made from chalk, a mineral derived from the accumulation of trillions of microscopic planktonic coccolithophores. A type of phytoplankton, these – like their photo-synthesizing brethren – have a protective shell or exoskeleton around their bodies. Looking like tea-strainers, the scales that surround coccolithophores allow water and vital chemicals access to the cell

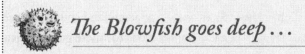

The Blowfish goes deep . . .

WHEN THE SEA SNOWS

The term 'marine snow' is a fancy metaphor for the particulates that fall to the ocean floor, a kind of monsoon of death; yet this blizzard of waste isn't as grim as it may sound, for it provides a vital food source for millions of creatures and keeps carbon out of the atmosphere.

The dead bodies of plankton, especially phytoplankton, make up a large proportion of marine snow. Accordingly, the seasonal abundance of plankton means that marine snow is also seasonal, with the deep ocean getting inundated during the spring and autumn blooms. Faecal matter also makes up a large component of marine snow, but this is not so much the waste from large fish – it is mainly the constant excretions of creatures such as tiny crustaceans called copepods feeding in the plankton.

Just because marine snow doesn't sound appetising to us doesn't mean it is shunned in the murky depths. Many deep-sea animals have evolved with the direct purpose of collecting marine snow through particulate and filter-feeding methods. Indeed, so nutritious are the dead bodies of plankton and even the faeces of other animals that particles of marine snow may be consumed and excreted numerous times over before they finally get to the ocean floor.

As the particles fall, they tend to coagulate with sand, silt and other detritus; and as they get bigger, they fall faster, but even that doesn't mean they will definitely reach the bottom. Because it can take several weeks for a 'flake' of marine snow to complete the downward trip, bacteria have plenty of time to work on it, possibly even to consume it completely en route. If the marine snow finally does makes it all the way down, it can settle into a fine ooze, which in turn can be the beginning of an incredible transformation over millions of years, into rocks like chalk or quartz. Then again, even at rest on the ocean floor there are more creatures waiting to hoover up whatever edible particles remain.

beneath the protective layer. Each scale, or coccolith, is made from calcium carbonate derived from seawater and formed by the coccolithophore itself.

As the single-cell organism grows and divides, the coccoliths fall to the ocean floor, or the cell itself dies and takes the whole lot on a one-way trip. Either way, there is a constant rain of these calcium-based fragments falling to the ocean floor. Given enough time – and they need a hell of a lot, since each coccolithophore is barely one-tenth of a millimetre across – these deposits can build up into a thick layer. Give it even more time, along with some compression from heavier sediments settling over the top, and the result is chalk.

The White Cliffs of Dover started this process when dinosaurs roamed the Earth, and were later thrust to the surface when the Alps formed. It's amazing to think that right now micro-algae in the ocean could be creating the lands of the future.

Water slides . . .

It's not only on rainy, deforested hillsides that landslides can occur. Underwater landslides are quite common in the world's oceans, and they can be as dangerous and devastating to undersea life as any similar event on land would be to terrestrial inhabitants.

The underlying concept is the same. In areas around the continental shelves, there are significant slopes that descend to the deep ocean below. But some may have an incline of just 1 per cent. When sediments build up on these slopes over time, they can reach critical mass before sliding down far below. Underwater landslides are actually a very important natural process: they move sediments and organic matter like carbon into the long-term storage and recycling facility that is the deep ocean. But there's risk and danger involved for any sea life that happens to be in the way. As huge volumes of debris rapidly tumble or get stirred up into a suspension again, clouding the water, undersea habitats can be completely destroyed.

There are other reasons, apart from this gradual sediment loading, why an underwater landslide might occur. Earthquakes, volcanic eruptions, hurricanes and the collapse of a weaker substrate beneath the sediments are just some of the other causes. As far as humans are concerned, underwater landslides can weaken coastal areas, damage undersea cables and disrupt oceanic mining and drilling efforts. For the most part, it's all hidden beneath the waves. But not always. About 8,000 years ago, the Storegga slides off Norway shifted 3,500 square kilometres of sediment down into the Norwegian Sea. This event was so intense that it caused a local tsunami, which slammed across the North Sea and hit the east coast of Britain.

... and bubble-baths

As familiar on British beaches as the slightly thuggish seagulls and obligatory ice-cream sellers are the flecks of light-brown foam kicked up along the waterline by the encroaching waves and onshore breeze. Sea foam, or spume – which is frankly a much better name for it – occurs thanks to the constant agitation of the ocean through wind and waves. It is, essentially, organic waste, the broken-down proteins, fats and sugars produced by many different forms of marine life. If the water is calm, you can see the dissolved organic matter as faint slicks on the surface. They are often concentrated at the meeting of currents, known as fronts; but when stirred by constant wave and wind action, they foam up into bubbles which are remarkably tough and hard to burst. The spume is then washed or blown up the beach, where microbes in the sand can feast on it. Sometimes, large algal blooms offshore can create spume at nearby beaches so intense that it can impede visibility or even be a danger to humans because of the irritating chemicals that certain algal strains contain in their bodies.

Spume is a by-product of the ocean and not one that really makes much dynamic impact; but those of us who love our aquariums are *very* keen on spume, and we make it ourselves. In marine aquariums, a device called a protein-skimmer can drastically reduce nitrogenous waste in the water. The idea is simple: water from the aquarium passes into a chamber where a strong pump vigorously aerates the water. This causes bubbles to form, and the resulting waste can be collected and removed, ensuring that the tanks and their inhabitants stay in tip-top condition.

The survivor: seaweed

Often dismissed as unsightly and smelly, seaweeds are the ocean's vegetation. And yet they are not plants at all; they're algae. They possess neither roots nor flowers, and lack the sort of tissues that your standard terrestrial plants have. However, to attempt to classify seaweeds any further would take a great deal of effort. They are extraordinarily diverse – a real pain for taxonomists – and debate rages over their finer details.

Seaweeds have unrivalled success when it comes to ocean ecosystems, thanks to a kaleidoscopic range of adaptations. For a start, the absence of a root system means they can grow almost anywhere, so we see everything from small encrusting growths on rocks to acid-boring seaweed that penetrates mollusc shells. Flexibility in how to respond to the water is just as important, and this is where seaweed's famous floppiness comes in. Having flexible stipes and flowing blades (the flat main part of the seaweed) means they can move with the turbulent flow of the ocean, surviving the worst the weather can throw at them without breaking. In fact, in storms the rocks to which seaweeds are attached can give way before the seaweeds themselves. If you're a seaweed, ensuring you get as much light as possible means you have to have some method of supporting a floppy blade, and many species have gas-filled bladders to raise them up towards the surface.

Able to colonize the ocean as well as intertidal areas, seaweeds can contain chemicals that stop them from freezing in the winter or baking in the summer sun at low tide. It's the chemicals given off by heated seaweed that give the coast its signature smell – and, believe it or not, those same chemicals happen to play an important role in the formation of rainclouds too.

Generating more heat than light?

What is light? It's just the rapid vibration of a particle travelling as a wave: energy in its purest form. The photons that make up light radiation react with whatever they hit, which, in the air, is not very much, until they reach the Earth.

In water, it's a different matter altogether. The first problem is that a lot of light doesn't even make it into the water in the first place. Depending on the angle of the Sun's rays, light can reflect off the water's surface and travel away in a different direction. For the photons that do penetrate the water's surface, everything changes. Instead of flying along at nearly 300,000 kilometres a second, they suddenly collide with water molecules, and this slows them down and slightly skews their direction (depending on the angle of entry).

As light descends in water, it also starts to dissipate as heat energy. The photons possessing the lowest energy are always the ones to go first, since they're already pretty close to heat themselves in terms of wavelength, and this means that red light starts to disappear from the visible spectrum. The deeper it goes, the weaker light becomes, until only the highest-energy blue wavelength remains; even then, it will eventually hit enough H_2O molecules to be lost as heat. At around a kilometre, it's all over. Sunlight cannot penetrate deeper than this, and beyond it lies an area that no photon has ever visited.

Super-charged sunbathing: photosynthesis

Photosynthesis is crucial for life, and the plants and algae that indulge in it provide the starting point for nearly all known food chains. I'm not going to go into the chemical reactions of photosynthesis, because frankly ... it's boring. You just need to know that carbon dioxide + water, with sunlight = food and oxygen. Job done!

Only a few, unique and isolated parts of the Earth rely on energy derived from somewhere other than the Sun. Even so, photosynthesis isn't all that easy to achieve and many adaptations have evolved to increase its potential wherever possible. Take seaweeds, for example. These macro-algae have modified the methods of sunlight collection to fit their lifestyles. As previously mentioned, sunlight rapidly diminishes in water, with the red end of the spectrum going first. So seaweeds directly under the surface or in rockpools tend to be bright-green, but, as the water depth increases and the wavelengths of light diminish, they become brown and then red. This change in the pigments, associated with photosynthesis, has a purpose: to maximize sugar production with all the available wavelengths.

Photosynthesis is such an attractive option for creating food that many animals have managed to hijack the process for themselves, by taking on living algae as lodgers. In this way, the algae can continue to do their full-time food-processing job, and the host creature, be it a coral, anemone, jellyfish or even a sea slug, can live life knowing it has food on tap whenever it wants it.

The psychedelic sea: oceanic colour-changers

The colours in the ocean can be truly breathtaking, from the bright and vivid corals to the enormous and beautiful variety seen in marine animals. Typically for the ocean, everything is in constant flux, and the colours of sea creatures are no exception.

The natural ability to change colour is perhaps best known in the chameleon, but the masters of colour change are fishes and inverte-brates. Rather than relying on blood to initiate a colour change as does a chameleon, which is a slow business, fish and cephalopods also use nerves, generating an instant colour change. The cells responsible for producing this sudden makeover are called chromatophores, and they work in a wonderfully simple way.

If you close a colourful parasol and then point it horizontally at a friend, they will see little white dot at its end; but open it up, and the full array of colours appears. That is how chromatophores work. They are bags of pigment, which can be relaxed and expanded out between layers of the skin to reveal their colour, or quickly contracted to reveal the colour of the flesh beneath. From this basic premise, many different colour-changing cells have evolved. Iridiophores, for example, are cells of silvery crystals that produce iridescent blues and greens, while melanophores create blacks and browns, and cyanophores give out shades of blue.

The kings of colour change have to be the cephalopods. Not only do their nervous systems control chromatophores, they also go one step further in having muscles directly attached to the colour cells themselves. This means they can put on the most amazing displays and adopt the most cunning camouflage seen in the natural world. Suck on that, chameleon!

A nose for the water: streamlining

Fluid dynamics is a subject so packed full of equations and diagrams that you can spend a lifetime of study and still not understand it. So let's stick to the essentials.

Water is actually not that easy to move through: it's heavy and can't be compressed. Nor can it be separated easily, so it constantly surrounds whatever is moving through it. Slap water with the palm of your hand and it feels as though you are hitting something solid. Much better is to jab the water with the tip of your finger because you can slide right in. To put this a little more technically, if you make an easy and linear path for water to follow, you can move through it with less force and more speed: this is streamlining.

Streamlining is why most fish are shaped as they are, the shape we call fusiform. They have a sharp nose that allows them to cleave through the water. Once a creature is moving in a direction through water, the molecules line up into a laminar flow, hugging the body passing through them in clean lines. It takes effort to break this laminar flow. This is good news for fish swimming forwards, but not when they want to change direction, so fish have fins that can be used to change the laminar flow at a moment's notice. Some fish, such as sharks, have amazing scales that can project a laminar flow just slightly away from the body while also generating a convenient layer of turbulent, unrestricted flow directly next to the body, allowing them to change direction easily.

A fin for all seasons

While many people may not have given the fins on a fish much thought, evolution certainly has. Not only do fins provide fish with the means to move through the water, but their position, shape and arrangement are specialized to their environment. It's possible to tell a lot about a fish's lifestyle and behaviour just by looking at its fins.

In the basic fin set-up, there are single fins for locomotion and stability, and paired fins for steering and finesse. Imagine your standard fish: the single caudal (tail) fin provides forward thrust, while the dorsal and anal fins act like a keel to stabilize it. The paired pectoral fins stay close to the body unless being deployed for fast turning, and the same can be said for the paired pelvic fins, which only spring into action if the fish needs to manoeuvre quickly. Although some serious species-specific modification then goes into fins, that's essentially the big picture.

In large predators that ambush their prey, such as pike, the dorsal and anal fins are enlarged and extend down to the caudal fin. While providing increased stability, they now also act to supercharge the forward thrust of the fish by helping increase the surface for the caudal area to work with. By contrast, a pufferfish may not look as though it's using its caudal fin; instead it constantly beats its paired pectoral fins like a manic hummingbird. This allows it to bob in and out of coral with perfect accuracy; but if threatened, it will still rely on that caudal fin for its main escape thrust.

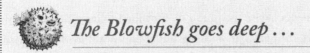

The Blowfish goes deep...

HOW DO YOU LIKE IT?
WET OR STICKY?

If you haven't already guessed, I'm not a big fan of maths. Certainly, it's very clever and important, but, well, I'd rather avoid it. But that's not an option when you're talking about a bit of physics called the Reynolds number.

The reason that it appears in this book is that it's all to do with fluids – whether they flow in a smooth (laminar) or more higgledy-piggledy (turbulent) way, and how that affects the nature of objects within a fluid, such as fish in the sea. Certain factors such as mass, drag and surface area all affect the equations used to produce the Reynolds number, which may then be small or large. In marine life, a small Reynolds number of say 0.02 means that the animal or object is dominated by the viscosity of the liquid, as if it were living in treacle. A high Reynolds number of perhaps 20,000 would result in the animal or object being in constant motion, even at rest.

This distinction is therefore very important for the creatures of the ocean, because some rely on a low Reynolds number and others a high one. Plankton, for example, don't want to sink into the depths when they stop moving; they would much rather stay in the upper levels of the sea where they can photosynthesize or feed. Luckily, their small size and other attributes, such as long spikes and drag-inducing flaps, serve to lower their Reynolds number, and they can remain comfortably stuck where they are. On the other hand, if you're a fish, or even a whale, the prospect of coming to an immediate halt every time you stopped finning would be really annoying. However, streamlined bodies and a higher mass all make for a greater Reynolds number, so that one fin stroke will give a glide of a certain duration without any additional effort as the fish exploits the more fluid part of the equation.

There. It's worth noting a nifty bit of maths when you can ... even if you *still* don't understand it!

Things get weirder when you look at gurnards, whose pectoral fins have adapted into 'fingers' for walking along the seabed, or a sunfish, whose entire body appears to resemble an entire fin. Either way, the fins of a fish can tell you a lot – if you know what to look for.

A question of scale(s)

Scales, or their absence, play a vital role in a fish's life. Each type of fish has its own unique set of scales, and each type of scale performs a unique role.

Although we automatically think of fish as scaly, some have significantly reduced scales, or even seemingly invisible scales (such as the moray eel). In some fish, highly modified scales have turned into spines, as with the porcupine pufferfish, or even into bony plates like those of seahorses or boxfish. Scales do not grow on the outer skin of the fish – they are not like a shell – but rather they originate in the epidermis as human hair cells do. This allows for scales to be lost, shed and replaced constantly, without the need to moult in the way reptiles or arthropods might. As far as appearance goes, most bony fish tend to have cycloid or ctenoid scales, which look roughly circular or toothed, respectively. These kind of scales grow as the fish grows, exhibiting circular growth rings, like those of a tree, and just like a tree they're very useful to scientists when attempting to chart the ages of fish.

A great deal of evolution has gone into honing scales to fit their roles perfectly, with streamlining being a key consideration. No fish have taken this further than the sharks and rays, whose scales, so different from those of bony fishes, resemble teeth in their composition, with internal dentine, blood vessels and an enamelled surface. Such placoid scales are shaped to provide advanced hydrodynamic properties, so much so that when human swimmers took inspiration from them for special 'shark-skin' swimming suits, the kit was banned from competitions for giving an unfair advantage: the suits achieved too much drag reduction.

Getting a skinful: the lateral line

Fish can feel the water around them, and I mean really *feel* it around their bodies and respond to the physical signals it carries. Starting on the head of a fish and running down each side of its body is a sub-dermal canal, open to the surface via pores that appear at regular intervals allowing water in. Dotted along the canal's internal length are neuromasts – multiple hair cells that combine to form a sensory node, which, when deformed and distorted by the movement of water past it, sends a signal to the brain.

This is what is known as the lateral line, and there is a great way for you to experience how it works. If you're waiting on an Underground platform, you can feel the whoosh of the air through the tunnel from the oncoming train, so you don't need to see it to know it's coming. It's the same for the neuromasts in the lateral line. As water pressure changes around the fish, whether caused by currents, the tail flick of another fish, or the onward rush of a predator, water is relayed down into the lateral line, sparking off a neuromast and enabling the fish to respond with the appropriate action. It's the lateral line that allows fish to form schools so effectively and, in the case of deep-sea fishes, to detect other animals in completely pitch-dark conditions.

In a way, therefore, the lateral line also acts like an extra ear, since sound underwater is merely waves of pressure. Fish such as herring have taken this notion to extremes, for their lateral line actually interacts with their internal ears to give them an ingenious ability to detect sound over a wide range of frequencies.

Home security systems: Mauthner cells

If you've ever wondered how fish seem to go from 0 to 100 miles per hour in a blink of an eye, avoiding predators or the lunge of your rockpooling net, then I shall tell you the secret. It lies in clever Mauthner cells.

The vast majority of fish have these two huge nerve cells running down either side of the body almost all the way to the tail. As the cells reach the brain, they cross over, so that the cell body for the left side of the fish is located in the right side of the brain, and vice versa. When one of these Mauthner cells is triggered by information from associated sensory structures, such as eyes, nares (nostrils), lateral lines, etc., it immediately inhibits its twin cell from firing and instead unleashes its own nervous impulse. This action potential then stirs the muscles into what's known as a C-Start escape, where all the muscles down one side of the body contract as one (thus forming the fish into a C-shape) before firing forwards in a huge burst of speed.

This relatively simple mechanism is very successful, and fish will even adapt this behaviour to moments of burst feeding. The reason why the cells cross over is to ensure the fish moves the right way. For example, if a threat is detected on the right-hand side, then you need the left-hand side of the fish to contract into a C-Start escape and power away. If the Mauthner cells didn't cross over and excited the muscles on the same side as the information they received, they would catapult the fish directly into the path of any oncoming danger.

Take a breath: gills

Gills aren't just underwater fish lungs. Yes, they are the site of respiration, which allows fish to swap dissolved oxygen for carbon dioxide. But they also play an important role in the animals' biochemistry and metabolic reactions.

Not every ocean inhabitant has gills. Those that still breathe air don't bother with them, and neither do the smallest and more basic creatures. Jellyfish, for example, can rely on diffusion across their body tissues to deal with all their respiratory and metabolic needs. However, the more active and more complex underwater creatures all have gills of some form, and the basics are the same irrespective of species.

A gill is formed of many thousands of thin plates – lamellae – situated on branching gill filaments that are arranged to maximize water flow over the entire gill's surface. A blood supply is present and passes through the filaments, travelling through the lamellae in capillary beds that lie just a few cells away from the seawater around it. This close proximity allows dissolved gases and other chemical compounds to pass across the incredibly thin membrane in both directions.

Gills drastically increase the surface area available for respiration, which is highly useful, as oxygen is found in much lower concentrations in seawater than in air. To doubly ensure that fish can extract as much oxygen as possible from the water, the blood flow in their gills opposes the directional flow of water. This counter-current mechanism ensures that every haemoglobin molecule is loaded with as much oxygen as it can possibly carry before leaving the gill and travelling round the body. Gills play a further crucial role in the excretion of nitrogenous waste, hormones and the control of salt within the tissues, with nearly as much fish wee being excreted from the gills as comes from the kidneys.

Time to get bladdered!

Buoyancy in water is a really useful thing to have, not least because being able to float while perfectly still, without expending energy in swimming, is a supremely valuable gift. Fish manage their buoyancy in a wide variety of ways, but by far the most effective and widespread method is use of a swim-bladder.

The idea is simple: it's an airtight sack within the body of the fish, which can be multi-chambered and filled with gas, and so counter the weight of the fish in the water column. Pressure, however, affects gases quite dramatically. Air pockets are halved in size with each 10-metre increase in depth, so the fish needs to be able to add and remove air from the bladder as needed. This requirement has led to the evolution of two basic styles of swim-bladder: physostomous and physoclistous.

Physostomous swim-bladders retain a connection to the lumen of the gut, meaning that the fish is able to gulp down air and fill its swim-bladder, or expel air by either burping or farting. This kind of bladder allows for rapid rising through the water column as any expanding gas can simply be voided without hurting the fish. By contrast, physoclistous swim-bladders lose their connection to the gut and instead are filled via a gland that can excrete gases into the sealed space of the bladder using some very clever biochemistry. The gas is reabsorbed by blood vessels in another part of the bladder called the oval window, decreasing the bladder's volume and allowing the animal to sink.

Physoclistous swim-bladders are extremely useful for fish at depth that cannot keep swimming to the surface to fill their swim-bladders. However, they do not allow for rapid ascent through the water, and such fish that rise too quickly – cod caught in fishing nets, for example – appear at the surface with their viscera exploding out of their mouths because of their now vastly overinflated swim-bladders. It's a very nasty way to go.

Time to light up

Bioluminescence is one of the most astounding phenomena of the ocean. Vital for deep-sea living, it allows creatures to create the light in the darkness that is essential for hunting, mating, camouflage, communication and defence.

The organs responsible for bioluminescence are called photophores, and their structures are extremely varied, depending on their location on the body and the uses to which they are put. However, there are essentially two main types: those where the light is created by photocytes, and those that use cultivated bacteria in special sacks. In the first type, nerves trigger a cellular reaction in which an enzyme, luciferase, breaks down a substance called luciferin, creating light. In the case of bacterial photophores, special chambers – either open to the ocean or linked to the gut – fill with bacteria that constantly produce light.

With the bacterial method, the animal can't switch off its light – it can only hide it with a shutter or by rotating the light into an opaque internal pocket. One potential hazard from carrying lots of bacteria is the threat of infection or bacterial overpopulation, so fish using this method tend to have only a few photophores, but they are tailored to do multiple jobs. By contrast, marine animals using the enzyme method tend to have a wide and varied distribution of photophores across the body.

The photophores themselves can get extremely technical and sophisticated, the most advanced of them looking structurally very similar to eyes, with a reflective layer, a focusing lens, colour pigments and filters allowing for some wondrous adaptations and uses in the deep ocean.

All ears

A sense of hearing may not be something you immediately associate with fish. After all, they don't have massively visible lugholes! Nevertheless, the ability to detect sound is vital for fish and in the ocean more generally, as sound travels far better through water than it does through air.

Fish in the bony category, the teleosts, have internal ears that perform functions similar to our own, in that they can detect sound waves, and allow a fish to align and balance itself accordingly in the water column. The sense of balance works much like our own: fluid in canals lined with motion-sensitive hairs shift and pitch as the fish changes orientation. As the fluid moves, it activates the hairs and sends information to the brain about what movements are going on. Fish have three such canals, arranged at right-angles to each other because fish live in a medium where any kind of orientation is possible.

In order to detect sound, each canal has a large swelling called an ampulla associated with it, containing a small calcium carbonate ear-stone, or otolith. It rests on a bed of sensitive hair cells, which transmit any fine movements of the otolith to the brain. The system works because, while a fish's body is generally a similar density to seawater, the otolith is more dense than the tissues around it, and so it vibrates differently to the rest of the fish, translating pressure waves into brain waves – and so detecting sound.

Some fish even have a specialized amplifying system called the Weberian ossicles. These are a series of fused bones in the neck, which directly link the swim-bladder to the back of the internal ear canals, rapidly transmitting any vibrations within the swim-bladder to the sensitive otoliths.

The water babies

The critical role of distributing and fertilizing eggs has seen a dizzying range of aquatic adaptations, all with their own pros and cons. In fact, there are far too many different behaviours to mention here, but we shall have a quick look at the three big ones.

In broadcast spawning, the spawners (egg-layers) tend to breed in large shoals, and the eggs are fertilized by numerous males as they are released from the females. In the pelagic sub-type, the fertilized eggs are then carried away by the current, which is highly useful for spreading the population. Broadcast spawning ensures many females and males can mate and so maximizes the number of potential eggs fertilized; but leaving your eggs to the whims of the ocean can also mean a high mortality rate.

Benthic spawners avoid the risks of losing offspring to currents and tides by laying heavy eggs on the seafloor, or by sticking them to seaweeds and rocks. These spawners will sometimes build small depressions, or spawning areas, in which to lay their eggs. Benthic parents, who can be pairs (like salmon) or a single female with multiple males (like cod), avoid the risks of losing eggs to the ocean; but they do – literally – place all their eggs in one basket. So if conditions change, a whole brood could be lost.

Brooders are those fish that in some way carry their young with them. Seahorses are a famous example: the male carries fertilized eggs within a special brood pouch. Other fish might carry their eggs or young fry in their mouths to keep them safe. Such parental devotion does mean you're limited as to how many offspring you can have at any one time, but the upside is that you can protect all of your eggs all of the time, thus ensuring that no predators can get at them. Unless, of course, the predator gets you instead!

Shore

You might think of the coast as a place filled with happy memories of sandcastles, snorkelling and ice creams, but there is in fact far more to the interface of land and sea than the picture postcards suggest. For the animals and plants that inhabit the shoreline, this is a warzone: the site of a daily battle to survive and thrive in this ever-changing and most challenging landscape.

No two shorelines are alike: there's the tropical heat of the Equator at one extreme, the iceberg-strewn gravel of the polar wastes at the other. However, one factor is supreme everywhere: the tide. The regular mass movement of water is forever shifting the boundary of what is, or is not, property of land or sea. The effect of the tide may be greater in some areas than others, but everywhere there is a constant ticking rhythm that all intertidal life must obey. While temperature is relatively stable in water, it is far more variable in air, so any animal or plant looking to exploit the shoreline needs to be highly adaptable, responding quickly to a change in the wind or the splash of a wave. The power of the ocean is another factor that cannot be resisted, as waves break on the rocks of the shore with enormous force. Even a small wave contains enough energy to lift rocks and stones, while a large one can crush shells and skeletons. Then there are the whims of the weather. You might not think that rainfall poses a significant threat – coastal plants and animals are often wet in any case – but the sudden influx of fresh water can in fact interrupt and damage the delicate biochemical balance of organisms living in a saline environment. Snow or ice can send destructive ice crystals deep into vital tissues or cause flexible fronds to become brittle and snap under the slightest breeze.

Very few environments on Earth are as dynamic and demanding as the coast, and that goes for the land too. Not all beaches are sandy: many different kinds of coastline exist and each has its own dedicated army of specially adapted lifeforms to survive in the challenging conditions. Large rocks and cliff faces are a perfect beachhead for life looking to stay put, boring in or gluing themselves to hard surfaces in order to bear the brunt of what the ocean has to throw at them. Sand, on the other hand, may look good and feel nice beneath our feet, but its lack of stability causes great problems for anything large looking to settle and take root. Beneath the surface, meanwhile, there is a whole unseen world, as the spaces between tiny sand grains provide a unique environment for predator and prey. Other shorelines have a stranger aspect, as twisted trees encroach into the silts and sediments – arboreal inhabitants that are just as heavily modified as the creatures that live in or on them.

Once the stage on which terrestrial life began, as our distant ancestors crawled from water to land, the coasts and shorelines of planet Earth remain both rich and challenging, just as they were all those eons ago.

Life among the sand grains

We might think of a sandy beach as a nice place for a picnic and a stroll, but for a whole host of animals it is the universe where they spend their whole lives. Thanks to the irregular shape and size of its grains, sand has lots of interstitial (in-between) spaces: basically, it doesn't knit together tightly, so there is a maze of microscopic pockets where thriving

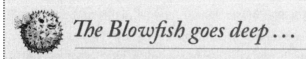

The Blowfish goes deep …

LIVING BETWEEN THE TIDES

Life on the shoreline is dictated by the tides. You might think that either dry land or salty sea would bring the greatest stability and therefore create a bloom of life, but in fact the diversity that tides bring creates a mass of opportunities to be exploited.

The tidal range – the vertical distance between low and high tides – plays a vital part in how intertidal animals are distributed. A smaller tidal range means that there is a smaller area between the low- and high-water marks (intertidal zone), so there is greater competition for life between the organisms crammed into that tiny space. A larger tidal range, on the other hand, means that there is a greater area for life to colonize and a wider range of conditions to exploit. Algae and animals furthest up the beach need to be able to withstand the longest periods of exposure – sometimes many hours – to the terrestrial elements, whereas those at the low end of the beach might only be exposed for a few minutes each day, or perhaps an hour on a spring tide.

You can see the distinct zonation created by the tides by looking at something as simple as lichen, barnacles and seaweed. Visit a beach in the UK that has a decent tidal range, and at the very highest reaches of the water you will see tar lichen, a black lichen capable of surviving salt spray. Next, where the high water always reaches regardless of the state of the tides, barnacles start to come in, along with particularly hardy seaweeds such as spiral wrack. Move further down the shore and you'll see serrated wrack and other species that are less tolerant of desiccation. Finally, as you hit the low-water mark, where the shore is only occasionally exposed by the tide, you'll find large brown kelps beginning to dominate.

ecosystems develop. These spaces are such a great place to live because they are very environmentally stable. The temperature is relatively constant, as is the salinity for the most part. Organisms are protected from the sun and elements above, while also hidden from larger predators. Sand is also extremely permeable to water, so each wave brings in fresh supplies of organic carbon which soak in from above.

No surprise, then, that everything from bacteria to anemones, from molluscs to isopods, are found in the plethora of small animals (meiofauna) that exploit this small and claustrophobic environment. Most are slim, have small or no eyes, and have body pigments to make best use of the dark. Many larger marine species also use the safe spaces of the sand to lay their eggs, which allows the larvae to settle straight into gaps; others have planktonic larvae which nestle straight into the sand once they have travelled far enough from their parents.

Needless to say, a rich ecosystem like this doesn't go unnoticed. Larger members of the meiofauna, such as polychaete worms and copepods, fall prey to wading birds and benthic (bottom-dwelling) fishes, while smaller inhabitants have to worry about being guzzled up by lugworms or actively hunted by fearsome arrow worms.

Rock-bound microcosms of life

Some of my happiest memories are of clambering over slippery rocks to squat down and view the awesome miniature world trapped within a rockpool. You might think that life is relatively easy for the rockpool-dwellers, isolated in their own sea of tranquillity. But this couldn't be further from the truth: living in a rockpool is very, very hard! The water of your rockpool home may be refreshed daily by the tide, but just how much water you get and how long you have to wait to get it depends on the distance your pool is up the beach. And it is the length of time before a pool is refreshed by the ocean that directly determines which creatures can live there.

Once a pool is exposed by the retreating tide, many abiotic

(non-living) factors begin to change. The oxygen content of the water drops as it is consumed by biological activity in the pool. The water temperature rises too, further reducing the amount of oxygen in the remaining seawater and putting organisms under increasing metabolic stress. With rising temperature comes evaporation, and that leads to an increase in salinity. Throw in some seasonal factors on top of that and things get even tougher: in summer, the hot sun rapidly increases the rate of oxygen loss and the rise in temperature and salinity; in winter, rainfall can send temperature and salinity crashing down in the space of one heavy downpour. Then, as the chemical profile of the pool reaches a critical and potentially dangerous state, come the next high tide, one single large wave can reset all these chemical factors in an instant!

Such a sudden change in temperature and salinity should cause a massive biological shock to any animal hit by it. Extraordinary, then, that many of the most dominant rockpool creatures are invertebrates – animals that are unable to regulate their internal temperature and chemical balance. As any fishkeeper will tell you, these are the animals that are most difficult to acclimatize to new water conditions, yet in a rockpool they are wrenched from one extreme to the other without warning. And as if all that were not enough, there are a stack of biotic factors to deal with, as your once-safe underwater home is suddenly unprotected by the waves and exposed to all sorts of predators, such as gulls, racoons and even baboons.

Sea urchins: spiny grazers of the coast

Coastlines can get a bit messy, with all sorts of green slimes and algae building up on rocks and other places. To keep things looking neat, what you need is a good clean-up crew. Enter (very slowly) the sea urchins!

Found throughout the oceans in a variety of shapes and sizes, most sea urchins follow a similar design pattern. A hard, round outer shell (test) is covered in defensive spines and lined with sticky tube feet, while

Sea urchin

underneath lies a mouth in direct contact with the ocean floor. They may be simple animals without a recognizable brain, but they are very sensitive to touch, smell and light. In the coastal shallows, sea urchins are valuable grazers, responsible for keeping rocks clear of algae and other slimy encrustations. They are so good at this grazing job that, when their natural predators are removed, they can strip areas of the coast completely clear of all vegetation.

Living in the rich shallow waters is great for ensuring a steady supply of greens to munch, but it also puts you in line to be munched yourself. Not the nippiest on their tiny tube feet, sea urchins need a solid defence, and this is where those spines come in. These are certainly sharp, making contact with the animal difficult, but there is much more to them than that. Each spine is moveable and can be independently controlled, so when the animal is threatened from a particular direction, the spines can be directed to face the aggressor. In some species, the spines are sharp enough to penetrate human skin, where they are designed to work their way inwards, and – if not removed quickly – they may require surgery to extract.

Flavoursome filter-feeders: mussels

Life isn't all sweet for the common mussel. When not appearing on the plates of the world's diners, these familiar bivalve molluscs often act as lab rats, appearing on the dissection tables of the world's marine biology students. Personally, as one of those responsible for many a dissection, I'd *never* eat one ... I know their secrets and, trust me, ignorance is bliss.

Mussels

Mussels are hardy and widespread filter-feeders, drawing water in through one siphon, passing it over the fine filtering mess of the mucus-covered gills, and then ejecting it through another siphon. They are so good at this business that they can work through 3 litres of water an hour; massive mussel beds, kilometres long and populated by millions of individuals, can act as biological filters for bays, inlets and estuaries. Mussels are not often exposed by the tide, but they still feel the full force of the waves at times, so they need an effective method of attaching themselves to rocks. Using their muscular foot, they bind themselves to a surface with byssus – long hair-like threads of a strong and super-sticky substance the mussel creates within its body.

Seeking safety in the sand: cockles

Mussels are visible on rocks and reef beds, clams and quahogs can be seen on the shallow seafloor – but what about cockles? I'm sure you've heard of these shelled beasties, but would you know where to find them? In fact, these small bivalve molluscs live in the sediments of sandy beaches, out of sight and out of mind. Feeding in the same way as mussels and other filter-feeding bivalves, cockles must have access to seawater, so they live only a few centimetres down in the sand, and when the tide is up, they move towards the surface to feed.

The cockle moves by means of its large muscular foot, which it uses as an anchor towards which it pulls the rest of its shelled body. The foot is extended in the desired direction to its maximum reach, then the animal pumps blood to the very tip of the foot, causing it to expand. Now locked in position in the sand, the cockle contracts the muscles associated with the foot, thereby pulling itself towards the stationary anchor point. This may seem a rather slow and laborious way of getting about, but you'd be surprised how quickly bivalves can move through the sand when they have to (anyone who has gone digging for razor shells will testify to this).

Moving to the surface, the cockle extends both its siphons, inhalant and exhalant, and gets on with the business of filter-feeding. Having your fleshy body parts exposed to the sea while the rest of you is hidden

Cockle

is a hell of a risk, and shrimps, crabs and flatfish will all take a decent bite given the chance. Because of this, the cockle is extremely sensitive to chemical cues in the water that suggest predators are nearby. As the tide recedes, the aquatic predators leave too, but it's not over for the cockle, as the animal now pulls itself down deeper into the (relative) safety of the sand, hoping to go unnoticed by hungry wading birds, such as the oystercatcher and its long, probing beak.

The unassuming assassin: dog whelk

You probably wouldn't give a dog whelk the time of day: just another boring old snail. Admittedly, the standard-issue dog whelk isn't exactly riveting to look at: a small whelk that measures just 3 centimetres when fully mature and comes in a variety of muted colours, from cream to brown to golden yellow. And while not *the* common whelk, it is *a* common whelk: found throughout the intertidal zone, dog whelks can withstand a wide range of temperatures and salinities, allowing them to access the high shore if necessary and even to work their way up into estuaries. So far so boring. But there's boring and there's *boring* – as in drilling a hole through someone's shell and sucking up their innards through your snout . . .

Because the unassuming dog whelk is also a *murderous bastard*.

The main driving factor for dog whelks is food, and they accumulate in large number when conditions are good. Feeding mainly on mussels and barnacles, they basically have two techniques to get at the goods. The first is to ram the long proboscis (feeding tube or snout) through a gap in the shell of the prey, excrete paralysing saliva, and then begin to feed on the hapless victim. The second involves using acid created by the dog whelk's foot to soften the shell and then use its radula – the long feeding belt of sharp, rasping teeth – to chew a hole through to the meat within. Either way, the end result is the same: the proboscis is extended and the radula then goes to work on the shell or flesh of the animal, ripping it to shreds. The combination of paralysing saliva, boring radula and dissolving acid results in a meaty soup the whelk can slurp up in its own sweet time. And it does like to take its time: it can take three days to access, shred and consume a mussel. During this time, whelks are themselves at risk of predation or exposure at low tide, so they prefer prey that they can despatch in the shortest time possible.

Razor shell: the motoring mollusc

Not a huge surprise here, but razor shells get their name from their striking resemblance to a razor – a cut-throat (or straight) razor, the old-fashioned kind with a blade that folds back into the handle. Probably better not to try and shave with one, though, or you'll end up stinking like a sweaty mollusc ...

Living in the sand and filter-feeding from the water above, the razor shell is found from the low-tide mark all the way out to 60 metres depth. Sometimes living to ten years and growing to 20 centimetres or more, they are real long-term members of the beach community. Most of all, though, the razor shell is the Ferrari of the bivalve world. Open at both ends, its foot always has easy access to the sand beneath, and when threatened, it can dig down at a rate of 1 centimetre a second. Just like cockles, they use their muscular foot to form an anchor point, to which they then pull themselves by contracting muscles in the foot. In the case of razor shells, that long thin shell is perfect for cutting through the wet sand, so much so that they can burrow down 70 centimetres if needed. It isn't all down to streamlining and good footwork, however. The razor shell also uses muscular contractions to jet water down to 'fluidize' the sediment, briefly turning it into quicksand and allowing for an easier dig.

The razor shell is the bivalve of choice for the discerning beachcomber. Essential gear includes a spade and strong muscles as you dig to outpace the racing razor. Or you can rely on a subtle plan of attack, to lure the fella out. At low tide, the razor shell's siphons leave a keyhole-shaped depression in the sand, a sure sign that a razor shell lurks beneath. If you pour salt into this depression, you'll find the shell rapidly appearing at the surface, significantly disturbed by the huge change in salinity. This allows for some pretty easy collection – you just need to know where to look in the first place.

Ice, slice and a nice nibble: sea lemon

A sea lemon sounds like something you might want to put in your gin and tonic on a beach holiday. But probably better not, as sea lemon is actually the name shared by a wide range of sea slugs. As slugs go, mind, these are real beauties. Flat, fat and oval, most sea lemons reach around 12 centimetres long; some are yellow, but not all – they range from white to brown, and occasionally you get one with black spots, or even a rare variety which is red. Technically, these slugs belong to a group called nudibranchs, which means 'naked gill' and refers to the exposed gills found on the back of these gastropod molluscs; in the case of sea lemons, the tuft of frilly gills is at the rear end, ringing the anus. At the slug's front end, there are two large horn-like projections called rhinophores. Very often ribbed or ruffled to increase their surface area, these are like noses on stalks and are used to detect chemical signals in the water, from potential prey, predator or mate. These are the sea lemon's key sense organ, so they take very good care of them, rapidly withdrawing them within protective pockets inside the head at the first sign of trouble.

These super-cool slugs feed on sponges. They are able to withstand limited exposure on the low shore, where they hide in cool, damp crevices or under thick fronds of still-wet seaweed, waiting for the tide to return and allow them to start feeding once again. They lay the most delicate rings of eggs that look very much like prawn crackers – a nice nibble to go with your gin and tonic.

Plough snails: South Africa's beach cleaners

You never know what the next tide may bring, but it's a good bet that amongst it all there's a free meal to be had. The incoming waves often bring something dead and rotting up the beach, where scavengers of all kinds race to devour it. Now, racing can be a bit tricky if you're a snail, and you can easily miss out on a decent feed. But that doesn't mean you can't give it a bloody good go ...

The plough snail is a dedicated scavenger found on the beaches around the coast of South Africa. At 6 centimetres in length, with a streamlined spiral shell, this whelk spends most of its time buried in the sand with just its long sensitive siphon sticking out. At the first sniff of decay, these snails make a mad rush (well, a mad snail rush) for the body, even if that means travelling up the beach and away from the water. For this snail, time is of the essence: take too long, and either the meal will already be gone, or you'll get cooked in the hot sun and die in the attempt. Answering the need for speed, these snails use their greatly enlarged and highly expandable foot as a sail to 'surf' the waves still driving up the beach. Once they have got as far as they can go this way, they use their big foot to scoot rapidly (for a snail) over the sand, following the scent trail left by the carcass. When they finally make it, they feed as fast as they possibly can before the external conditions become too much for them, or the tide returns and steals their lunch away. These caretakers of South Africa's beaches seem to have a particular fondness for dead jellyfish and siphonophores. But, when it comes to it, they'll scoff pretty much anything they can catch up with.

How to cling like a limpet

To our terrestrial eye, the humble limpet may appear static and lifeless in its conical shell, but underwater they come alive. Living in the inter-tidal zone, limpets are subjected to all that water and land can throw at them. Essentially a snail in an uncoiled shell, a limpet has a large muscular foot (like other gastropod molluscs) that holds it firmly in place when exposed by the tide, and moves it around when submerged. At the business end, a rasping radula (a sort of conveyor belt of tiny teeth) is used to graze the rocks for bacterial and algal films.

There is a huge diversity of limpets, all evolved to graze, but uniquely adapted to their particular place on the shore and the harshness of the environmental conditions they have to endure. For example, limpets that suffer high wave action tend to have a low-profile shell, while limpets that are slightly less hammered by waves grow taller and more conical in shape. Apart from the action of the waves, another big problem for limpets is water loss, so the temperature when they are exposed to the sun at low tide is a key factor. The common limpet has developed an excellent method to help reduce water loss. When the tide is up, the limpet grazes as far and wide as possible, but as the tide turns, it always comes back to the exact same spot (its 'home scar'). Over time, the shell of the limpet grows to perfectly match the contours of the rock, and the rock itself may be worn away to match the shape of the limpet. The result is a perfect seal between rock and shell, allowing the limpet to keep hold of that precious water during the ordeal of exposure at low tide.

Ragworms: the fisherman's fearsome friends

If you're a fisherman, chances are you've tried your hand using ragworms as bait at some time or another. Pulling the limp body of a ragworm from a bait pack probably won't give you much idea just how excellent a predator this bad boy is. But for those of you who have dug your own raggies ... Well, I just hope you've still got all your fingers.

Ragworms are very active polychaete worms. They have many segments, a head with multiple eyes and other delicate sense organs, and large fleshy appendages (parapodia) for swimming through water and burrowing in sediments. My personal favourite is the king ragworm, a greenish-coloured worm that lives and hunts in sandy burrows around temperate shorelines and even up into estuaries. Its constant scrummaging through sands and silts helps turn over the sediment, allowing oxygenated water to reach deeper into the substrate and so extending the range of habitats accessible to other creatures. These beasts can grow to 40 centimetres, while some specimens from Welsh beaches have been reported at up to 90 centimetres – at which point they really would present a danger to your fingers. While the king ragworm is known as an omnivore, feeding happily on bits of seaweed and scavenging too, they have a set of jaws that would be the envy of most out-and-out predators. Hidden in the throat of the worm, there is a surprisingly large set of black fangs, which are ready to spring forward and skewer prey at lighting speed . . . Mind those fingers!

Follow the poo: lugworms

It is the misfortune of the humble lugworm to be one of the classic test subjects for marine biologists. And what decades of poking, prodding and probing have shown is just how closely linked the lugworm is to the health of a beach environment.

Measuring not much more than 20 centimetres in length and dark-brownish in colour (basically, worm-coloured), lugworms are segmented (like earthworms) with paired tufts of branching gills and a highly extendable balloon-like throat. In terms of appearance, then, these worms aren't anything to write home about. Thankfully, though, you won't have to look at them much (unless you're a fisherman digging for bait) as they spend pretty much their entire lives buried in sand.

What you are much more likely to see is their poo. The tell-tale sign of a lugworm on a beach is a densely coiled lump of sand a few centimetres away from a small depression with a hole at its centre. The sand coil is the worm's faeces, and on some beaches individual piles of the stuff can stretch as far as the eye can see. You can't see the worm itself, however, which lives at the bottom of a U-shaped burrow connecting the pile of poo to the associated depression and hole. Feeding almost constantly, the worm wriggles its body in such a way as to draw water down from its tail end, over its gills and past the head; the water then rises back to the surface through the sand the worm is feeding on – this moistens the sediment directly in front of the worm and allows for easier chomping. The lugworm obtains nutrition from taking large mouthfuls of sand and processing the grains inside its body for any edible micro-organisms, such as bacteria, diatoms or detritus. It's the constant munching and removal of material at the head end that causes the depression and hole in the sand above. Once processed, the cleaned sand is excreted as the worm reverses its tail to the surface to defecate.

Without the constant action of countless millions of lugworms, many beaches across the temperate zone would become anoxic and stagnant just a few centimetres below the surface.

Barnacle: has super-penis, can't travel

Barnacles may not be at the top of anyone's Top Ten Greatest Sea Creatures, but there's actually a lot more going on under the bonnet (well, shell/carapace) than you'd think.

First, it's important to remember that barnacles aren't molluscs (like mussels and limpets), but crustaceans (like crabs and lobsters). You might not guess it, but these immobile, rock-like creatures are actually tiny shrimps lying on their back in a reinforced house, using their hairy legs to filter out particles of food from the water. Barnacles are experts at colonizing any surface the waves touch. Many intertidal species attach themselves high up on the shore and can tolerate massive shifts in environmental conditions, surviving – in the space of a single wave – being almost cooked alive in their own shells by the hot summer sun to being drenched in cold seawater.

One widely rumoured fact about barnacles is that they have really big penises. Well, this is certainly true of the common species *Semibalanus balanoides*, which grows to about 1.5–2 centimetres at most but has a monster penis around 7 centimetres long! Such extravagant tackle is one solution to the problem of spending one's life stuck to a rock, which can make dating difficult. This particular species is hermaphroditic (it has both male and female reproductive organs), so each barnacle uses its super-penis to fertilize all the other individuals around it before it is fertilized in turn. Now that sounds like some serious partying.

Blowfish diet: goose barnacles

I have had the 'pleasure' of eating fresh goose barnacles not once, but twice. The fact that I went back for more (admittedly, in two different countries) perhaps says more about me than their gastronomic excellence. Still, the significance of these curious crustaceans extends well beyond the kitchen: the taxonomic framework we use to classify goose barnacles is based on the work of one of the greatest scientists, Charles Darwin, and his famous theory of evolution by natural selection was influenced by years of work studying barnacles.

Goose barnacles are certainly strange things that don't look at all like the barnacles we are all familiar with. The living, feeding part of the barnacle is on the end of a long fleshy growth called a peduncle – it is a rather spooky-looking arrangement that resembles an ornate fingernail on the end of a black and scaly finger. Still, you can tell it's a crustacean when the plates covering the hairy thoracic limbs open up and the limbs are thrust into the water to feed. These barnacles are usually found anchored on wave-battered rocky shores, where the flexible stalk allows them to flow with the rushing water, ensuring they are always in the best position to harvest the passing plankton. Some species actually float free in the ocean, while many different kinds are known to colonize whales, boats, floating logs and the like. One species even excretes its own organic air-filled float which has much the same consistency as polystyrene.

The strange name 'goose barnacle' is, perhaps not surprisingly, linked to the bird known as a barnacle goose. As the bird is migratory, people never saw it nest or lay eggs, so they came to believe (apparently on the basis of shape and colour) that the goose barnacles they found washed up on the beach actually were the barnacle goose's eggs. Well, that's the story anyway ...

Smashers and spearers

You may be familiar with the brightly coloured peacock mantis shrimp, which is founds on tropical reefs, but there is in fact a large number of different species of mantis, some of which form large colonies just off the coast. These are extraordinary crustaceans, with a wide array of unique and defining characteristics.

For one thing, these feisty little shrimps must have the finest vision of any animal. Each of the two large eyes has its own dedicated nerve bundle that acts as a mini-brain, essential for decoding all the incoming information, as the mantis shrimp has trinocular vision (trinocular vision, that is, *in each eye*). Also, their full-colour vision is much fuller than ours, as they have sixteen different types of light-sensitive cone cells; they are also able to detect ultraviolet wavelengths and polarized light.

When it comes to the hunt, mantis shrimps tend to wait inside their burrows, watching for prey to pass by, before rushing out and attacking. Broadly speaking, there are two main groups of mantises – smashers and spearers – defined by their way of dispatching their prey. In each group, the front claws are highly modified, with a special muscle arrangement that allows for a super-rapid strike (so rapid that it produces a shock wave, with a cavitation bubble in its wake). In the case of the smashers, the end of the claw is a large bulbous club, which can be fired forward so quickly as to crack a crab's shell – or aquarium glass. In spearers, the claws resemble the grasping forelegs of the praying mantis insect; shrimps of this kind hunt soft-bodied prey such as fish, which are easily impaled on the spiked claws and dragged back into the burrow to be consumed.

Sand-bubbler crabs

Stripping anything that is even mildly organic from sand isn't the worst way to make a living. The main downside is that you may have to spend every available minute of the day feeding just to scrape together enough to get by.

Across many of the beaches of the Indian and Pacific Oceans, there lives a family of small crabs that spend their lives scouring the sand for anything remotely edible. No bigger than 1 centimetre across the shell, these crabs live in burrows in the sand, taking refuge in them should any predator come by or when the tide has risen. As soon as the coast is clear, the crabs set to work. The sand-bubbler has special mouth-parts that are coated in fine spoon-tipped setae (hairs) to filter out any possible organic matter. The sand is initially shovelled into the mouth with the claws, where it is kept moist by water from the gills. Once the first major sorting of coarse sand grains has been done, a round waste pellet is produced, dropped and booted away by the crab. As it prepares for another mouthful, the various different mouthparts further sort the finer inorganic particles for edible morsels. The crabs are dependent on tiny organisms that live on or between the sand grains, so they need to process a *lot* of it – so much, in fact, that they can produce sand balls at a rate of six to eight a minute as they comb the area around their burrows. As they feed, they walk sideways away from the burrow, but they always ensure that all the waste pellets are kicked *behind* them, so that the path back to the safety of the burrow is kept clear in case of danger.

Christmas Island red crabs: do exactly what it says on the tin

We usually just think of crabs as living in the sea, but you'd be surprised just how many terrestrial crabs there are. However, just as many marine mammals whose ancestors left the land for the sea still return to terra firma to pup, so land crabs still require water to spawn their eggs. And for one particular species, that means a trip to the beach.

The Christmas Island red crab is a red crab found on Christmas Island ... well, no one said *all* science had to be tough. Reaching about 12 centimetres across the shell (carapace), these crabs spend 99 per cent of their lives living deep in the humid forest of Christmas Island, hiding in burrows and feasting on fallen leaves, fruit and decaying matter. When the wet season starts, the entire population leaves the safety of the trees and heads for the coast, where they gather in their millions. The males appear first, and after a bit of scrapping with potential rivals, they dig burrows in the best spots on the beach. The females then appear and mating occurs in the burrow, after which the males promptly scarper back to the forest. The females remain at the beach until they have laid their eggs and the eggs have developed enough to be released. On a suitably gentle tide, the females walk into the water and, with a quick shimmy, release all their eggs, before rushing out again for fear of drowning. The eggs hatch almost instantly upon hitting the water, and the larvae are then swept out to sea to develop in the plankton, just like those of any regular crab. A month later, long after the females have followed the males back into the forest, the beaches of Christmas Island are bright red again, this time with miniature crabs, one tenth the size of an adult, which begin their own long journey towards the safety of the forest.

Ooh, what a big claw you've got . . .

Fiddler crabs are best known for one big thing (and it isn't their skill on the violin): a single massive claw. And in the world of fiddlers, size really matters.

Fiddlers are found along the tropical beaches, mudflats and saltmarshes of the Indian and eastern Pacific Oceans and certain areas bordering the western Atlantic. Like many other beach crabs, they feed on the sediments they live in and on, sifting out edible particles and scavenging on larger lumps of waste. The real interest comes with that huge claw that the males sport (females have a matching set of smaller claws). In most species, it can be either the left or the right claw, and if it is lost during a fight with a rival male, the remaining normal claw metamorphoses into a new 'fiddle' on the next moult. Fighting tends to be limited, however, as most disputes are settled with lots of waving. The male crab sits at the entrance to his burrow, and raises and waves his large claw; this is a sign to other males to keep away and to entice females, who like nothing better than a nice big claw and a flashy display.

Some species, though, are known to be all mouth and no trousers. If two evenly matched males fight, the loser is likely to lose his major claw. If a male ring-legged fiddler crab loses his big claw, he grows a new one that is just as big but without the extra mass needed to make it a good fighting claw. This is then waved about in the usual way, apparently displaying great strength, but actually it is all bluff. It does the trick, however, as stronger but smaller-clawed males are cowed and receptive females are wowed.

The house-proud hermit

You might think that hermit crabs are cute little things you find on the beach, but you'd perhaps think twice before getting too cuddly with the largest member of this crustacean family: the robber crab. One metre across and weighing 5 kilograms, this hermit crab gets so big that as an adult it can't carry around a shell anymore. It is protected, instead, by its own hardened exoskeleton – not that it needs much protection, with claws that are strong enough to rip open coconuts. On the whole, though, hermit crabs are quite small. Some (like the robber) are found on land, but most live in the sea, and in whatever environment they live, they are important scavengers, feeding on fallen and decaying matter and grazing on organic growths and algal films.

The hermit crab's main claim to fame, of course, is the borrowed shell it carries around. The shell is held by the crab's curled abdomen and supported by two backward-pointing legs, while the other legs are used for walking. In many species, the claws are asymmetrical and fit tightly together, forming a strong 'door' over the shell's opening and blocking entry to hungry predators. No surprise, then, that in the hermit-crab world the shell is a seriously big deal and there is fierce competition to get a good one. Like other arthropods, these crabs must moult to grow larger, and over time their stolen mollusc shells get too small or become weakened by the elements. The only time a hermit crab leaves its shell is when it has to move to a new one. Hermits, both terrestrial and marine, are known to form disorderly mobs around new shells, and they are sometimes so keen to get at an empty shell that they walk right past the mouth of the predator that has just discarded it.

Puffers and archers

Rivers, estuaries and fjords are water bodies where fresh and salt water meet, mixing gently to create a brackish water environment. Living in water that is fresher than seawater but saltier than fresh water presents particular challenges to organisms, but, as usual, life has found ways to exploit these special conditions.

One brackish-water specialist – a personal favourite of mine – is the green spotted puffer, a species that begins life in fresh waters before developing and maturing in saltier conditions. Like all puffers, the green spot is a vicious little predator, dispatching worms, snails and shrimps with abandon. The change in water chemistry from fresh to salt causes a lot of the particulate matter suspended in the fresh water to clump together and drop out of the water column, producing a steady fall of organic morsels for feeders below and a rich plethora of small invertebrates to feed even the hungriest puffer.

Another well-known brackish-water resident is the archer fish. This sharpshooter can jet water out of its mouth to knock insects and other grubs from low-hanging branches. Amazingly, adult archer fish are able to accurately hit prey at the first attempt, so they must be taking account of the way light bends when entering water. This is a learned behaviour, as juvenile archer fish seem to spit wildly at anything edible and it takes them a while to get their eye in.

The sticking power of the lumpsucker

Not a full-time member of the coastal community, the lumpsucker, or sea hen, only makes an appearance when it's time to breed. Growing to an impressive 60 centimetres, the lumpsucker is a deep-bodied rugby-ball-shaped fish with multiple warty ridges and pop eyes. Usually found in deep water down to 300 metres, the lumpsucker eats whatever it can get its warty mouth around, including shrimps, jellies, crabs and smaller fish.

Normally grey, blue or nearly black, come the breeding season the males turn a shade of orange in their bid to attract females, and this is when they move into the coastal waters. Males dig nests and display in the hope of convincing a female to lay her eggs there. If he's lucky, a female lumpsucker will lay a large clutch of eggs, before promptly disappearing back into the deep and leaving the male to fertilize the brood. However, the male doesn't leave – he stays to defend the eggs from predators, as well as to ensure they get a healthy supply of fresh oxygenated water by constantly fanning them with his fins. The attentive fathers are known to head-butt the clump of eggs to make sure there is good circulation throughout, and they eat any damaged or diseased eggs to ensure the rest remain healthy. Sometimes, these nests can be in very shallow water – so shallow that they are above the low-water mark and even gentle wave action could be a real problem for the protective father. Not so for the lumpsucker, as the pelvic fins have fused together to form a suction disc, which keeps them affixed to the rock no matter what. After a month or so, the eggs hatch and the tiny baby lumpsuckers spend their first few months developing in the lowest rockpools and shallow intertidal waters, before following their parents back down into the dark depths.

Fish out of water, part 1: capelin

There are many fish to be found within the coastal and intertidal zones, and it is fair to say that *most* of them stick to the water. After all, the whole needing-water-to-make-gills-work thing is, generally speaking, an important guideline for fish to follow. However, there's something to be said for getting onto dry land – not least, you can take most of your predators out of the picture – and there is one particular fish that has taken this idea to heart. Capelin are a small sardine-like fish, reaching around 20 centimetres in length, which form a crucial link in the food chains of the Subarctic oceans. Just like sardine, they are heavily preyed on, so they have to mature quickly and breed en masse. And it's the breeding bit which really sets them apart.

Capelin which visit the North Pacific and Newfoundland coasts are one of only three species known to spawn out of water. Now, don't get me wrong – we are not talking about fish laying their eggs in the car park at the top of the beach. Males and females congregate in the lapping waves right on the shoreline, where they wait for larger waves to drive them up on the beach where spawning occurs. The eggs are sticky and quickly settle into the damp sands; here they are exposed to warmer temperatures and have access to a higher concentration of oxygen than they would in seawater, so they develop quickly. As they hatch, the fry are then carried back into the ocean by the same high tides that brought their parents to the beach a fortnight earlier.

Fish out of water, part 2: mudskipper

Mudskippers are the fishy kings of the intertidal zone: truly amphibious fishes that spend more time out of water than in it. Most intertidal fish have to reduce their activity and simply wait out the low tide in safety, but not the mudskipper, which feeds, fights and frolics in the open air.

The first obstacle for any fish out of water is the need to breathe. The mudskipper takes large gulps of air and holds them over its moist gills, which are stiffened so that they do not collapse and lose their surface area. To maximize oxygen uptake, gas exchange can also occur through the lining of the mouth, which is heavily packed with blood vessels. One problem the mudskipper has to deal with is that – unlike its fully aquatic cousins – it cannot constantly excrete dangerous nitrogen-based waste products like ammonia from its gills or anal vent, for to do so would waste too much water. In order to detoxify what would potentially be dangerous levels of ammonia in its blood, it actively turns the harmful chemical into amino acids and other safer biological compounds.

The mudskipper's body is specially modified for life on land. The eyes are positioned at the top of the head, giving good all-round vision, while its strong pectoral and pelvic fins are used like legs to walk about on the mud. It is when threatened that the mudskipper really lives up to its name, dashing and skipping over the ground, with vigorous beats of its long tail, to the safety of the water or its burrow.

Flatfish and the intertidal feeding frenzy

When a returning tide starts to flow up a beach, there is a great shift of activity as crabs, shrimps, isopods and other invertebrates that were hiding out in the soft, damp sand emerge to feed. They haven't got long, as predators from deeper water are waiting for the tide to rise far enough for them to safely enter the shallows and hunt.

There is one type of predator, however, that can access this bounty of food almost immediately, without waiting for deeper water to return. Flatfish, such as plaice and dab, are perfectly suited to hunting in these very shallow waters and can be found right up to the surf line, where it is easy to corner prey against the beach. They are so keen to have first dibs on this exclusive buffet that they actively ride the tide to get up the beach quickly: rising higher in the water column, they use their body as a sail to bring them in, then drop to the bottom to avoid being swept back. Rather than swimming, flatfish crawl along the sand using specially modified fin rays, which allow them to literally walk right up to a potential victim.

Excellent camouflage from chromatophores (colour-changing cells) allows flatfish to completely blend into the sand or silt beneath. This isn't so important for hunting – it's more about not being hunted. Coming into such shallow water puts these fish at risk of being spotted by avian predators, anything from a tenacious gull to a deadly sea eagle, which could bring a swift end to their feeding festivities.

The major drawback with this intertidal feeding is that it doesn't last long. As the tide rises higher, more predators can access the beach and competition becomes fierce. Also, it is only possible to feed efficiently on a rising tide, so flatfish species like plaice, as they grow larger and get hungrier, tend to migrate offshore into deeper water where they can feed more frequently.

The turbocharged tarpon

A fine-looking fish with a reputation for giving a good fight on rod and line, tarpon are big mouths and muscle-bound bodies with some fast fins attached. Reaching 2 metres in length, weighing 120 kilograms and living to a ripe old age of 55 years, tarpon are superb piscine predators. While these fish can survive in fresh water as well as in marine conditions, it is the brackish water habitats of tropical coastal environments, especially mangroves, where they really rule the roost.

In mangroves, slow water flow between roots, high temperatures and mixing of salt and fresh water can lead to very low levels of dissolved oxygen and stagnant conditions. This means that everything has to slow down, or potentially suffocate, but the tarpon cheats by breathing air. It has a specialized internal plumbing system in which the gut is connected to the large swim-bladder, and the fish can fill this with air by taking big gulps at the surface. The swim-bladder contains four long rows of spongy tissue, creating a large surface area with a good blood supply; functionally similar to the mammalian lung, this is where gas exchange takes place. Fuelled by a decent gulp of air, the hunting tarpon can outstrip nearly everything else in the stagnant swamp and will eat fish, crabs, shrimps and even insects which they snatch from the surface. The tarpon is the only marine fish known to respire in this way, and although the gills are the main site of gas exchange when conditions are suitable, it is likely that even then the tarpon uses its bladder as a sort of turbocharger for bursts of activity.

Versatile and deadly: bull sharks

For fish, moving from salt water to fresh water, or from fresh to salt, is physiologically very taxing. Few fish manage it with any great aplomb, and even the most famous – salmon – slowly disintegrate as their bodies shut down during the time in their freshwater spawning rivers.

There is one fish, however, that can move from ocean to river, and back again, without blinking an eye. The bull shark can grow up to 4 metres long and weigh over 300 kilograms; it is a strong, stout species and can, on occasion, prove to be highly aggressive (it is sometimes said to be the most dangerous fish in the world). Also known as the Zambezi shark, this animal is not just capable of surviving in brackish waters, but can move right up into freshwater rivers (like the Zambezi). In Australia, many freshwater inlets and canals have resident populations of bull sharks; there was even a recent story that during floods in Brisbane a bull shark was seen swimming down a flooded street.

The problem for a saltwater fish moving into fresh water is that the salts in its body draw water into its tissues via osmosis. In theory, the animal could swell up like a sponge and the salts essential for its biochemical functioning could be fatally diluted, or its cells could simply burst under hydrostatic pressure. The bull shark has developed multiple physiological techniques to deal with this. Its gills actively pump any salts found in the surrounding water back into the bloodstream. The kidneys go into overdrive and start to produce large amounts of very watery urine, helping to eliminate the excess freshwater intake. Finally, the rectal gland, which normally works to excrete extra salt absorbed while living in the ocean, slows or even stops functioning altogether to ensure no precious salts are wasted.

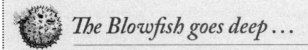 *The Blowfish goes deep . . .*

FAKE NEWS: SHARK ATTACK!

Despite what the movies and the media tell you, shark attacks on humans are vanishingly rare. You've probably got a better chance of being hit by a rhino or a Reliant Robin – or both simultaneously. However, if you *do* want to minimize the already-remote chances of an attack, understanding how sharks behave near beaches would be a good place to start.

You get the most movement in the oceans around dawn and dusk, as the shift from night to day, and from day to night, produces a hazy twilight that is the perfect time for many predators to hunt, especially sharks. Coastal sharks, such as tigers, blacktips and lemon sharks, cruise up and down a beach, parallel to the shoreline. As the Sun rises higher, they tend to move further offshore onto reefs and better hunting grounds. Swimming close to the surf line allows a shark to trap potential prey between itself and the shallow water of the beach; usually, it slowly cruises past several times to assess the target before striking. This behaviour also ensures that any carrion washed in with the tide can be devoured before it is dumped out of reach on the sand.

You might think that the nets used to protect bathers on at-risk beaches are meant to prevent sharks from approaching. Well, they are – though not by putting up a barrier but by killing them. The wide-mesh nets are designed to trap, and eventually drown, sharks, though there is also a huge bycatch, including many whales and dolphins. Erecting barriers perpendicular to the shore would disrupt sharks' natural hunting pattern and could be a much better deterrent than the long walls of death currently used by local authorities that have little understanding of how sharks actually behave.

Common cuttlefish: ink but no stink

You may only know this animal from its remains – the cuttlebone – washed up on the beach, but its original owner, the common cuttlefish, is a cephalopod mollusc, related to octopuses and squid, and an intelligent and calculating hunter of the coastal shallows.

The cuttlebone is a large structure made of calcium carbonate that runs down the back of the cuttlefish's mantle cavity. This slab was once, in the distant evolutionary past, the animal's shell, but it has since migrated beneath the skin and is now used as a buoyancy aid. Filled with tiny chambers, the cuttlefish can control the amount of gas in the cuttlebone and float motionless in the water as needed. The cuttlebone may be all you'll see on the beach, but go out into the surf of a fertile, calm bay and you can find these animals hunting in the shallow weeds and rocks. Like a squid, the cuttlefish has eight arms and two elastic feeding tentacles, but it is stockier and not so streamlined, and doesn't perform such great feats of long-distance swimming. It uses two long fringing mantle fins to hover and scoot around, relying on its siphon for propulsion only when escaping predators, at which point it usually jets a squirt of ink too.

Those of you in the know may have noticed that the Latin name of the cuttlefish genus – *Sepia* – is the same as the tone/filter available on many phone cameras. In fact, cuttlefish ink was first used as a writing pigment by the ancient Romans and Greeks, whose word for 'cuttlefish' was '*sepia*'. Still, the way the cuttlefish uses its own ink is much more fun. A squirt of ink not only creates a cloud of black in the water column, allowing the animal to disappear into the murk; but it contains analgesic chemicals, like those that numb your throat when you have a cough sweet. These chemicals numb the chemosensors of an attacking predator, preventing it from smelling its way back to the retreating cuttlefish. In some cases, loose iridiophores (metallic iridescent colour cells found in the skin) are also ejected with the ink, causing sparkles of light that further confuse and distract a predator.

A water snake that eats crabs: the crab-eating water snake

The intertidal mangroves and swamps of the tropics provide a livelihood for aquatic animals that have managed to crawl from the sea and take up residence, but they are also excellent places for terrestrial animals to get their feet wet ... well, if they have feet. One particularly cool hunter is the crab-eating water snake, which lives and hunts in the tropical mangroves and shallow coastal waters of South-East Asia and northern Australia.

Crab-eating water snakes do what you might expect them to do – they eat crabs – but this is actually no mean feat for an animal without feet (or limbs). Fiddler, ghost and mud crabs all feature on the menu, and each one has the potential to deliver a nasty nip to delicate eyes or tongues. There is even evidence that larger crabs may attack the snakes as a potential food source, so size certainly matters in the mangroves. The crab-eating snake is rear-fanged and its venom is mild but strong enough to paralyse the targeted crustacean. Hunting at night and often catching a crab in its burrow, the snake has a strong bite, which is needed to penetrate the tough shell and deliver its venom. Once the crab has been incapacitated, the snake attempts to eat it, but is restricted in what it can swallow by the size of its gaping mouth. So the snake secures the crab by pressing it down into the mud with its body; then it shreds it, pulling off legs and claws, or – in the case of soft, newly moulted crabs – using its sharp teeth and mobile jaws to saw off chunks of flesh.

The sea lizards of the Galápagos

Aquatic lizards are pretty thin on the ground . . . and in the water. Turtles, terrapins and crocodiles are dominant in tropical freshwater habitats, while sea turtles have mastered the oceans, along with a few crocs that enjoy the beach life. However, there is another reptile that has managed to take advantage of the plenty to be found in the shallow coastal waters: the marine iguana.

Reaching an impressive 1.5 metres (in the case of males – females are slightly smaller), marine iguanas live on the warm tropical islands of the Galápagos, but feed in the relatively cold waters that rise from the south. Heat is obviously a serious issue for reptiles – they are ectothermic (cold-blooded), which means that they rely on the Sun to give them the energy they need to function. That's not a problem when you're basking on rocks, but a pretty big issue when you're being smashed by bloody cold salt water. Quite a surprise, then, to learn that these lizards feed on the wave-drenched rocks of the shore, furiously grazing on the red and green algae that grow there. Powerful muscles and sharp claws give them great purchase on the wet stone, but still they keep one eye on the waves to ensure they are not battered by an incoming breaker.

Even more surprising is that some larger iguanas actually take to the water on purpose. Usually diving to 1 to 5 metres (though occasionally as deep as 15 metres), they feed on the algae that is thicker and more abundant beneath the waves. It seems to be only large males that engage in this behaviour, probably because their greater body size allows them

Marine iguana

to withstand the cold water for longer and to avoid becoming so chilled that they are unable to climb out again. Even a dive of a few minutes can drop the body temperature by 10°C or more. Once a dive has been completed, the lizard has a good break, basking in the hot sun to warm up and reaching an optimum 36°C, before jumping back in and starting all over again.

The killer croc of the coast

The largest of all living reptiles – a true dinosaur if ever you saw one – the saltwater crocodile can grow up to 7 metres in length and weigh over a tonne. Like other crocs, the saltie is a consummate predator and can eat whatever it can overpower (they also represent a real danger to any human who wanders too close). Found on the coasts of northern Australia and throughout Indonesia, in coastal lagoons, mangroves, estuaries and even sandy beaches, these crocodiles are excellent swimmers and have been sighted far out at sea, travelling between islands or accessing different beaches. They can cruise at 3–5 kilometres an hour, but move much faster as they burst forward towards prey. They are essentially ambush predators, and most animals they attack won't know much about it: when those massive jaws slam shut, with the most powerful bite on the planet, it is pretty much all over. Once caught, the prey is quickly dragged underwater, where it is drowned before being ripped apart and consumed.

There can be few other coastal predators that have such a powerful effect on the populations around them, on land and sea alike. A saltwater crocodile is as much a threat to a buffalo as it is to a shark, and will prey on monkeys living in mangrove trees as readily as it will the large crabs that live beneath them. Right at the top of the food chain, you could argue that the saltwater crocodile is actually *the* top predator of the shoreline. While sharks might take fish or seabirds from the shallows, and orcas can breach to catch a sea lion, only a saltie is going to follow you from sea to land and back again.

Cracking the coast

Coming back to land to breed remains a necessity for seabirds. Even albatrosses, which spend the rest of their lives on the oceans, have to lay an egg somewhere dry at some point. So when seabirds do get together, they can have a truly dramatic effect on the coast: they change landscapes, and even create new ones, all because of their need to be safe during the vital breeding season.

Puffins are small seabirds that lay a single egg and are very vulnerable to predators. So when they come together to breed on exposed cliff tops, they dig burrows down into the soil, often using the same burrow year after year. These burrows provide protection not only for the egg, but also for the adult puffin, which can easily take cover from large predatory gulls or skuas. Puffins are so hyperactive in their tunnelling that they are sometimes responsible for serious erosion and landslips, causing whole sections of costal cliffs to fall into the sea.

Whether birds dig burrows or just nest directly on the sand, their colonies have an impact on the land they inhabit, bringing vital biological productivity from the ocean to the land and shore. Many small islands in the South Pacific would be barren rock without the regular return of nesting seabirds. The influx of guano, feathers, shells, dirt, dust and dead bodies provides a fibrous and nutritious base for any seeds caught in feathery plumage or carried to an island by the wind or waves. Once plants begin to establish themselves, the island ecosystem can start to grow. In seabird colonies in the coastal regions of the northern landmasses, eggs and defenceless chicks become prime targets for animals such as Arctic foxes, and without this seasonal bloom, the foxes' own cubs would struggle and die.

Beaks on the beach

The interface between water and land is an area of astonishing biodiversity, with a huge range of rich pickings to be had in and on the sand and mud. Among those that take advantage of this feast are the wading birds of the shoreline. Found on coasts throughout the world, many different species of waders are specially adapted to exploit a whole array of different feeding opportunities.

Wading birds generally have long, thin, featherless legs, which allow them (you've guessed it) to wade, happily moving through a range of different bodies of water with different sediments, on mudflats and in tide pools and sandy shallows. Probably the most distinctive characteristic of waders is the beak. Take a look at the curlew, sandpiper, oystercatcher and knot, and you'll see that their beaks are all markedly different in shape. This variety may seem strange – after all, many of these bird species are found together foraging on exactly the same stretches of shoreline – but actually it is the perfect way to exploit the full bounty of the beach. Each beak is suited to a different type of prey, so the curlew, with its long, thin, curved bill, can prey on worms and invertebrates deep down in the sediment, while the sturdy, short bill of the knot is used to strike open the valves of small molluscs and to crack the shells of crustaceans. With such a diverse cast of characters, the waders are the real winners when it comes to picnicking on the beach.

Pink posers of the Caribbean

Not all wading birds are drably camouflaged, and in the Caribbean there is a famous wading bird that really struts its stuff! In low-lying coastal areas, salt lagoons and brackish lakes can form. Filled by the ocean only on the highest of tides, these large pools become isolated ecosystems. In the tropics, the Sun bakes down on these bodies of water, and evaporation soon causes the salinity to skyrocket, creating a hostile environment for nearly all life. However, a warm, salty lake with seemingly no predators is too good an opportunity to pass up, and small amphipods, polychaete worms and brine flies take advantage while they can. Although predatory fish may not be present, predatory birds certainly are, and of these the flamingo is the most lethal.

Moving smoothly through sediments and shallow water on its long legs and webbed feet, the bird uses its long neck to reach down and sweep large areas of the surface water. The downturned beak has rows of fine keratinized plates within, which act like a sieve to strain out potential prey from the water. Flamingos graze over vast areas of the lakes, swinging their heads from side to side and using their tongue to pump water in and out of the beak at a serious rate, five or six times a second. It's just as well, as a Caribbean flamingo need to consume around 32,000 brine fly chrysalids, or 50,000 larvae, a day!

Flamingos are known for their bright-pink plumage, but they don't actually start out that way. They only turn pink by consuming a natural dye called canthaxanthin, which is found in the bodies of brine shrimp and other planktonic organisms they feed on. The coloration probably plays a part in courtship, as a very pink flamingo would have to be one that had fed very well indeed, therefore making it a good choice as a potential mate.

Murder on the beach

The coast will always play a vital role in the lives of those marine animals that retain an unbreakable link with the land. Pinnipeds such as seals and sea lions, for instance, still need a beach and dry land to give birth

Sea lion

to their young. This can sometimes give their pups a great start in life, as young born on remote islands may come into the world in the absence of large land predators. However, danger is never far away.

Southern sea lions that congregate on the isolated beaches of Patagonia have been subjected to an incredible, but deadly, predatory behaviour. Just at the time when the pups are starting to bulk up and have begun swimming in the shallow waters skirting the beach, a pod of orcas (killer whales) arrives. It is the same pod that appears year after year, and they have developed a unique hunting tactic especially for the occasion. Needless to say, any sea lion out in deep water in the presence of an orca is dead meat, but surely a pup playing in the shallow surf must be safe from these 8-metre-long, 6-tonne beasts? Not so: these orcas have learned that by rushing the beach at great speed and catching a wave where possible, they can aquaplane right up into the shallows and grab a seal, even if it means beaching themselves in the process. Once there, the massive mammal thrashes around in an attempt to get back to the water and refloat itself. It's damned risky behaviour that takes younger members of the pod many years to learn, but it's worth all the effort, as it means they can bag themselves an otherwise inaccessible meal. The bonanza doesn't last long, though, and soon the pups are fully weaned, the orcas move on, and the breeding colony disappears back into the sea.

Northern beach bums

Walruses spend most of their time hunting along the coastal ice floes of the extreme north and have adapted well to polar life. One handy adaptation is the extraordinary blubber layer and thick skin which protect them from the cold. Shutting down blood vessels and capillary beds in the outermost layers of the body helps reduce heat loss, but it leaves the animal looking very pale, and even white in the coldest conditions. After a winter of hardship, when temperatures rise and the ice begins to melt, walruses can no longer haul themselves out on sea

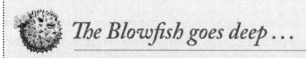

The Blowfish goes deep ...

BEACHING WHALES

Of all the animal stories that appear in the news, few arouse greater interest and anxiety than cetacean strandings. It doesn't matter if it is the beaching of a single individual or a mass stranding of hundreds of animals, such events always cause great concern among the public. But why would a whale or dolphin beach in the first place? These animals are excellent navigators: how do they get it so wrong?

Well, the truth is that there are plenty of theories and no one knows for sure. Taking human influence out of the equation, beaching may occur when an animal is weak or dying – a natural occurrence that has always happened (and an important event for coastal scavengers and land predators alike). One possible danger is that an old or weak animal might lead others into trouble: the leader of a pod might become sick and wander off course, taking the healthy pod members with it; or the healthy members might attempt to help a weakened animal that strays into danger and become stranded too. Another theory is based on the fact that particular beaches around the world are associated with multiple stranding and beaching events; it is suggested that the local geology of these beaches may somehow confuse a cetacean's navigation system, leading it to think a bay is deeper than it actually is or that there is a clear passage through it.

Then there are factors that involve human agency. Apart from obvious problems such as entanglement in fishing gear and pollution, naval sonar is often brought into the picture. Some researchers claim that high-powered sonar used to map oceans or search for submarines may damage the sonar abilities of whales and dolphins, or even cause them to panic and swim into shallow waters. Exactly how or why all this might occur is not clear, so more study is needed.

Whatever the explanation, the sad reality is that stranding events rarely have happy endings. While some animals do make it back out to sea with or without human help, for others the beach becomes their final resting place.

ice, so they seek isolated beaches instead. The summer is a perfect time to relax and soak up some sun, so as the walrus's body temperature rises, the external blood vessels open up again and the whole animal turns bright pink! There's no better time for walruses to rid themselves of that scabby layer of year-old skin, so they now spend much of their time rubbing themselves on just about any hard surface they can find, from their neighbours' tusks to the gravel and shingle beneath them. Moulting is doubly important for male walruses, as it allows them not only to get rid of harmful skin-feeding parasites but also to look their best for the ladies.

Foraging for rockpool riches

When the tide recedes, a real feast of animals is left behind on the rocks. Snails and other molluscs clamber over seaweeds, crabs and blennies scuttle around in pools, and occasionally you get a real bonus when a small octopus or even a shark's egg is stranded. For me, nothing beats getting your head down, bum up, and searching for all the cool critters you can find trapped in and around rockpools. But I'm not the only one who likes these wonderful environments: there are many other animals that make daily excursions to the coast when the tide is low, to take a chance on this seashore 'lucky dip'. And – unlike me – these foragers don't practise catch-and-release.

In the northern United States, coastal racoons regularly patrol the beaches, using their highly sensitive hands to 'feel' for a meal. Their sense of touch is so refined that they can detect the difference between a rough pebble and a ridged clam shell without even looking. Racoons are also adapted to deal with cold temperatures, so they can plunge their paws into the chilly salt waters for minutes on end without losing sensitivity. A bit of intelligence goes a long way too. Cape baboons on the Cape Peninsula in South Africa spend a great deal of time searching in rockpools at low tide. Here, learning how to deal with armoured crabs or spiny sea urchins is key to getting a good feed, so younger members of the troop watch and learn while the older, more experienced monkeys go about their business.

Feeding behaviours like this provide a vital link between otherwise isolated food chains, allowing the rich productivity of the oceans to find its way into the flora and fauna of the land.

Brown bears on the beach

The highly fecund ecosystems of the temperate shoreline attract many terrestrial visitors: after all, there is quite a feast to be had on the coast if you know what you're looking for – or sometimes, what you're smelling for.

In Alaska, the massive brown bear is in a race against time to eat, fight, mate and sleep, all before another harsh winter comes along. Bears are famous for snaring fish during the salmon run, but they are also among the world's great opportunists and can sniff out a meal anywhere. Along the Katmai coast, before the salmon arrive, bears start to gather. Every day the large tides uncover great expanses of beach that hide a tasty bounty. Burrowing bivalves, such as soft-shelled clam, Alaskan surf clam and Nuttall's cockle, are all found in the damp sand, just waiting for the tide to return. Bears are known to pace over the beach, head low, sniffing out the bivalves from beneath the wet sand with their super-sensitive snouts. They then dig the shellfish out and seize them in their powerful jaws. At this point, it would be simple enough for these huge bears to eat the whole damned thing, but many don't, preferring to use their hefty 10-centimetre-long claws, with surprising dexterity, to prise open the shell and eat only the flesh within. This high-protein seafood diet is perfect for the bears, as it means they can stay close to where the salmon run will start and saves them from having to resort to vegetation in their efforts to bulk up.

Coastal Seas

Head out from the beach, through the shallows and away from the shore, and you enter a world of vibrant change and fascinating interplay. Before the ocean expands into the infinite blue, there is a zone packed with life, from the tops of the waves to the rocks below: it is the coastal zone of temperate seas. They are filled with an unrivalled energy, and they form a habitat where every possible niche is contested.

To be more technical, the area we're talking about is located between the very low water mark, where the tide never exposes the world beneath, all the way out to the edge of the continental shelf, where the earth below plunges away down to the true ocean depths. These wide and relatively shallow waters offer a fertile environment for life to thrive. Here, winds and storms can churn everything up, disrupting the tempering effects of deeper water but in the process stirring up nutrients and ensuring that most organisms can freely travel from the bottom to the surface, according to need. It is in these coastal seas, too, that globally important events such as the spring plankton bloom occur, sparking a chain of events essential to the health of the whole planet.

The rich and productive coastal zones are home to some of the largest and most awe-inspiring animals ever to evolve on planet Earth, from predators to planktonic feeders. Size isn't everything, though, and the drive to survive has created a plethora of evolutionary marvels which inhabit even the smallest nooks and crannies. Indeed, at the bottom of the green waters we find biological cities covering the sands and sediments. Here, on the cold-water reefs and seaweed-dominated floor, a mystical world lives its life mostly hidden from our eyes.

The coastal seas were, for obvious reasons, the watery places that humankind first started to explore and exploit. They offered not only great shoals of fish, harvested for the table, but the water needed for industry. They became great trading and transport routes, as vessels preferred to hug the shores – despite the threats of rocks and sandbanks – rather than risk the vastness of the ocean beyond. No wonder, given the coastal seas' importance and bounties, that people soon claimed them as their own, and these waters became 'territorial' – objects of competition.

Inevitably, the coastal seas have suffered not only use but abuse. But gradually, as science has grown wise to the delicate balance of marine ecosystems, and observed how the essential components of healthy and diverse oceans can be observed in even the smallest creature, there has been greater enlightenment. With that knowledge and huge efforts, our closest shallow seas have proved easier to protect than the distant high seas; and where countries have shown a dedication to the cause, life has made a startling comeback. Today, the temperate seas surely provide a template for how resilient the waters of the world truly can be.

To look into the rich green coastal waters is to appreciate the beating heart of the world's oceans, as robust as it is delicate, a wonderfully vital place – and a stone's throw from the shore.

A year in the life

The temperate coastal seas are some of the most challenging environments in which any animal can make a home. Yet here we find some of the greatest variety and biodiversity thanks to the constantly shifting pattern of the seasons. Let's spin through a year and see how it goes.

Winter brings its raging storms and howling winds. These may not seem like a good thing, but they are, for they help to churn up the water column, bringing nutrients into the shallow waters. Winter is merciless, too, as waves smashing against the shore strip away weaker animals and algae that have attempted to make a home there, scouring the stones and rocks for the season to come.

In spring, as the waves die down and the Sun stays in the sky long enough to heat the water, a thermocline appears in the ocean. This barrier between warmer and colder water keeps the surface waters stable, allowing phytoplankton to bloom in such numbers that whole swathes of the planet can be seen turning green. In turn, the phytoplankton bloom unleashes a mad rush of aquatic life, and everything from sardines to whales to copepods starts to eat as much as possible. This is also a pretty good time to breed, if you can get your eggs and larvae into the water column in time for them to make the most of the bounty while it lasts.

The early summer brings longer days, but the larder starts to empty. As the thermocline gets stronger and stronger, and the deep nutrient-rich waters can no longer resupply the shallows, the phytoplankton bloom starts to dry up, as grazers take their toll. Seaweeds and other photo-synthesizing organisms make the most of the sun, however, and grow as much as they can before 'breeding' towards the end of the season.

Enter autumn, and as the sun weakens and bad weather starts to ruffle the oceans, there's a resurgence of the phytoplankton – just not as impressive a bloom as in the spring. This is also the time when many creatures that have spent the spring and summer feeding in the plankton begin a different lifestyle, attached to rocks (like barnacles) or perhaps settling on the bottom (such as crabs or flatfish). And finally, when winter approaches, the encroaching storms and low light toss the plankton around so much that no decent blooms can form. Larger fish species tend to migrate offshore into calmer, deeper waters, whereas smaller ones might find wrecks or reefs to shelter in until the Sun starts to rise sufficiently again in spring. And so it goes on, the waterwheel of the temperate shallow seas.

Sea of green: phytoplankton

The deep green seas around northern Europe and the UK might not have quite the tourist-brochure appeal of the clear blue of the tropics, but that characteristic hue is because they are stuffed with life. Such coastal seas are the workhorses of the ocean, thanks to tiny green organisms called phytoplankton.

Like plants (but not plants as we know them), phytoplankton take in carbon dioxide, produce oxygen, and in the process make edible sugars for themselves. They also come in a staggering array of different shapes and types, though they are dominated mainly by diatom and coccolithophore varieties. Both types build 'tests', the hard shells that protect their cellular structures – the diatoms favour silica for the job, whereas the coccolithophores use calcium. As these algae multiply and grow, the tests are shed and slowly sink to the seabed below, where over time they are accumulated into the fossil history, eventually producing such geological marvels as the White Cliffs of Dover.

Phytoplankton's rapid growth and extravagant consumption of CO_2 are critical for Earth's climate. We have phytoplankton to thank for giving us most of the oxygen we breathe, as well as for trapping carbon dioxide and eventually sinking it to the bottom of the ocean. This 'carbon sequestration' is a fundamental element in balancing the greenhouse gases in our atmosphere.

Greedy grazers: zooplankton and copepods

The world has rules. Where there's muck there's brass, where there's grass there are grazers, and where there's phytoplankton there's zooplankton.

While phytoplankton are the primary producers of the ocean's food chains, zooplankton (meaning 'animal plankton') are the primary consumers. Everything from fish eggs to arrow worms, from barnacle larvae to jellyfish – all are zooplankton. There are so many different kinds of zooplankton that predator–prey relationships even develop among them: in other words, they eat each other. Zooplankton that spend all their life within the plankton are known as holoplankton, while those that spend only part of their life cycle floating in this mad mass of marine life are meroplankton. Both play a critical role in managing the overall abundance of phytoplankton and, therefore, in phytoplankton's effect on the climate.

Copepods are a good example of holoplankton, spending their entire lives feverishly creating feeding currents to trap the smaller diatoms and other phytoplankton in a one-way trip to their mouths. Indeed, they feed and breed so successfully that, uninhibited, they'd soon completely outstrip all the photosynthesizing members of the plankton. Now that would be a real downer for us oxygen-breathers on land! Thankfully, it would be fair to say that nearly everything in the ocean enjoys a good copepod lunch. Salps, jellyfish, fish larvae and fry all target the ever-present copepods and keep the pod population in check. Without this grazing on the grazers, we'd all be in trouble – and fast.

Browns, reds and greens: multi-talented macroalgae

Choose crispy seaweed in a Chinese restaurant and it will not only be crispy but vibrantly green. But the seaweeds in the sea are not always green (or crispy – and for that matter, crispy seaweed isn't even seaweed). In reality, shades of brown and red also define these much-maligned macroalgae.

The brown seaweeds, including kelp and bladderwrack, are usually found in colder waters, where nutrients are plentiful and seas can be rough. It is for this reason that their holdfasts (the tendrils they use to attach to the rocks) tend to be highly developed and very strong. Being brown allows them to maximize the spectrum of light they absorb, ensuring they can exploit areas of low light and/or great turbidity. Green seaweeds tend to look more grass-like and include species such as sea lettuce and gutweed; they grow rapidly, so a profusion of them can indicate too many nutrients in marine systems. The green ones are also usually soft and tasty and a major target for grazing creatures, which is a good thing too, because fast-growing hair algae can quickly swamp reefs and rocks, snuffing out other slower-growing life.

Finally, you have the red seaweeds, such as dulse or Irish moss. These venerable algae are the most ancient of the lot, and were probably around 1.25 billion years ago. They colonize and exploit any surface they can find, in any way they can. Some species deposit calcium carbonate, just like corals or shell-dwelling molluscs do, in a process that is still poorly understood. The reds are critical for the establishment and health of cold-water reefs, because of their slow deposition of limestone.

Seaweed – slimy and clingy? Maybe, but amazing and important all the same.

Giant kelp: gargantuan grower

Famed for its great abundance along the western coast of America, all the way up to Alaska, giant kelp could easily be one of the fastest-growing organisms on the planet. Its rapid growth rate has made it vitally important to the oceans – and more than a little useful for humankind too. But how fast are we talking? The answer is so fast that you could probably *see* it grow, as it puts on 60 centimetres a day to reach an overall length of up to 50 metres.

This astonishing growth requires plenty of sunlight and is helped by the fact that kelp lives in nutrient-rich waters. By definition, such waters tend to be more turbid, with some intense wave action, so to keep itself aloft giant kelp has small gas-filled bladders on each of its blades. At its

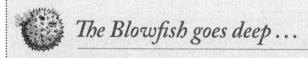

The Blowfish goes deep . . .

CASCADE TO CATASTROPHE? WHY KELP NEEDS SEA OTTERS

Giant kelp grows super fast, but that doesn't make it invulnerable. In fact, looked at another way it's a prime target for disaster. In recent years, poor water conditions in El Niño years have brought about the decimation of some kelp forests at the hands – or rather the mouths – of sea urchins, which feast on the seaweed's holdfasts, destabilizing the algae until eventually they are ripped away. The urchins are also partial to new kelps just beginning to grow. The result of this urchin all-you-can-eat banquet can lead to a trophic cascade.

'Trophic' refers to the position that any living organism holds in the food chain, so simple food chains have few trophic levels, such as grass/cow/human. Complex food chains have many trophic levels, and this means more species, greater diversity and all-round better ecological health. A change in just one single factor can greatly disrupt things. In the case of giant kelp, the first trophic cascade occurred when a keystone species, the sea otter, was hunted for its pelt back in the days of the fur trade. Sea otters loved to feast on sea urchins, thus controlling their population; as the otters disappeared, the urchins went rampant and gorged on the kelp. Then, the loss of the kelp meant the loss of many other species, leading to a complete breakdown in the ecosystem and the formation of very low-energy urchin barrens. Recovery began with the reintroduction of sea otters, which started to gobble up the urchins again, with the benefits being felt by the kelp, which, once returned, allowed many other species to re-establish.

Nowadays, although the becalmed waters during an El Niño event are a danger to kelp, there's another looming threat in the shape of orcas (killer whales). As the orcas' normal fishy prey disappear from the ocean, they are beginning to look more and more to sea otters as their lunch and dinner. Indeed, predation by orcas is just as effective as the actions of the old fur trappers, and great urchin barrens are starting to take hold again in the Pacific North-West.

base is its holdfast – as close to a root as you'll get with algae – gripping the rock like a hand and chemically bonding with it to provide the kelp with powerful support, as the waves and currents buffet it above.

Thanks to its turbocharged growth rate and large size, giant kelp has long been harvested for food; but, as more and more is learned about the magical properties of macroalgae, its uses have multiplied, and today you can find kelp as a binding agent in chemical processes and appearing in biofuels.

Snarfing through a sieve, or how to filter-feed

Life at sea is, for much of the time, the art of feeding – and one of the most effective, but hardly classy, methods is filter-feeding. Hugely successful among ocean creatures large and small, it's a method unique to the aquatic world and one so brilliantly simple that it cannot fail.

Let's begin with the obvious. The first thing you need is . . . a filter. In creatures such as barnacles or the seaweed-encrusting sea mats (bryozoans), this comes from external body modifications, which, in these two cases, are feathered, hairy limbs and dedicated feeding appendages respectively. The filter, regardless of type, can then be waved or wafted into a column of water, capturing whatever microscopic food can be found there. Not all filters are on the outside of the body, though. Salps, or sea squirts, are the masters of the inhalation method: cilia associated with the gills beat to draw water into the body, which passes through a net-like mucus-coated structure called the pharyngeal basket, trapping anything edible in the sticky film, ready to be consumed.

Fish are pretty good filter-feeders too, having fine rake-like structures in front of their gills to collect particles. These gill-rakers are most prominent and developed in dedicated plankton-feeders such as herring. Fishy filter-feeders have a great advantage over the barnacle or sea squirt in that they can move in search of new and better feeding grounds. Sometimes this means just following a nutrient-rich front that has formed in the water column; at other times, it can mean great migrations to chase the seasonal plankton blooms in higher latitudes.

At the very top end of these diners are the various species of filter-feeding baleen whales. With perhaps rather worse table manners than other filter-feeders, they take huge great mouthfuls of ocean, before sieving the water out and retaining any prey caught up in the process. In their case, baleen, a unique material resembling thick, strong feathers, lines the rim of the whales' mouths and acts as the filter.

Sex and death: the jello-pocalypse!

You may not think that often about jellyfish. But don't be sniffy about them: they could wipe you out. Primitive creatures they may be, but they have the power to cause an oceanic apocalypse.

Here's how. If we take the standard moon jellyfish – about as widespread as a jellyfish can get – and describe a day in its life, the population expansion is truly terrifying. Jellyfish split via a process called fission, and they do it *once a day* under the right conditions. So, the adult population has a daily chance to double its numbers. But that's not all. Before they split, most jellyfish will have been able to breed, sending out millions, even billions of eggs and sperm into the water. This happens every day in summer, assuming the conditions are right.

Just follow one fertilized egg on its journey, and you'll see how the possibilities of Armageddon unfold. A fertilized egg, or planula, can swim thanks to cilia on its outer surface, and it motors along until it finds a decent surface to settle on. Once attached, it transforms into a scyphistoma, which is a polyp much like an anemone, and it uses its stinging tentacles to start feeding from the passing water. This polyp is nomadic too. It travels over the rockface using its sticky flat disc of a foot, and as it wanders some of its cells get torn off in a process called pedal laceration. Wherever this flesh is left, there grows a brand-new polyp! And we're not done yet. Next, after winter has died down and spring is coming, all these polyps undergo strobilation or budding, a process whereby the polyp starts to look like a large stack of tyres. In fact, these tyres are brand-new baby jellyfish, and each one will bud off in turn. Some polyps produce fifteen to thirty jellyfish this way, each one with the chance to reach adulthood and start the rampant reproduction cycle all over again.

OK, they breed like crazy. But why would that threaten the world? The reason is that if too big a bloom of jellyfish were to occur – and rising temperatures combined with crashing fish stocks are ever favouring the jellyfish – they could hoover up so much plankton that they disrupt the amount of carbon dioxide consumed in the ocean. The result? Increased greenhouse gases and a sped-up global meltdown of ice. And it could be fast. Realistically, one *very* good jellyfish year could mean curtains for us.

Aquatic architect: the sand mason worm

Gardeners, anglers and schoolboys may love them, but worms in general have a muddy, slimy, not-so-hot reputation. But in the oceans, and especially in the shallow coastal seas, worms have evolved a staggering array of forms, all of which play key roles in the oceanic ecosystem. Some aquatic worms have even created structures to protect and support them as they feed on the plankton, living in tubes built from mucus and from sediments such as sand or silt. The honeycomb worm is a prime example, and its large colonies can be found attached to rocks in such numbers that they look like reefs.

However, the top prize in architecture has to go to the sand mason worm. This fine fellow builds a truly amazing tube from sand, silt, stones and shell fragments. The worm begins by seeking out potential building materials with its long sticky feeding tentacles, which are then retracted and repurposed to create the single vertical tube. The attention to detail and size of particle is impeccable. Put a tubeless sand mason worm into an aquarium filled with differently coloured and variously sized materials (e.g. big blue sand, small red shingle, yellow shell pieces), and you will see a most colourful yet clearly structured tube develop.

They're filter-feeders, too. At the top of the tube is an outcrop of small thin branches, which are always orientated at right-angles to the current. They slow the water, so that edible particles start to fall out of suspension onto the sticky tentacles that the sand mason lays along these branches.

Superpowered super-soakers: sponges

The simple sponge, a staple of the kitchen, the bathroom and the ocean, is easily overlooked. You might find it hard to get excited about sponges, but they're much more interesting than you'd imagine. For a start, they've probably been around for countless millions of years, as one of the first large, multi-celled creatures ever to exist on Earth: that says something about their durability. They have one overriding job, which is to pump seawater through their bodies, extracting whatever edible particles they can find. But they achieve it in two very impressive ways.

First, the filtering process is itself highly effective. A sponge's most active cell is a collar cell (choanocyte), with a long tail-like flagellum that whips water into a minute current. Put enough of these collar cells together and you have a very strong current indeed. Moreover, the tails of the collar cell are ringed with microvilli, the small cellular extensions that give the cell its high-collared appearance. It is these microvilli that extract potential food particles from the passing water and absorb them into the cell, where they are then processed and the nutrients shared with nearby associated cells.

Second, and despite appearances, a sponge is always moving, its cells constantly shifting position to allow for maximum water movement through the body's channels. Some amazing time-lapse footage has revealed how sponges shift and twist to ensure they remain at full filter-feeding tempo at all times. This ability also happens to bring with it a kind of superpower. If you take three distinct and separate sponges, whizz them up in a blender, and pour the resulting soup into an aquarium you'd have quite a mess; but, given time, the three individual sponges will gradually re-form from their original cells.

The truth is that sponges are not passive blobs, but extremely active and even deadly predators – certainly to plankton.

Sea squirts: our long-lost cousins?

You could be forgiven for assuming that nothing is more alien to the evolution of the human race than the weird aquatic filter-feeding bags we call sea squirts. So it may come as a shock that you're actually rather closely related to them. Tunicates, to give them their proper name, belong to the phylum Chordata, which contains all animals that have a backbone and dorsal nerve cord at some stage of life – and that includes you.

Sea squirts can exist singly or in colonial growths, or as free-swimming colonies: salps. The single units can be extremely striking in colour, ranging from dark purples and orange to vibrant, iridescent blues, and their bodies contain many organs that we humans possess. OK, we may not have the sea squirt's large inhalant siphon, which draws water down into the pharyngeal basket and filters out the edible particles. But in a sea squirt you'll find a heart, stomach, intestines, gonads and an anus. This last voids into the exhalant chamber, where waste is removed along with the outflowing water. Colonial sea squirts have a very similar body plan, except they share a common exhalant siphon, while free-floating salps abandon the exhalant siphon altogether, instead just pumping water through their tube-like bodies.

Sea squirts create new sea squirts by means of budding and sexual reproduction, and some species have a larval stage resembling a tadpole. It is the larvae that possess the defining feature of all chordates: a very basic spine known as a notochord. It's bizarre to think that larvae which appear extremely animal-like should somehow end up as the multi-coloured fleshy blobs with two big holes we call sea squirts.

Armed with harpoons: sea anemones

You're never likely to find any anemones in the fossil record – their soft boneless bodies have made sure of that. But you can bet your life that 'nems (as we aquarists like to call them) have been around for as long as their close cousins the jellyfish and corals – and that's a very long time indeed.

Put simply, an anemone is a squishy, fleshy sea sock, a tube open at one end and closed at the other. The open end is the mouth, surrounded by tentacles, and the closed end the foot, or pedal disc, which holds the animal in place or allows it to travel somewhere else. It relies on muscular contraction and relaxation to manage the amount of seawater in its body cavity, and on hydrostatic pressure to give it form. What most people know is that anemones sting, and for this purpose they use their cells called cnidocytes. Now, not all cnidocytes *sting* as such – some are sticky threads that coil round and trap prey. But the big stinger is the nematocyst, which comes in different versions in different species, but has the same single function: kill, and kill quickly!

The cell of the nematocyst is under immense osmotic pressure, enabling it to discharge in two milliseconds or less, firing a barbed harpoon at whatever happens to be in its way. Some types of barb might struggle to get through human flesh, but others can penetrate crab shell: it all depends on what the particular anemone species likes to eat. Once the barb punctures the prey, it latches onto the tissues and holds firm. At this point venom and digestive toxins are released from the barb and its thread, which uncoil inside the prey. At least, for the unfortunate victim, death or paralysis is swift: the delicate-bodied anemone cannot afford to risk being damaged by a wounded prey that thrashes around or fights back in its death throes.

Cloak anemones: high fashion that's just a killer!

If you like anemones, you'll love the amazing cloak anemone. Where will you find it? Intimately entwined around a hermit crab.

The story of this aquatic odd couple starts this way. First, the anemone attaches itself to the appropriated mollusc shell that a hermit crab has adopted as its new home. But over time, the shell is dissolved and the anemone will create new hard armour for the crab. This means that the lucky crab, unlike other non-cloaked hermit crabs, never has to look for a larger shell as it grows, and so there is no chance of it abandoning the cloak anemone in a potential house move. The tentacles of the cloak anemone do not stick out into the water column, but curl underneath the crab, trailing on the seafloor and hanging below the crab's mandibles – in other words, perfectly positioned to collect any food particles dropped from the crab's feeding.

They get along just fine. Indeed, so keen is the anemone to defend its host and its home that when the unlikely pair are threatened, the anemone releases sticky white threads (acontial filaments) through small holes in its column. They're coated in the same stinging cells as the anemone's tentacles, providing a decent deterrent to any small predator that comes too close. The bond between hermit crab and anemone is so tight that you will not find a cloak anemone anywhere else except on the shell – or *as* the shell – of a hermit crab.

Permanent lodger: the immortal bryozoan

At sea as on land, long-term lodgers are known as epiphytes, and they can be any organism that lives or grows on another plant or algae as a means of physical support. Don't get me wrong: they're not parasites, because they don't denude their hosts of anything. They are much more acceptable, and in the marine world many creatures can decide to live as epiphytes, including sea squirts, anemones and hydras. Other examples include polychaete worms living in hard spiral tubes, or growing proud

The Blowfish goes deep . . .

FROM WRECK TO REEF

Humankind has provided its own lodgings for aquatic life, in the form of the countless wrecks littering the watery world. While there are plenty of ships lying at the bottom of the deep ocean, it is the coasts and shallow seas that have claimed the most vessels. Whether running aground on hidden reefs, forced onto the rocks by storms or poor navigation, or sunk in the heat of battle, each shipwreck brings new life to the water.

In the days of wood and sail, ships themselves were a source of food for specialized feeders, including the notorious shipworm. This modified clam, once the scourge of the Royal Navy, can drill so effectively into wooden vessels that it gave Isambard Kingdom Brunel the inspiration for a tunnel-boring shield, allowing for the first tunnel ever built under the Thames. When iron and steel took over from wood, wrecks became more permanent fixtures of the seafloor, enabling great colonies of soft corals to establish themselves, exploiting the wrecks' stability in the shifting sands of the temperate regions. In calmer tropical regions, the detritus of ships offered anchorage to wandering corals seeking a new home, and new reefs could form – and pretty quickly too. The sunken relics of American–Japanese naval warfare from the 1940s are now bright and colourful places of marine diversity. Like the poppy fields of Flanders, the war reefs of the Pacific are vivid examples of how one sort of life emerges from another sort of death.

In terms of fish, we are only just now beginning to understand the importance of wrecks when it comes to commercially important species such as pollack or cod. We know, however, that wrecks provide a sanctuary for small juveniles to grow and develop before joining the main shoals. We know too that wrecks are a great place to hide from large predators such as seals and sharks, and that they provide an added bonus of storm protection during the chaotic winter months.

from the host in leathery stalked colonies. The master of the piggy-backing lifestyle is, however, the tiny bryozoan or sea mat.

Bryozoans establish their squatters' rights on large seaweed fronds, appearing as a thin lace netting. Each chamber is a single animal, barely half a millimetre across. Known as a zooid, it is made up of a protective cover, a stomach, reproductive organs, some simple muscles and an exotic hand-and-mouth combination called a lophophore, which enables it to feed. The lophophore resembles a long tube, ringed at the top with tentacles and in the centre a mouth. It reaches out into the water column, trapping fine edible particles on the mucus of the tentacles, before cilia beat the food down into its mouth. Larger particles are physically transported to the mouth by the tentacles themselves.

Amazingly, the bryozoans seem to have stumbled on a way to cheat death. Although they age and start to break down, rather than just melt away, leaving an empty chamber in the colony, they form a so-called brown body. After a while, the bryozoans are reborn from this brown body, renewed and rejuvenated, ready to take up feeding duties once more.

It's a cod-eat-cod world

When it comes to fish, cod have been important to us since around AD 700, when the Vikings salted and stored them for long winters or traded them with other cultures. They may not seem the most dynamic creatures in the oceans, but in many ways cod is king.

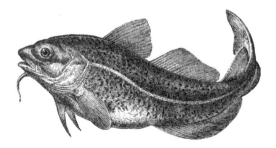

Atlantic cod

Before the overfishing of the North Sea and North Atlantic, cod could reach a metre or more in length and weigh in at more than 10 kilograms: the largest ever landed was very nearly 100 kilograms and almost 2 metres long. You don't get to be that kind of size without having something going for you, and in the case of cod it is its predatory viciousness and dietary unfussiness. Pretty much anything it can get its massive head and mouth around will do. In the case of larger adult cod, this often means smaller fish, including juvenile cod.

For the most part, a cod tends to stick near the bottom of the sea, using the sensory barbel protruding from its chin to search for dinner in the form of crustaceans or molluscs. The fish migrate to find suitable feeding and spawning grounds, with older cod often leading the way. This discovery is important in fisheries management, for if too many large adult cod are removed, the smaller adults can struggle to find the right environment that is critical for the population's survival.

As for mating, cod are as aggressive as any rutting stag. Large males fight for the best territories within the shoal and entice females into breeding, through displays and deep grunting noises. Eggs are spawned and float off into the plankton, but it is three to four years before those babies – at least, the babies that make it that far – rejoin the main school as breeding adults.

Safety in numbers

What's the difference between shoaling and schooling? Is there even a difference? Well, yes there is, and it can mean life or death to the fish involved.

A relatively loose, but still identifiably concentrated group of individuals performing slightly different tasks – feeding, fighting, milling about, etc. – is *shoaling*. Fish more or less doing the same thing but at their own pace – leisurely feeding in the water column or idly grazing on the reefs or rocks – could also be described as shoaling. By contrast, *schooling* is where a group of fish responds as one to the same stimulus, acting like a giant super-creature. Knitting together in a tight ball when threatened by a predator, or synchronized swimming, all at the same speed and in the same direction – both are examples of schooling. Fish can feed in schools, too, as when herring arrange themselves in very specific patterns to catch copepods.

What are the benefits of this highly social behaviour? Put simply, protection of the crowd. Moreover, fish of different species can shoal or school together, in which case you would say it was a school/shoal of *fishes* as opposed to a just one single species, which is then a school/shoal of *fish*.

Humble herring, fantastic farter

What could be humbler than a herring? This ubiquitous fish has been fundamental to the diet and culture of northern Europe for 5,000 years, even longer than the cod. Its meat has been smoked, salted or pickled, and its bones have been invoked to describe a much-loved floor and textile pattern. Relatively small, quick-growing and rapidly reproducing, herring provide good fishing for hungry predators, not least because of their shoaling behaviour and proximity to the coast.

Biologically, the herring is very much your standard fish, but it has evolved some pretty nifty adaptations to counteract the fact that it is everyone's favourite snack. To be great at defensive schooling behaviour, which herring are, requires effective communication. Herring do this in

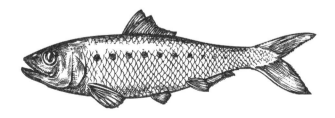

Herring

a truly admirable way: they fart. Their swim-bladder is connected to the lumen of the gut, which means air can be forced out via the anal vent. In this flatulent way, herring can 'talk' to each other and appraise the current situation. For a start, the taste of the fart is critical, since it can express fear at the presence of a predator, and so knit the school more tightly together for protection. Also, if you're going to speak in farts, you'd better have a damned good way of listening, and herring have Weberian ossicles, fused bones that connect the swim-bladder to the inner ear and auditory system. In this way, the swim-bladder acts as a huge amplifier to any pressure waves (i.e. sound), and a herring quickly picks up the latest gastric gossip from its neighbours or the tell-tale sounds from hunting predators.

One more thing that herring have going for them is their tremendous reproductive skills. They can breed in such huge numbers, and reach maturity so quickly, that there's little chance they'll fall off the aquatic menu any time soon.

Into the ring: humpback versus herring

If you're one of the larger ocean predators and you're partial to a bit of herring, you have a number of options. While a small shark or tuna will happily chase and nab a single herring from a shoal, that's not going to work for all the predators, especially if you want a really big portion. Whales and dolphins like herring very much, and some whales have a very effective method of catching literally tonnes of the fish.

Humpback whales adopt a feeding behaviour known as bubble-netting, and it's so successful that it allows each whale to consume more than 2 tonnes of fish each day during the height of the season. Once the whales have located the mass herring shoal, they dive below it, form themselves into a ring and start to blow air out of their blowholes. The air creates a kind of disorientating curtain, and the herring above are too scared to swim through it; instead, the fish school together in the middle of the bubble ring. Now the whales, still exhaling, start to rise, swimming in a spiral towards the surface. The herring, too, are driven upwards, still too scared and confused to attempt to pass through the wall of bubbles. At the last moment, the whales open their mouths and lunge at the concentrated fish ball in one go. Each whale gets a massive mouthful of herring, before they quickly reset themselves to start the process all over again. Bubble-netting doesn't just work on herring: whales and dolphins use it on a wide variety of prey, and it is extremely effective.

Mudwrestling with mullet: bottlenose dolphin

When it comes to problem-solving and hunting, there aren't many food sources that dolphins can't access. They are, after all, generally considered to be pretty smart. One particularly interesting method of fishing can be seen in the habits adopted by bottlenose dolphins in the mudflats off the coast of Florida. These mudflats are too shallow for any bubble-netting, so for the dolphin it's time for Plan B.

The target here is mullet, a famously annoying fish to catch for any human angler; but the bottlenoses have a plan. Working as a pod, they detect and home in on a suitable feeding school of mullet, and then perform a very well-drilled procedure. Upon approaching the group, one dolphin quickly jets away and rapidly swims around the mullet, deliberately stirring up the area's fine sediment in the process. The cloud of mud hides the rest of the oncoming dolphins, but they do not rush blindly through. Now all the dolphins, including the original trailblazer, line up in a row at one side of the mud circle, open their mouths and just wait. The mullet, terrifyingly aware of the predators but totally unable to see them, and completely unwilling to swim through the mud, start to leap up out of the circle, like corn popping out of the pan. And now the dolphins pounce, snatching the desperate mullet out of the air. The mud soon settles and the rest of the mullet escape, so the dolphins re-form for Round 2 – and this time a different leader will make the first, critical move. It's altogether a pretty nifty bit of organization.

Shady sharks in suits

The evolutionary race between predator and prey began at the dawn of time, and its cut and thrust is as dynamic today as ever. One theatre of battle is the effort to make oneself invisible. The coastal seas harbour multi-coloured environments, from brown kelp forests to patchy crimson rocky reefs. This isn't the endless blue of the open oceans, and here the same animal can hunt on the bottom or at the surface and so needs to be adaptable to these different conditions. In the oceans' more dynamic animals, it's often a matter of employing colour-shifting chromatophores to match whatever is around. But even simpler is the counter-shading that most fish employ. From mackerel to mackerel sharks, counter-shading provides very effective methods of both protection and deception, depending on whether you're in the role of predator or prey.

The great white shark is a perfect example. Its top half is a deep blue, but its belly is white, so if you are underneath it and looking up to the bright surface above, the white underside will be indistinct, blending in. Equally, if you're looking down from above onto the shark, its dark blue back will match the deeper waters below. Some fish take counter-shading a step further by actively augmenting it with photophores, special cells that are capable of emitting light. The photophores line the ventral side of the fish and match the radiance of light penetrating from the surface. This literally makes the fish disappear from any prying eyes below.

My greatest love: GWS

By any reckoning, the great white shark (GWS) has to be right up there with the most amazing, wonderful animals on the planet. This stunning creature might give you bad dreams, but it's an ocean *without* them that would be the real nightmare.

Let's list its capabilities. For a start, the GWS has all the skills and advantages that sharks and rays typically have. Its skin is made of dermal denticles – small scales, analogous to teeth, all directed down the body of the animal, which bring great protection and unreal hydrodynamic properties; its sense of smell is acute and can guide it to wounded prey up to 5 kilometres away; its ears and lateral lines are tuned to pick up pressure waves from fin strokes and thrashing of potential prey; and its head is covered in small pores (ampullae of Lorenzini) that detect the minute electrical signals all life produces, and which can guide it across oceans by detecting Earth's magnetism.

Now the GWS starts to ratchet things up a little, for it's the epitome of a top ocean predator and able to do things no other shark can. First there's size. The largest predatory shark on the planet, a female might reach 6 metres in length and weigh in at more than 2 tonnes. Then there's velocity: in bursts, it can reach an attacking speed of nearly 50 kilometres an hour. Like other members of the mackerel shark family, it has specialized blood vessels around the core body muscles, eyes and brain, which keep the most essential parts of the animal functioning at a higher temperature than the surrounding seawater. This allows faster reactions and enables the GWS to travel to higher latitudes and into colder, richer waters looking for prey. And when it comes to prey, naturally enough only the best will do for this super-predator, so adult GWS target blubber-rich seals and other marine mammals.

Seals: marvels of mammal modification

Even though seals are on the great white shark's menu, we needn't feel too sorry for these mammals: they have a great deal going for them. In general, the evolutionary journey out of the sea and onto the land must have been very difficult indeed, and a hard transition to reverse: just try diving into the ocean and see how far you get without fins or scuba kit. And yet numerous mammals have managed to make the journey back into the water and not just survive, but thrive, and seals are a masterful example.

Seals have a huge range of adaptations to allow them to exploit the water below. You often find them in rich seas, which are also cold, so most seals have developed a thick fur coat. The fur helps to trap a layer of air between the cold water and the warm seal body – exactly the same principle as a wetsuit. But the mainstay of a seal's insulation is its thick layer of blubber just beneath the skin, so plentiful that it can be 50 per cent of the animal's full body weight.

Next, seals have flippers, modified feet and paws for propulsion underwater. Some species use primarily the hind-flippers, some favour the fore-flippers, but either way seals are fast and agile enough to chase down fish and outmanoeuvre sharks. To sense danger and target prey both in and out of the water, seals have very large and well-developed eyes: underwater they're tuned to low light conditions with a tapetum lucidum, a reflective layer at the back of the eye, adding to the sensitivity. If conditions are too poor for eyesight, a seal can rely on something else – its vibrissae. These hypersensitive whiskers can pick up the smallest vibrations, since they possess ten times more nerves per whisker than any terrestrial mammal's. Indeed, the vibrissae are so good at their job that they enable some seals to follow in the wake of others in complete darkness.

Finally, at the business end of a seal is its crunching teeth, designed to tuck into crab, oyster, sea urchin, fish and squid. The dentition of something like a crab-eater seal is a wonder to behold – ample evidence that seals are fearsome predators.

Beach birth: the sea turtle

Some animals, while masters of the seas, are still tied to land for critical life stages. This means that even the most ocean-going of them has to come back to the coast at some point to mate, breed or lay eggs. In the case of sea turtles, it's laying eggs, and the outpourings of cute, turtle hatchlings are familiar from many a documentary film.

The basic idea seems simple enough: mate in the water, climb up on land, dig hole, lay eggs, scarper ... and hope that at least one baby makes it to the ocean. However, it's a far more complicated issue and one that is threatened by natural predators and our own constant demands on the planet. The first difficulty lies in the fact that there are two kinds of egg-laying: mass aggregation and the slow-release method. For the former, the whole breeding population of turtles must be in exactly the right place at the right time. Usually at a spring tide, when the Moon is at its fullest, hundreds of egg-carrying females crawl out of the water, drag themselves up a beach, dig a hole and lay as many eggs as possible, before covering the eggs and returning to the sea. These events usually happen over a couple of nights, but the number of turtles can be so great, and good beach space at such a premium, that many buried eggs are dug up by the next expectant mother. The slow-release method, in which turtles come and go over the course of a few weeks rather than arrive en masse, seems a lot calmer by comparison.

These different methods of egg-laying offer different survival strategies to the young hatchlings. Mass laying means that at hatching (usually at a subsequent full moon) so many offspring appear that any predators in the water, or on land, are totally overwhelmed. They can eat till they are full, but the vast majority of baby turtles will still reach the sea. The slow-release method relies on a very different logic for turtle survival. When clutches hatch over a given period, and babies run for the water at night or during the day, there are certainly predators around, but the slow release doesn't attract a constant large threat of massed birds, sharks or crocodiles.

The hazards, however, do not end with turtle-eaters. With sea levels rising, many nesting beaches are started to get flooded, and entire clutches drown. Also, human coastal developments tend to have bright lights, which confuse and attract baby turtles away from the safety of the water. Considering that their survival chances to adulthood are just one in a thousand, baby turtles need every bit of help they can get. At least the cuteness of the sea turtle gives it some pulling power when it comes to the public, and there are now conservation efforts worldwide aimed at protecting beaches that are critical for breeding.

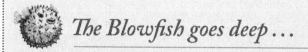

The Blowfish goes deep…

SUICIDE SWIM: THE PACIFIC SALMON

Are salmon the craziest, most self-sacrificing fish on the planet? You might think so, from all the footage showing their desperate struggle to leap upstream, against all odds, to spawn. But such an effort is worthy of profound respect. Of the two sorts of salmon, the Atlantic and the Pacific, the latter has a particularly amazing life cycle, some of which is spent in coastal waters.

All salmon spend their adult lives feeding and growing in the open sea, where they are excellent predators – and a favoured prey for sharks and orcas. When the time comes and the salmon have reached maturity, they return to the freshwater rivers in which they were born to breed. The homing mechanism that enables them to do this still isn't fully understood, but it is most likely a combination of three factors: the phases of the Moon, a form of GPS (thanks to iron deposits in the brain), and a very keen sense of smell. Once the salmon have reached the coast, they gather in holding areas while waiting for rains to swell the rivers and allow them passage upstream. And with the rain, the salmon start to move, entering the rivers as large, well-fed silver-coloured fish; but along their extraordinary riverine journey, they undergo significant physiological changes.

For starters, the salmon now stop feeding and have to contend with being in a freshwater environment, a combination that has the effect of literally eating the salmon alive. It's therefore a race against time to get to the spawning grounds and breed before the adults dissolve away. Male salmon tend to reach the destination first, where they compete with each other for the best spaces. Depending on the species, the males shift colour from silver to a deep red, can grow humps on their backs, and form a hook (kype) on their jaws. As the males settle their differences, the females come along and pick the best spots for laying. A resident male then fertilizes the eggs before a female gently buries them in the gravel. This process occurs throughout all the rivers and streams, with some salmon species travelling 1,500 kilometres to reach their preferred spawning grounds.

Once all the drama is over, 99 per cent of the adult salmon die, and the creatures of the surrounding forests enjoy one hell of a feast. The salmon eggs hatch into alevin, small fry hidden in the gravel but sustained by yolk sacs. When the yolk runs out, the fish emerge to feed as parr, which spend between one and five years growing in the river (depending on species and how well they feed). On reaching a given size, they move further downstream and begin the transformation into adulthood as smolts, grouping together in shoals as they feed and grow in the coastal waters. Eventually, the smolts move away into deeper seas and better feeding grounds, where they develop into full adults. And in four to six years, they will begin the arduous journey back to kick off the deadly procreation process once again.

Big and beautiful: the basking shark

The second-largest fish in the sea and a truly mysterious animal, the basking shark is a wonder of the coastal temperate seas. It can reach up to a massive 12 metres in length – and it is the largest shark in the UK's coastal waters.

These majestic giants appear with the first plankton blooms of spring and swiftly make the most of the edible bonanza, only stopping as the autumn draws in. Unlike its wide-mouthed cousin, the whale shark, the basking shark is much more streamlined, with a long nose and round, cavernous mouth. Its gill slits almost encircle the head, so that, combined with its plankton-stripping gill-rakers, virtually every move catches a mouthful of food with minimum effort. Although it's clear what these huge beasts feed on during the spring and summer months, little is known of their winter lives and habitats. The theory goes that after moving further offshore and heading into deeper waters to avoid storms, they continue to munch on deep-water blooms of plankton in the cold murk.

However, the basking shark has a predator too: man. Being slow, steady and easy to spot, especially at their dinner time, basking sharks have become targets for fisheries keen to harvest their huge livers (for oil) and large fins (for traditional Asian foods). At least the basking shark is now protected in the UK; but elsewhere, the lure of its large fins puts this gentle giant directly in the crosshairs.

Lopsided bottom-feeders: the funny flatfish

Flatfish are sometimes treated as a bit of a joke. From plaice to flounder, brill to dab, these funny-shaped animals look as though they've been trodden on, with their silly upward-pointing eyes and weird mouths. But appearances deceive. When it comes to predators along the ocean floor, you won't find more dangerous characters.

The first thing to know is that they aren't born flat: they hatch out in the plankton, where they look like any other fish larvae. It is only with time that they sink to the bottom and metamorphose into flatfish proper. This happens as one eye (the left or the right, according to species) migrates over the top of the head and establishes itself on the other side of the skull. In effect, flatfish are lying on their sides, and because of this the dorsal and ventral fins are highly developed, stretching the length of the fish's body. Often the first few fin rays of the pelvic/ventral fin are overdeveloped to act like fingers, which can be used to creep along the bottom and dig in the sand for potential prey. The mouth is usually quite large too and can be snapped around prey at great speed; indeed, flatfish will eat anything they can stuff into their mouths, from small fish and shrimps, to large crabs, lobsters and squid. The biggest of all flatfish, the halibut, will happily feed on cod and pollack, and on other flatfish as well.

Owing to their position on the bottom of the ocean, flatfish are amazing at camouflage and have a very well-developed set of chromatophores, which allow them to perfectly mimic the colour and hue of the surrounding bottom. Even so, certain species prefer particular substrates such as sand or mud. They are so effective at concealing themselves that their prey never knows what's hit them.

John Dory: silent assassin of the ocean floor

Another scourer of the ocean floor is the John Dory, one of my favourite fish, not just because it makes for good eating, but because of the way it gets its own dinner.

Zeus faber, to give it its scientific name, is a decent-sized fish, reaching the best part of 70 centimetres in length and weighing up to 7 kilograms. Mottled brown in colour, it is a serious ocean-floor predator. On each side of its laterally compressed body is a large black spot, which, according to legend, is the thumbprint of St Peter, giving the John Dory its alternative name: St Peter's fish. Less fancifully, this spot probably mimics an eye, helping it to deceive its prey when it's on the hunt.

The John Dory's real eyes are large and sensitive, and combined with an array of other senses they equip it well to stalk prey such as squid and other smaller fish. It approaches its target incredibly slowly, using its highly developed swim-bladder to maintain the most perfect stability

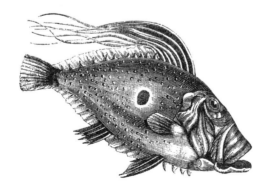

John Dory

in the water column: think of those images of shuttles docking at the International Space Station. The John Dory can glide at any angle, on any plane, including upside-down, and steal up close. But that is just the prelude to its next dramatic move. Using the marine equivalent of a long-range sniper rifle, it nabs its victim. The John Dory's mouth can shoot forward extremely quickly, stretching for more than one-third of its own body length, to create a tube. And that's how the unlucky prey ends its life: sucked down the tube before even being aware of the John Dory's existence.

Crab-cruncher extraordinaire: the wolf fish

While the John Dory likes to suck down its prey, the Atlantic wolf fish prefers to crunch. Sporting a body that is somewhere between an eel and a blenny, the wolf fish is a large and grim-looking creature, whose body ends in a massive and well-developed head, featuring a large mouth and fearsome gnashers. At the front are between four and six large canine teeth, capable of inflicting some serious damage. Further inside the mouth and down into the throat lies a meat-grinding apparatus of pharyngeal teeth, ready to pulverize anything chopped up by the fangs at the front. Typically, it is hard shellfish such as crabs, urchins and mussels that get smashed to pieces in this way.

The angry-looking yet weirdly charming wolf fish makes its home in very cold waters, even surviving in temperatures below 0°C. They can do this thanks to an antifreeze in their bloodstream, which stops the formation of ice crystals. Their preferred habitats are rocky burrows and holes, not just because they offer the perfect hunting ground, but because they provide protection for a fish that doesn't like to be too active. And these creatures of habit can often to be found in the same burrows year after year. It's a routine that is very useful when breeding, for once the eggs have been fertilized and laid onto the rocky bottom, the male wolf fish stands guard until the young are developed enough to fend for themselves.

Although the wolf fish appears an unlikely poster child for marine conservation, the species is a critical indicator of the health of the seabed. Where wolf fish are found, it's a sign that there's a rich environment to sustain it, which in turn is perfect for fish like juvenile cod and pollack.

Blue-blooded piss artist: the common lobster

A popular roamer of the ocean floor is the common lobster – and many of us will have tasted its meat. But it's also widely underestimated and misunderstood. So there's no better time to set the record straight and big it up a bit.

First of all, whatever cartoonists might have you believe, it's not red. The common lobster is a wonderful shade of deep blue-green, turning red only when heated, as the chemical bonds in the shell start to degrade. It's not just the shell that's blue – it's also a lobster's blood. Lobsters do not use iron as the primary oxygen-binding element in their blood, but opt for copper instead, the classic choice for many invertebrates.

Now let's look at those claws. Living on the ocean floor, in a variety of different environments, lobsters have to be adaptable, so why not go for dual-purpose claws? It's very handy to have one large, heavy claw like a nutcracker for crunching hard shells or snapping bones, and another slimmer, thinner claw to act like a brutal pair of shears, trapping slippery fish or stripping flesh from bones. Add in a formidable set of mouthparts, and there's not much a lobster can't, or won't, eat.

As you might guess, a lobster's claws are its first line of defence, and anyone looking for a fight usually ends up in a bad way. But when it comes to disputes *between* lobsters, the adversaries – conscious of the potency of each other's weaponry – generally battle it out in another way. Male lobsters will jet pee at one another from a gland just under their antennules ('little antennae'), in a pissing contest where potential rivals can settle their differences without coming to blows. You definitely don't want to get in the middle of *that* fight!

Sea lampreys: vampires from prehistory

The jawless and very, very ancient lamprey is the stuff of legend. It was said to have caused the death of England's Henry I, who enjoyed the flesh so much that he was laid low by a 'surfeit of lampreys'.

Lampreys have been around for 360 million years – and they may have hardly changed at all during that time. Lacking the mandibles we see in bony fish, lampreys are none the poorer for it. In fact, they're extremely good at what they do, which is . . . sucking blood. Look directly at a lamprey's mouth, and it's the toilet plunger from hell: a wide disc containing concentric rings of hooked teeth, with a vicious barb at the centre. When this mouth comes up against the side of a fish, it sticks tight and starts to feed on the victim's blood, slime and other fluids. Because its mouth is busily glued to prey, the lamprey has evolved pouched gills that allow it to breathe without having to draw water through its mouth.

Adult lampreys, at sea, can reach over a metre in length, and they feed on literally any fish big enough to sustain their size and appetite. When it comes to reproducing, they return to rivers and lakes to spawn, after which their jobs – and their lives – are done. The spawning adults die. The eggs are laid in areas of decent water flow, because when they hatch, the baby lampreys (ammocoetes) burrow into the sediments and start to filter-feed from particles washed downstream by the current. After

Sea lamprey

several years, the ammocoetes metamorphose into the adult form and make their way back down to the ocean, or sometimes to lakes, and start their grizzly vampiric ritual all over again.

Starfish: disgusting manners, perfect party tricks

Masters of the global seas, starfish are found worldwide and in a staggering variety of shapes and forms. They are able to exploit nearly any ecosystem you could imagine, from deep down on the seafloor and around hydrothermal vents to rich, shallow coastal waters. It is these latter species that have developed the most colourful behaviours and lifestyles.

Take the bog-standard common starfish. This five-armed orange warrior is a vicious predator of mussels and has a gruesome method of feeding. When a starfish commences its seafood lunch, it first humps its body directly over the mussel's shell, using its arms to anchor itself to the surrounding surface. Next, the starfish starts to pull on the shell in an attempt to open it, alternating between arms and so maintaining a constant pull without tiring itself out. The unfortunate mussel cannot boast such endurance, and once the mussel's shell is opened even fractionally, the starfish starts phase two of its merciless operation. It forces one of its two stomachs out of its mouth, on the underside of its body, and into the tiny gap in the doomed mussel's shell. Once there, digestive acids and enzymes are released and the mussel is literally dissolved in puke. The resulting sludge is then transferred from the first stomach up to the second stomach, inside the body of the starfish. Here the food is broken down further, before being absorbed.

If you're a starfish, living in the busy, bustling coastal waters ensures you always have a decent food supply; but you can easily become a food supply too. Starfish are not the speediest of creatures and are often waylaid by passing crabs or other predators of the seabed. If the starfish isn't consumed whole, it will frequently lose a limb or two in the battle, ripped off like segments peeled from an orange. Here's where starfish perform their most famous but still baffling feat. Not only can they regrow lost limbs, but lost limbs can regrow them! Yes, a single limb left on its own can develop into a brand-new starfish. For now, the starfish keeps its secret – we still don't fully understand how this is possible. But it's one hell of a party trick.

Cuttlefish: clever little cross-dressers

If octopuses are the masters of disguise, squid the flying predators of the ocean depths, cuttlefish are . . . well . . . like the blokes who work at a construction site: hardworking yet roguish, chatty, and covered in high-vis colours! Cuttlefish are essentially stockier, more relaxed versions of squid. Bearing all the standard cephalopod biology, cuttlefish have the two hunting tentacles that squid have, but which octopuses lack. If the squid is the cephalopod sports car, then the cuttlefish is the family hatchback. But if that makes them sound too boring, they have their own unique feature, and one beloved by beachcombers: the cuttlebone.

This calcium carbonate float lies along the back of the cuttlefish in the area known as the mantle. Squid have a thin spine of calcium carbonate called a gladius, but this acts as a support for the body tissues and not much else. The highly developed cuttlebone is for buoyancy. It allows the cuttlefish to float perfectly still in the water column, slowly hunting its prey.

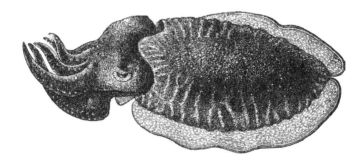

Cuttlefish

The Blowfish goes deep...

ALL THE SPECIAL PLACES: ESSENTIAL FISH HABITAT

It's not only sea turtles that need a helping hand from humankind. To better understand, protect and conserve marine life and fish stocks, we need to identify Essential Fish Habitats (EFHs). This is a term scientists use to describe any environment that provides a vital link in a fish's life cycle. It could be a place where eggs hatch, or a key feeding ground on a migration route; inland, it could be a single river or estuary where fish might assemble before breeding, or out in the ocean it could even be a piece of palm tree, marked as a suitable surface for laying eggs. The problem is that it can be very difficult to establish what Essential Fish Habitats are, and how to best protect them.

In the shallow and productive coastal seas, Essential Fish Habitats can be numerous and easy to access. In a perfect world, we'd preserve the entire ocean, taking just the fish we needed and leaving the rest untouched; but since that hasn't worked out, science and fishing must work together for a compromise. Identifying areas of EFH has become a key component in the establishment of Marine Protected Areas and No Take Zones, proving a boon to local fish populations. By preventing adult fish from being caught before they can breed, or by diverting bottom-trawling vessels away from kelp beds, the key stages of life in these areas are protected for the generations of fish (and indeed fishermen) to come.

Unlike octopuses, which virtually live like hermits, cuttlefish are highly sociable, interacting and communicating with their fellow cuttles, especially when it comes to mating. A large brain has allowed cuttlefish to develop complex mating rituals, which include pulsing and colour change, shape-shifting of the skin, body posture and even, in some species, the use of photophores to signal, like lasers at a disco. All this mating behaviour can get a little out of control, with large males fighting over females. In certain species, such as the giant Australian cuttlefish, small males even cross-dress as females to bypass the big bullies and sneak a sexy liaison with the opposite sex.

The eggs of cuttlefish are quite stunning, too, like bunches of engorged black grapes. All in all, these smart and sassy little cuttles really have a lot to boast about. Ponder that the next time you buy a cuttlebone for your canary.

Diver's delight: the tompot blenny

A well-known species found around the coasts of Europe and the UK is the tompot blenny. It's a smallish fish measuring 15–20 centimetres, but one with more charisma than you would believe. Brightly coloured, with ornate tentacles sticking up from its head and a large, slightly goofy mouth, it's a favourite of scuba divers. Like all blennies, they lack a swim-bladder, so they hop, skip and jump along the sea bottom with much wriggling of their long bodies.

Tompots are territorial. They will inhabit holes on rocky reefs, where they can take up residence for many years. Like any good householder, they can be very protective of their patch, zooming out to investigate wandering crabs, other blennies and even human divers. The large mouth and strong jaw have a single row of sharp teeth, which are used to munch a variety of creatures from the seabed, including, quite surprisingly, sea anemones. Tompots don't care about anemones' stinging tentacles, and are as content tucking into these as they are consuming hard-armoured crustaceans.

That's about it for the tompot blenny – except to say that to dive with one (or many, as is often the case) is a really special event. The blenny acts like a lord of the manor, bustling to and fro, investigating you and any other creature it may find. Good things really do come in small packages.

The lesson of Lundy Island

Coastal seas have always been the salty waters most exploited by humans. Long before we had steam- and diesel-powered ships to ease travel across the great oceans, men in small boats worked the few miles just out from land. When industrial-scale fishing arrived, the richest areas of the sea were also the closest, and they took a hell of a hammering.

Thankfully, ocean habitats have a great ability to recover, if only we let them, and Lundy Island off the coast of North Devon is a prime example of what can be achieved if we just give things a chance. In 1986, the island became a marine reserve because of the vast array of aquatic fauna and flora that surrounded it. However, it wasn't until 2003 that the first No Take Zone was designated, east of the island. This meant that no fishing whatsoever was allowed. In no time, samples collected from the zone were showing that life was returning with gusto. By 2008, significant differences were appearing in the size of lobsters found within the No Take Zone compared to the smaller ones found outside it. The positive effects spread to all the wildlife in the Lundy area.

Although some local fishermen still gripe about not being able to fish in the zone, in 2010 Lundy was designated the first Marine Conservation Zone in the UK. It remains a shining example of what can happen when fishing is relaxed and Earth's coastal seas are allowed to do their thing again.

Coral Reef

oral reefs are perhaps the most famous of all ocean environments. After all, you can hardly walk down the high street without seeing some display or packaging that has hijacked the retina-busting beauty of these havens of colour, variety and otherworldly enchantment. Yet reefs are not only gorgeous to look at, they are full of mystery: they are the rainforests of the ocean, continually revealing secrets that force scientists to redraw the boundaries of biology.

Now, it won't have escaped your notice that coral reefs aren't exactly widespread. Tropical reef-building corals can only live within strict environmental parameters, so you only find them in very select places around the globe. You might then think that coral reefs are isolated and independent systems, looking after themselves and their own space. Wrong! These tiny, bustling oases of life play a vital role in the lives of countless animals, from whales to cuttlefish, from sharks to snappers. While some of these may be visitors for a day or a week, other creatures never leave the reef, and it's in these cases that we see some of the more extreme examples of aquatic evolution, in both physical and behavioural adaptations to the unique conditions of the reef environment.

Coral itself is very ancient, a marvel of evolution that combines the benefits of both active feeding and harnessing the Sun's rays to grow and prosper. There is an enormous variety of forms of coral, each busily filling a precise and delicate niche on the reef. Competition for food, living space and sex are just as vital to corals as they are to any other animal, and these slow-growing colonies do all they can to ensure they remain bigger and better than the competitors around them.

But this lifestyle comes at a cost. Given enough time, coral can come to dominate an entire swathe of ocean floor, but it can be severely damaged in an instant by some environmental event, leaving it weakened and vulnerable to external threats.

Despite their fragile nature, corals are not just found in sunlit tropical waters but have made their home in the deep ocean and turbulent waters of the temperate zones. Here they are as critical to life and their associated food webs as they are in the tropics. And while they might not have quite the immediate visual impact of their tropical cousins, cold-water reefs still have a magic all their own.

Given their beauty, diversity and fragility, it is no surprise that studying coral reefs is, for some, the pinnacle of marine biology. At the same time, there is a great urgency to understand and protect as much as we can before we start to lose these extraordinary and intricate cities beneath the waves.

Masters of reef-building

Coral reefs and all the highly complex ecosystems interconnected with them would not exist without . . . well, coral. To put that another way, if you replaced the coral with a large rocky mound, you wouldn't get the same effect: it is the life of the coral itself that is the cornerstone of these incredibly rich and delicate worlds.

Corals themselves are related to jellyfish and anemones; collectively, these animals are known as cnidarians, and among the many character-istics they have in common, the most crucial is that amazing battery of stinging cells. The biggest difference is that they are colonial sedentary polyps (a polyp is a single animal, like a fleshy sock with a mouth and tentacles at the open end), rather than free-swimming medusae (the pulsing bells of jellyfish) or large, roving, singular polyps. However, it is the way corals live and grow that makes them so vital to the marine world as a whole. Certain species of coral polyp have the ability to synthesize calcium carbonate (limestone) from the surrounding seawater and to deposit it as a supporting structure for the continued growth of the animal. Although this process is not entirely unique to corals, they certainly seem to be the masters of it, and the fruits of their labour – most famously the Great Barrier Reef, the largest organic structure on the planet – are clearly visible from space.

Reef-building is hugely important to the animals that are associated with coral reefs. The extraordinary complexity of coral growth virtually provides a city for these creatures to inhabit: shelters, caves, nooks, hunting grounds, cleaning stations, grazing opportunities – all are provided within the coral structure. But as far as the reef-building corals themselves are concerned, it's all just bricks and mortar: they build to outcompete their next-door neighbours, not to provide a home for others.

The way in which corals feed is also critical to life in tropical waters. Whether reef-building or not, corals host inside their bodies zooxanthellae, microscopic algae which spread through the corals' tissues. These zooxanthellae are autotrophic ('self-feeding'): they are capable of creating sugars via photosynthesis, fuelling the corals' growth, even in waters considered to be very nutrient-poor. This means that corals can 'feed' during the day, thanks to the work of their symbiotic zooxanthellae, while at night, when coral predators and grazers are inactive, they can extend their stinging tentacles and feed on whatever organic particles and small organisms happen to be passing by. This versatile feeding method means that corals have been able to colonize and exploit environments that may be beautiful to our eyes but are very harsh on all other life.

The classic reef-builders: hard corals

Stony or hard corals are the ones we are all familiar with, famous for their reef-building activities. Found in a variety of different forms and sizes, there are thousands of different species, many of which are still little known to science. The thin living part of the coral exists on top of a calcium carbonate (limestone) skeleton, which is made by the coral itself and laid down over the life of the animal. The coral polyps live in grooves, troughs or cup-like structures, and every now and then the growth of the coral gets to a stage where it needs to start a new 'floor' above that of the old growth. So you end up with a hollow chamber capped with limestone beneath the growing polyps. Repeat this enough times and you get a labyrinth of old chambers going all the way down through the structure of the reef. The abandoned coral dwellings are perfect for other creatures to live in, be it bacteria specializing in breaking down organic matter or larger creatures like shrimps or worms that hunt in the limestone maze.

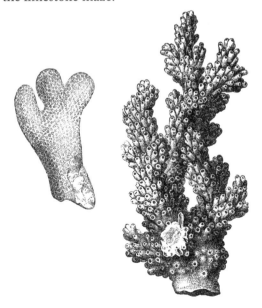

Hard corals

The hard corals themselves are often split again into two categories: large-polyp stony (LPS) or small-polyp stony (SPS). LPS corals tend to be much larger and bulkier growths, often forming the strong heart of the reef, whereas SPS corals include the thin branching or plating forms seen on the edge of the reef crest. They both feed in the same way – a combination of photosynthesis and particle-feeding – but LPS corals have a much bigger appetite. The larger polyps have bigger mouths, allowing them to swallow bigger meals, including prey such as small shrimps and copepods.

The not-so-classic reef-builders: soft corals

When you think of corals, you probably imagine a hard, spiky, brightly coloured thing that looks like a tree branch or a stag's antlers. But there is a different kind of coral that functions in a near-identical way to the hard or stony corals, but is soft and leathery. These 'soft' corals do not lay down a limestone skeleton like the reef-builders, but they do have small spine-like structures in their flesh called sclerites. These are often shaped like miniature toothpicks and provide support, as well as defence, for the soft coral. For many years, it was thought that soft corals are not reef-builders, but new research has shown that some species aggregate their sclerites at the base of the coral and cement them onto the rock below. So it seems that they are reef-builders after all.

Unlike hard corals, which grow within very strict water parameters, soft corals often live in areas of lower light and higher nutrient content. In temperate regions, soft corals dominate the underwater landscape, their feeding polyps extended ready to catch anything that floats by. In tropical waters, soft corals still feed just as furiously, but they also benefit from the internal presence of microscopic photosynthesizing organisms (zooxanthellae) which bolster their diet. The upshot of all this is that soft corals grow far more quickly than their hard reef-building cousins. This is important as many creatures, especially juvenile fishes and some clownfish species, make their homes in soft coral. And being soft doesn't mean that these corals are not beautiful, as they come in a variety of colours and can form large toadstools, plateaus or tree-like structures with their long, flowing branches.

The orderly chaos of the coral reef

When you dive down to a coral reef for the first time, you are likely to be blown away by the staggering spectacle: the breathtaking array of brightly coloured, bizarrely shaped living rocks, populated by a teeming mass of fish and other animals that are visually just as gorgeous. But actually, behind this apparently chaotic riot of colour, there is much organization at work, with different corals dominating different areas. So let's take a trip around a coral reef.

At the most seaward point and nearest the surface, you find the reef crest. This is the area most impacted by the elements, of both land and sea. Wave, wind, rain and sun all batter the crest 24/7, so the corals here tend to be some of the hardiest and fastest-growing. Staghorn corals, branching and tree-like, are masters of the reef crest, where they compete with algae for dominance.

Move below the low-tide mark at the reef crest, still facing seaward, and you come to the fore reef, an area that is still high-energy but slightly more stable. However, it often leads to a steep slope and serious drop-off into the depths below, so space for growth is tight. The fore reef is also characterized by branching corals, but there are also many plating varieties, such as vase coral. These plating corals grow fast, spreading like a German beach towel over a sun-lounger and snuffing out the light beneath.

Head back towards shore, behind the protection of the reef crest, and you enter the back reef. Here, wave action is much reduced and you see large round varieties such as brain corals start to appear. These particular corals are slower to grow than branching staghorns, but they pack a much more powerful punch when it comes to stinging. This means they can not only catch and eat larger food, but also fight more aggressively

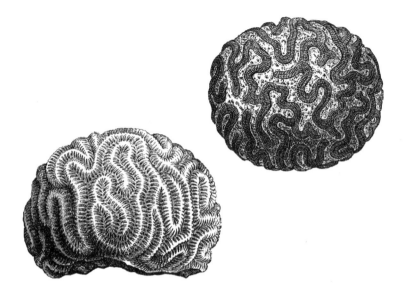

Brain corals

for space on the reef. It is corals such as brain and pineapple that really build the heart of any long-lasting reef.

Head further towards shore and you leave the reef proper and enter the lagoon environment. Here, conditions are much more stable than anywhere else on the reef, and calmer water means more sedimentation, so any corals found here tend to be ones used to getting buried frequently by sand. Often you find small patch reefs or bommies (coral outcrops) in this zone, with species such as elegance and mushroom corals living on the sandy bottom. Lagoons often have seagrass meadows growing in them, which help keep the reef proper free from pollutants and sedimentation.

While this is the basic layout of a reef, there is of course great variation due to particular local conditions. For example, areas with high wave action often have large rip currents scouring through the coral from the back reef towards the open ocean. These high-energy channels become dominated by filter-feeders such as sea whips and anemones. It is hard to believe that such daily commotion and uproar have to be weathered

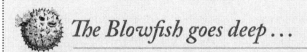

The Blowfish goes deep ...

REEF TYPES: FRINGING, BARRIER, ATOLL

Coral reefs grow and accumulate so slowly that you might easily think they had always been there. Certainly, the 10,000 years it took the Great Barrier Reef to establish itself is hardly rapid by anyone's standards. In reality, though, reefs have to adapt relatively quickly to changes in their environmental conditions, and in this process of adaptation three distinct forms are recognized: fringing reefs, barrier reefs and coral atolls.

The first stage of any reef is the settling of coral on something hard and stable in clean, shallow, sunlit waters. This usually occurs just off the shore of a landmass or island, and over time the corals develop and the reef starts to grow outwards from the shore towards the ocean. This is a fringing reef, where the corals surround the shoreline but may only be a metre or so from the beach.

Roll on the decades and the reef continues to move outwards until it has crept such a distance that a shallow-water lagoon develops between the shore and the reef crest. This is the barrier reef stage, which can persist indefinitely as the reef continues to grow but the shore does not move. Barrier reefs create a whole new environment as the lagoon area is protected from storm surges and the risks of the open ocean.

The final stage for a reef occurs when the original source of the establishment (the rock, island, sea mount, etc.) subsides into the ocean and the reef appears to be growing out of nowhere. This is an atoll; these occur most often where a fringing reef establishes itself on the side of a volcano that erupted from the ocean but subsequently fell back below sea level. Don't hold your breath waiting for the next atoll to show up, though, as formations can take tens of millions of years to develop.

by such delicate, slow-growing creatures. And yet, though you'd scarcely know it from just looking at a coral reef, there is definitely method behind all the apparent madness on display.

Sex! Sex! Sex!

When you are, basically, a living lump of rock, breeding can be tough. While coral polyps may wriggle about quite a bit to catch food or to fight off intruders, mature colonies are not exactly nimble on their feet. So how do you reproduce successfully if you are a coral? Well, asexual reproduction is extremely common for cnidarians (jellyfish, anemones, corals); simply put, corals sprout new polyps and that is how the colony grows larger. But to form new colonies in other areas requires a different technique altogether.

Corals can be male, female or both, and they produce sperm, eggs or a combination of the two wrapped together in a packet. Now it wouldn't be much good if a single colony randomly spewed genetic material into the water, as most of it would be rapidly consumed by neighbouring corals or nearby fishes. Any remaining eggs or sperm would probably only fertilize one another, so there wouldn't be much chance of the colony really getting itself and its genes out into the world. To avoid the wholesale loss of so many eggs and sperm and to maximize the chances of mixing with other corals, the reef spawns in one mass event, ejecting its love juice in a single evening and completely clouding the water in the process. Usually on a spring tide, this event is timed by the phases of the Moon and seems to be prompted by subtle cues of temperature and lighting intensity.

These mass spawning events are not just critical for the reef to spread and seed new areas, but can also provide a vital feed for animals that are tuned in to the sexy schedule. For example, whale sharks make oceanwide migrations to arrive at particular reefs just in time for the spawning. No one knows exactly how they time their arrival so precisely, but for the biggest fish in the sea to put in an appearance, the whole gig has to be pretty special.

The long road from blob to reef

Coral reefs are real slow developers, so unless you've got a lot of time on your hands – perhaps half a century or so – you probably aren't going to see a reef getting established. So here's a quick guide to the long, slow road to forming a reef.

First, you need a fertilized egg, called a planula. Thrust into the world during one of the reef's mass spawning events, this free-swimming, hair-covered blob is the start of the new coral. At the whim of currents and tides, the planula is carried to a suitable place to settle, where a blob on a rock metamorphoses into a single small polyp of new coral. Settling down is a big risk for the planula, so it checks that the parameters of its prospective new home are just right before it allows the transformation to take place: important factors include light, water flow, nutrient levels, pH, presence of other corals, and how much time it has left before its energy supply is exhausted. If it has settled in a good spot, the planula now races to grow as fast as possible, reproducing asexually to increase the size of the colony and give it the best shot at surviving the many hazards it now faces. Even something as simple as waves scouring the rock with sand could terminally damage the forming colony. As the colony grows, our budding young coral will be joined by more and more other corals, all set on exploiting the favourable conditions. Different corals take different roles on the reef and are willing to fight for their space to thrive: this is where the real turf war begins!

In its early stages a reef won't look like much more than some green or brown smudges on an outcrop of rock. But given a decent plot of land and a big slice of luck, something that looks like a proper coral reef will appear within fifty or sixty years.

More sex please, we're reef fish

It isn't just corals that time their breeding to occur as one massive event: many reef fish do this too. Generally, most reef fish, especially the slightly larger ones, keep themselves to themselves. This allows each animal its own space to forage, feed or graze without getting in one another's way. If they then chose to breed with their nearest neighbours, this would limit each individual's chances of getting the 'best deal' for its genes – which basically means mixin' it all up!

Using environmental cues like tides and the phases of the Moon, mass-spawning reef fish such as brown surgeonfish and two-spot red snappers gather in large tightly packed shoals on the edge of the reef. Often the males joust and jostle to get as close as possible to the gravid (egg-carrying) females, but the real fun doesn't start until the females are ready. At an apparently random moment, female fish rise rapidly up from the shoal, closely followed by the fastest and fittest males in the vicinity. As each female streaks towards the surface, she starts to expel eggs and the males do all they can to be the closest one to fertilize them. Once one female goes, they all start, and soon the entire shoal is in an orgy of eggs and sperm.

Now, there's one especially smart aspect to all this: another reason *not* to breed close to the reef is of course that corals, invertebrates and many other fish would just *love* to eat super-nutritious eggs and sperm – which would rather scupper the chances of the next generation. These mass spawning events, held on the edge of the reef during strong spring tides, ensure that, while some eggs meet their doom on the reef, most are carried out into the open ocean, where they can hatch in the plankton and develop into juveniles, ready to return to the reef on the next spring tide.

Cold-water reefs: oases of the deep

When you imagine a coral reef, you probably think tropical sunlit waters, but that's not the only place you can find them. Cold-water reefs, every bit as vibrant as their warm-water counterparts, thrive in some of the ocean's darkest and deepest spots.

Found anywhere it's dark, from cold temperate continental shelves all the way down to 2,000 metres or more, the corals that form cold-water reefs belong to exactly the same group as their tropical cousins. In fact, many deep-water corals look pretty much the same as those you find in shallow waters, except that their feeding polyps tend to be much bigger. This is because deep-water reefs do not rely on photosynthesis to get energy from the Sun; instead, they use their stinging cells to harpoon zooplankton, copepods and even small shrimp. These corals lay down calcium carbonate skeletons too and create large mounds of growth, which rapidly become focal points in the deep ocean. Many commercially important fish species, including halibut, cod and pollack, spend time on these deep-water reefs as there is such a rich diversity of prey in the form of shrimps, crabs and molluscs.

Because they are not powered by the Sun and live in waters sometimes as cold as 4°C, deep-water corals grow extremely slowly. According to some estimates, one particular coral on a Norwegian reef was 10,000 years old. This slow growth rate means these reefs can really struggle to recover from destructive fishing and mining practices. Considering how critical these deep and dark oases are to so much life we expect to find on our dinner plates, we had better start paying some serious attention to them before we lose them forever.

Colourful conversation on the reef

You will all know that reef fish are some of the most extravagant, vibrant, fantastically coloured fish you can find. But have you ever asked yourself why?

The first thing that springs to mind is probably camouflage – the idea that a reef fish's coloration helps conceal it against the backdrop of corals. And you'd be right, in part anyway, as *some* of the colours we see are intended to break up outlines and make fish merge with their background. But what you have to remember is that the fancy colours of reef fish aren't intended for *our* eyes. Fish eyes are tuned differently to our own and have the ability to see colours we cannot, including ultraviolet (UV) light. In the end, we can't know exactly what fish see, but we are starting to discover that there's a lot more going on here than simple camouflage. For example, fish can change colour in an instant, but whether you can see this change depends on what colour receptors and filters you have in your eye. This means that fish with the right filters are able to pick up colour clues and communications from other specific fish. It's possible that the bright colours we see on the reef are actually just one massive conversation happening before our eyes, with large cross-spectrum colours broadcasting health, fitness and vitality to all, while subtle, species-specific colours flash out in bursts like classroom whispers to those in the know.

Coral colour control: keeping the partners in line

If James Hetfield had been a coral, his Lars Ulrich would have been zooxanthellae: the microscopic organisms that live within the coral's tissues and boost its growth by creating sugars by means of photosynthesis. Now, the wavelengths of light that are least used and most reflected by the zooxanthellae are greenish-brown; indeed, the cells themselves are greenish-brown, so, in theory, the coral colony itself should also appear . . . greenish-brown. But if that's the case, why on earth are corals so crazy in their colours? How come we see blues, pinks, purples and lurid greens? The answer is that the bright coloration of healthy corals is actually an all-out attempt to keep the symbiotic algae inside their cells from running rampant and taking over the show completely.

When light is restricted or water conditions are less than perfect, you will often see light brown or brown corals. This is because the photosynthetic symbionts in the coral's cells are either being fully exposed to make the very most of all the sunlight there is, or because their population is increasing so much that it is flooding all available space in the coral's tissues. It might seem like a good thing to have lots and lots of sugar-producing cells living in your body, but if there are too many, they start to cause damage to the coral polyps.

So the coral has two options. They can eject the algae from their tissues to prevent further damage, leaving the white of the skeleton showing through the flesh (a process known as bleaching). Or – in the case of healthy corals living in ideal conditions – they can control the amount and type of light reaching their sun-loving partners in the first place. The coral conducts this light-rationing process through the use of specialized pigments and proteins. Chromoproteins are special proteins found in coral tissues that reflect light at given wavelengths, and it is these proteins and their reflected light that we see as red, blue, green, purple, and pretty much any other colour a coral can be. Most coral species have about two dozen types of chromoprotein in their cells. The other way to control the amount of light reaching the zooxanthellae is the use of fluorescent pigments, which absorb light at damagingly high wavelengths and then emit it again at lower, safer wavelengths. It is this group of pigments that cause corals to 'glow' under certain types of light.

The colour of corals is directly linked to their health, and sadly we have seen reefs worldwide starting to become blander and browner. Pictures and footage of reef dives from the 1970s now look like insane psychedelic dreams compared with the scenes we regularly see during the summer on reefs worldwide.

Giving nature a hand: artificial reefs

For a reef, getting started is really tough! Coral polyps can't get a grip on loose sand and suitable rocky outcrops might get swamped by algae before grazers can arrive and keep the space clear for coral growth. And it's a real shame, for there are many perfect spots in the ocean that would offer a nirvana for corals if only they could get started.

Thankfully, humans have stepped in to help out. Artificial reefs can easily be constructed and deployed in areas where coral would thrive but have trouble getting established. These false reefs can range from something as simple as a metal cage, to specially fashioned coral pods made from ceramics. And then there's the really fun stuff, when unique structures are used to create new reef environments. In Mexico, there's an underwater sculpture park where many different human forms are slowly being colonized by corals and nibbled by fish. Off Australia, many old boats are purposely stripped down to their safe, non-toxic bones and sunk in areas of current to allow passing coral planulae to attach themselves. Better still, in the South Pacific, among the coral islands where the US stormed Japanese-held areas during the Second World War, the skeletons of tanks, planes and boats have become thriving new areas of life and rebirth. In fact, the corals that settled in 1945 have now bloomed into near-mature reefs. Every year, their continuing growth eats up more and more of the structures they live on, and in time, we may hope, nothing but coral will remain.

Conserving corals – sustainably

Artificial reefs produce really positive results, but we can go one step further, giving reefs a serious head start by seeding them with life. Corals can easily be propagated by taking a small piece (frag) from a larger coral; these frags are then grown either on grids at sea (mariculture) on in aquariums (aquaculture). Many corals are grown in this way, for scientific study, in conservation efforts or for the aquarium trade.

A non-profit organization in Indonesia called LINI grows coral frags and then attaches them to specially constructed artificial reefs. They then create completely new reefs seeded with coral, and also help restore areas of previously damaged coastline. These seeded reefs establish themselves much more quickly than bare-bones artificial structures, and – in LINI's case – provide an income for the people who live and work there. By creating, seeding and protecting reefs, and then managing the associated reef fish and coral, LINI can sustainably harvest the coastline to provide fish and invertebrates for the aquarium trade worldwide. This is a cracking example of what can happen when conservation and consumerism come together to create a working model in which everyone, the sea included, benefits.

Clearing the waters: seagrasses and mangroves

There are not many true plants in the oceans – it's a pretty tough environment, after all. Try pouring salt water on your roses and see how they like it! However, there are two groups of plants that have a major impact on the health of tropical reefs: seagrasses and mangroves.

Of the two groups, seagrasses are the simpler, being essentially wide blades of 'grass' growing out from the sand. Many animals, including manatees, sea turtles and grazing fish, live on seagrass. But the benefits of seagrasses extend much further than this, as their shallow root systems spread like a net underneath the shifting sands, holding them in place. The upright blades cause yet more particles and sediment to settle and be stabilized by the mesh of roots. This filtering process provides excellent water clarity for photosynthesizers such as corals, which cannot survive being swamped by sediment for extended periods of time. Seagrass also grows at such a lick that it is a very significant player when it comes to taking in CO_2, happily sucking in tonnes of the stuff and keeping it stored safe in roots, rhizomes and further growth.

Mangroves are a more complicated set-up – a tropical coastal ecosystem consisting of different trees, shrubs and plants that are capable of dealing with salt water for limited periods of time. True mangrove trees are the ultimate masters of this halophytic lifestyle and have evolved a variety of ways to survive being partially submerged in salt water every six hours. To get started, mangrove trees need decent support in the shifting silts and rolling waves, so they grow a series of specialized roots that anchor them firmly in the sediment while also ensuring that most of the plant stays above the high-water mark; these aerial roots (pneumatophores) either rise from the sediment like skyscrapers, or hang drown from the stems like stalactites. As well as providing support, they are covered in pores that allow the plant to take in oxygen and avoid drowning when it is submerged by the rising tide.

Mangrove forests have always played a vital role in keeping nearby reefs healthy. Like the seagrasses, their extensive roots cause sedimentation to occur and so help keep the water clear for reef communities. In addition, the maze of tangled roots and branches is a perfect place for small fish and sharks to develop and hunt. Most of the fish we love to see on coral reefs would have spent their earliest days darting around the twisted legs of many a mangrove tree.

Shock-and-awe claw: the pistol shrimp

Although not a big hitter, the pistol shrimp packs one hell of a punch – such a blow, in fact, that one click from its mighty claw can stun or even kill a fish outright. Also known as snapping shrimps, the members of this crustacean family are small in stature, growing to no more than about 5 centimetres in length, but a large part of this is made up of one disproportionately mega claw. And this claw needs to be big, as it is packed full of muscles all lined up ready for just one job: to fire the pistol!

The specialized claw has evolved differently to the standard crustacean pincer. The larger main body of the claw has a deep pocket, into which an extension of the smaller moving hammer snugly fits. The hammer can be cocked nearly at right-angles, and when fired, closes into the main body of the claw at around 100 kilometres an hour. The water in the pocket is forced out at such high speed that it boils, briefly hitting over 4,000°C, before collapsing in on itself in a process called cavitation. The effect is so powerful that a small burst of light is emitted, so you could almost say that this shrimp is shooting lightning! All this clicking doesn't go unnoticed, and pistol shrimps are responsible for a lot of noise in the ocean, actually competing with whales for the title of loudest animals in the sea. This lightning pistol claw is used in hunting and communication. The pistol is highly accurate and the jet of super-heated water, followed by the cavitation shock wave, can stun or kill small fish or crustaceans.

The odd couple: pistol shrimp and goby

Except when breeding, pistol shrimps are usually solitary, living in burrows of their own construction, where they hide before rushing out to stun their next meal. However, while they may not be chummy with other shrimps, some species do form extremely close bonds with small fishes.

These so-called shrimp gobies form a loose group of small bottom-dwelling fishes whose mission in life is to seek out and bond with the aforementioned shrimps. Not all species of pistol shrimp are keen on this arrangement, but others are only too happy to welcome a goby into their lives – and into their burrows. This symbiotic association brings benefits for both parties. The shrimp has poor eyesight and relies mainly on its antennae for information about the world around it, but the goby has excellent vision and acts as a look-out for the shrimp. The latter is nearly always in contact with the goby, gently touching it with its long antenna, while the little fish communicates with its partner with gentle flicks and wafts of its tail-fin, enticing it out of its burrow or ushering it back in. The presence of a goby in the life of a pistol shrimp makes the shrimp far more adventurous in its foraging behaviour. And as for the goby, it gets full board and high-security lodgings inside the shrimp's burrow. While both animals can live apart, together they have a much better chance of making it in the big, bad world of the coral seas.

The humpback's coral calving

When you think of coral-reef residents, you could be forgiven for not immediately thinking of humpback whales. After all, they don't exactly fit in with the reef ethos: small, delicate, vibrant . . . Yet, without the safety and stability of coral reefs, humpback whales could be threatened with extinction.

Humpbacks do not feed on or near coral reefs – that takes place in the extremely rich waters of the higher latitudes, on the bounties of krill and herring. The coral reef instead provides an area for the female humpback to calve. It makes good sense: the turbulent waters of the rich temperate zones are wracked by storms, high winds and waves – not a good place to bring up a youngster, as even baby whales need lots of help in the first stages of life, with mother often holding baby stable at the surface for it to breathe and rest. Coral reefs provide the calm, shallow and warm seas needed for this delicate stage to occur. During their time on the reef, the mother herself does not feed, but she provides a constant supply of extremely rich milk to her offspring. Whale milk is nearly 50 per cent fat and has the consistency of toothpaste, and the idea is to get the baby as healthy and large as possible as quickly as possible. Immediately after their tropical maternity, mother and child make the long and arduous journey to the rich and rough polar waters. The migration from warm birthing waters to rich feeding grounds is one of the longest of any mammal, clocking in at 5,000 kilometres – hardly a trip you'd want to attempt on an empty stomach.

Cheating on your diet

Corals grow very slowly – a reef can take half a century or more to get properly established – and today they face ever-growing pressures due to climate change. Green filamentous algae, on the other hand, are not so hampered by human activities. Indeed, pollution such as fertilizer run-off can actually create supercharged conditions for growth in the reef environment, causing algae to quickly swamp a reef, covering living corals and obstructing settling areas that would otherwise be ideal for new polyps. What we need is some vegetarian fish!

Veggie-munching fish are key to a reef's survival, but most aren't strict vegetarians. Of all the known living species of bony fish, only 3 per cent are true herbivores, yet we see these grazers constantly munching pest algae. So what's going on? As fish graze on encrusting growths, algae and seaweeds, they are consuming not just the 'plant' matter, but the rich mix of small animals (meiofauna) that live within the complex

structures. Imagine eating a cabbage without removing the slugs first ...
it's a bit like that.

Thankfully, then, grazing fish such as tangs and surgeonfish act like
sheep on these underwater meadows of algae, grazing down to the bare
rock and allowing the corals light and space to grow. The overall health
and survival of the entire biome is dependent on the grazing of these
fish. When a reef is healthy, the amount of algae is limited – so limited,
in fact, that fish often defend a patch of reef as their own turf, patrolling
it and grazing where possible. Some fish, like convict tangs, move in vast
shoals over the reef, mobbing and overwhelming territories of other fish
and stripping them clean in seconds.

The passing of the parrotfish, or why tropical beaches are crap

I hate to pour cold water on your dream-holiday plans, but here's some
bad news: the white-sand beaches of tropical islands so beloved of
tourists are, basically, poo. It is likely that the tropical islands associated
with coral reefs are formed primarily from the digested remains of the
corals themselves. So how do you form a pile of crap so big you can
build a hotel on it? Well, it helps to have friends in wet places ...

First, any damage done to the coral adds to the pile. As branches are
broken off in storms, or snapped off by half-witted divers, they fall and
are buffeted about by the constant wave surge, over time being worn
down and degraded into sand. This is a rather slow process, however, so
holidaymakers who haven't got a few thousand years to spare will be glad
to hear that there are ways to speed things up. Any animal that grazes
on corals makes a difference, so specialized polyp-feeders such as melon
butterfly fish do their bit for the poo pile, one tiny bite at a time. Starfish,
sea urchins, sea cucumbers – all help in the slow disintegration of the reef.

But the really big hitters in the droppings department are the
parrotfishes, a stunning group of fishes that have a range of weird and
wonderful lifestyles, but all have one thing in common: a great big beak.

This beak grows throughout the animal's life and must be continually ground down. The parrotfish feeds on all sorts of organisms that live in and on the reef and rocks, ranging from sponges and encrusting algae to coral polyps themselves. Once a big chunk has been crunched off, it is ground down by a honeycomb of strong teeth in the fish's throat. This action, combined with subsequent digestive processes, ensures that, when the parrotfish takes a dump, it produces that wonderful picture-postcard poo we keep telling ourselves is sand.

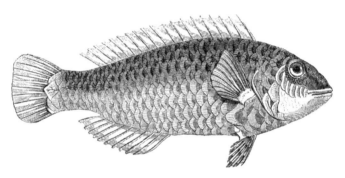

Parrotfish

The proud gardener

At first glance, the dusky farmerfish might not seem all that special – it is a fairly ordinary-looking damselfish. Its diet might not seem all that exciting either: it enjoys the usual mix of small crustaceans and tasty bits of plankton, and it likes grazing on algae. But not just any algae: it is partial to a very particular kind of red algae called *Polysiphonia* – and that's when things start to get interesting ...

The thing about *Polysiphonia* is that it isn't very good at outgrowing the filamentous green algae that plague reefs, so it very quickly gets swamped by its faster-growing neighbours. Now, the farmerfish doesn't like eating these green algae, as it doesn't have the right teeth or gut fauna to properly digest them. So, to ensure that there is always a supply of its favoured algae, the farmerfish protects, farms and grazes an area of reef. The fish spends many hours a day ripping up green algae that has invaded its patch and swimming away to spit them out. It tends the rock by scraping and grazing to ensure its favoured red algae has somewhere to grow. Any foreign grazers, including sea urchins and other damsel-fish, that show interest in the farm are viciously attacked and driven off. Even human divers have been known to receive painful bites and nips. The bond between farmer and its crop is so tight that they have become mutually dependent, and one is not able to thrive without the other.

Diver-crushing clams . . . not!

We all know about clams: massive creatures that live on the seabed, slamming shut to trap the leg of an unlucky diver. That's what cartoonists would have you believe, at any rate. In fact, the reverse is true, as these stunning shell-dwellers are extremely delicate.

There are a number of species of tropical 'giant' clams; these bivalve molluscs are filter-feeders, but – like corals – they host microscopic photosynthetic organisms (zooxanthellae) in their tissues, which provide them with much of their food. As they have to deal with all the stresses and strains of filter-feeding *and* have all the hassle of hosting hyperactive zooxanthellae, tropical clams have more complex bodies than the much simpler coral polyps. The wonderful colours you see on a clam's mantle are there to protect, control and promote the growth of its photosyn-thesizing symbiotic partners. The pattern on the mantle, unique to each clam, is a living map of the distribution of its sun-loving guests, with different colours indicating areas of greater or lesser light penetration to the tissues below. You'll find tropical clams all over coral reefs. The smaller rock-boring species are right among the corals, fighting for space, while true giant clams (*Tridacna gigas*) live on the open seabed or nearby lagoons. They can grow to well over a metre in length and weigh 300 kilograms or more – but they've never trapped a diver . . . not yet, anyway.

Nemo's world

Probably the most famous of all reef inhabitants, the clownfish is well known worldwide – and it's not just because of the animated journeys it supposedly makes in search of its offspring.

One of the things almost everyone knows about clownfish is that they live in anemones. This is true – they are often found living in the stinging tentacles of all sorts of different anemone species – but it is still not known for certain how they manage to live in anemones that would normally sting and kill other fish. One idea is that the thick layer of mucus the clownfish has on its skin either stops the stingers reaching the fish or, more likely, prevents the stinging cells being triggered in the first place. The other theory is that clownfish are accustomed to being stung and therefore have some sort of immunity to the stinging cells. Whatever the explanation, clownfish certainly make very successful homes in the deadly tentacles, and it isn't only the fish that benefits from the arrangement. For one thing, the clownfish's movement keeps the anemone's tissues well oxygenated and stops potential nasties landing on the flesh and settling there. For another, it is thought that the clownfish swimming in and out of the curtain of tentacles attracts other fish and so brings food to the host.

Clownfish are also well known for their mating behaviour. Much larger than the male, the female will only mate with him and tolerate his presence if he can keep up with some pretty demanding house-keeping duties. The male prepares a suitable space on a nearby rock that lies within the protective reach of the anemone. The female then lays her eggs, and after they have been fertilized, the male tends them with the greatest care. His job is to keep them free of fungi and other pests, while also providing oxygen by fanning water over them with his fins. Should his efforts not be up to scratch, the female will physically attack him, even to the point of killing him. Murdering your mate might seem like a bad idea, but most clownfish live in large harems, and beneath the female, around the very edges of the anemone, live

The Blowfish goes deep . . .

SEX CHANGE IN FISH

We often think of gender as something fixed that defines our lives, dictating what we do, where we go, how we dress. However, in the oceans there are many fish species where gender is much more fluid – being male or female is just one phase in a life in which things are always ready to change. Clownfish, for example, are protandrous. This means that males will develop into females if the right conditions arise. If the large female that presides over the anemone harem is lost for some reason, the dominant male gains weight and grows in size, and his testes develop into ovaries. This system has obvious advantages given the clownfish's lifestyle. Ovaries need more space within the body than testes, so growing into a big fish is the only way to fit them in. And one bossy female defending a small but desirable bit of turf means she can breed regularly, producing a small number of well-developed and carefully protected eggs, all containing her genes. The male clownfish, meanwhile, is essentially a pair of testes and acts as housekeeper. In this way, one small area of reef can become, effectively, a clown-fish production line for the DNA of the one large dominant female.

The reverse of this process, in which females turn into males, is called protogyny, and many species of wrasse found on the reef change sex in this way. The trigger for the shift is the size and condition of the fish. Growing big and powerful allows you to control a much wider area of the reef, which will doubtless contain a lot of fishes, including many suitable females. So ditching your large, biologically expensive eggs for small, cheap, mass-produced sperm is a great way of quickly spreading your genes across the whole territory you command. A female, even a large one, would have to wait a given time to replace the eggs she had laid on just one meeting. Not so for a male, where the large store of sperm can go a long, long way.

smaller male clownfish, just waiting for a chance to take their place at the top.

Whitetips on the reef

There are many dangers on the reef – lionfish, groupers, octopuses. But it is surely the most famous predator in the oceans that is also the biggest beast on the reef. Sharks are well-known inhabitants of reef systems, and while most species patrol the waters around the corals, some dive into the reef itself to hunt the fishes living there.

Whitetip reef sharks may not look like much: slender with a wide mouth and square body, they only grow to about 1.5 metres in length. During the day, they are often to be found in loose groups resting on the seabed, snoozing like dogs in the sun, but at night they come alive and become a hurricane of death sweeping over the reef. Often hunting in large groups, whitetips fire in and out of holes and crevices, flushing out fish and mobbing them as they emerge. They eat pretty much anything they can catch, from fishes to crustaceans and molluscs – whatever it is, if they can force it out, it's dinner! They are assisted in detecting prey by the amazing array of senses sharks possess, gaining a particular advantage in the dark thanks to their excellent low-light vision and electricity detectors (ampullae of Lorenzini).

Once dawn starts to break, though, the sharks move back to their favourite resting spots and relax in the warm waters, waiting for the dusk to stir them to action once again.

The reef service stations

Motorway service stations are handy places to stop off, spruce up, grab a bite and refuel. Well, on coral reefs cleaning stations serve pretty much the same purpose. To the inexperienced eye, these special places might not be obvious – you might not notice much difference from any other part of the reef. However, they are normally in areas of open, easy access with fewer large coral outcrops, and they are usually marked by the presence of large fish such as reef mantas, sharks and groupers.

That's not to say that access is restricted to larger species – the animals that operate these cleaning stations have a warm welcome for all visitors. Regular workers include parasite-feeders such as blue-streak cleaner wrasse and scarlet cleaner shrimp, which will diligently pick, scrape and nip anything edible from any fish, big or small. And there are part-time cleaners to be found here too, as many species of wrasse and tangs spend some time working the cleaning stations for an easy meal. Then there are the thieves, such as the false cleanerfish, which looks almost identical to the trustworthy blue-streak and uses its disguise to gain access to the delicate gills and scales of prospective clients. One big bite later and the false cleaner has a meal and the cleaning station has a *very* angry client.

Cleaning stations are vital to the overall health of a coral reef. Not only do they draw together the smaller fish and invertebrate cleaners themselves, they are also an important point of interaction between larger animals visiting the reef, such as turtles, manta rays and sharks. If cleaning stations are lost through bleaching events or destructive fishing practices, the biodiversity of the reef as a whole is greatly reduced.

Cleaning-station etiquette

There are all sorts of different workers on the reef, each carrying out its own specialized task. One of the busiest is the blue-streak cleaner wrasse, a small but boldly marked fish with a great work ethic. These fish are usually seen in pairs in the reef's cleaning stations, where they advertise their services by a special dance that involves hopping and plenty of fin extension. Once a likely client has moved into the service area, the wrasse go to work, using their strong mouthparts to strip parasites from the surface of the fish's body. This takes a lot of courage, as all are welcome at the cleaning station – everything from sohal tang to thresher shark. And services offered include a full valet: dental and gill cleaning work sees these tiny wrasse disappearing into what looks like the mouth of doom.

Luckily, there is an unwritten truce, and both cleaners and clients have to be on their best behaviour. Clients that decide to snap and munch on a cleaner are often shunned on future visits to the cleaning station, and it isn't just the blue-streaks that reject them. In the same way, if one of the wrasse got a bit carried away and took a bite of delicious protein-rich gill filament, it would find its services boycotted until the misdemeanour had been forgotten. Not all is fair at the cleaning station, though. Pairs of wrasse have been recorded deliberately chasing away a fish halfway through a clean, to make space for special clients such as turtles or sharks, which usually have a much higher parasite load and therefore offer a bigger feast for the cleaners.

Dirty dancing, pipefish-style

You wouldn't guess it from looking at them, but pipefish belong to the same family as seahorses and sea dragons. And even though their body shapes are dramatically different, all these fishes in fact have much in common. Perhaps the best-known 'fact' about this group of fishes is that it is the male which 'gives birth' to the young. Well, that isn't quite what happens. The breeding process is actually perfectly normal: the female lays eggs, which are then fertilized and protected until they hatch. What *is* pretty amazing is the way the pipefish mixes it up and makes a real song and dance of the whole breeding business.

Before pipefish breed, the male and female come together and proceed through a very elaborate and demanding courtship dance. Considering pipefish are masters of camouflage and prefer to spend their time lying motionless in weeds, the sudden change to conspicuous wiggling and jiving, all in plain sight, may make you wonder what on earth is going on. In fact, the idea behind the dancing is not to get their groove on, but to show just how fit and responsive they are. If either male or female fails to make the grade, mating is not likely to occur. But assuming everyone makes the right moves, the female lays her eggs, depositing them either inside the male's specialized brood pouch or on a special flattened area of skin on his belly. The male then fertilizes the eggs and goes about his business, while the female leaves him for a time. The male cares for the eggs until they hatch, usually around two or three weeks later.

Not long after the birth, the male and female meet and mate again. This is actually quite a smart move: as the female doesn't have to carry the eggs after they have been fertilized, she can go away, have a good feed and develop more eggs, which will be ready for fertilization by the time the male has hatched her previous clutch. That's why the dance at the start is so important, for if the male isn't fit enough to dance, then he isn't fit enough to carry the precious cargo of eggs.

Scourge of the reefs: crown-of-thorns starfish

There can't be a more hated member of the reef community than the crown-of-thorns starfish. This large starfish can grow to over 30 centimetres in width and have between fifteen and twenty arms. It gets its name from the fact that it is covered in large, sharp, toxin-filled spines which give it excellent protection against nearly all predators it encounters. And you wouldn't want to mess with it either: if you get stabbed by one of those spines, you'll suffer extreme localized pain, swelling, uncontrolled bleeding and nausea, and you may need the spine removed by surgery. However, it's not the effect these starfish have on us that's the big problem; it's the effect they have on coral reefs which we are not so wild about.

Crown-of-thorns starfish eat stony corals. They tend to emerge at night to feast on plating and branching corals, but they'll eat any stony coral and even soft corals if competition for food is high. The starfish feeds by climbing onto the target coral and extruding its extremely large stomach into all the nooks and crannies of the coral's surface. Digestive enzymes are then released and the dissolving coral flesh is absorbed into the body of the starfish, which can consume an area equal to its own body size every feed. Larger starfish feed both day and night, so the damage to the reef is extensive and prolonged. These starfish do have natural predators, including Triton's trumpet (a large snail) and the harlequin shrimp, although the latter can only tackle smaller starfish. And some corals have their own protection against the starfish, thanks to symbiotic partners which live within the coral itself: snapping shrimps, crabs and polychaete worms have all been known to defend their home coral from attacks by striking at the softer underneath of the crown-of-thorns starfish, usually causing it to move on and hunt elsewhere.

Now, crown-of-thorns starfish have been around for a long time. When in balance with the reef ecosystem, they can actually help maintain a wide range of corals, by stopping any particular species overgrowing its neighbours. The trouble starts when the starfish population explodes and they rapidly destroy parts of the reef habitat. These plagues are often due to overfishing of the starfish's predators, while recent research has shown that excessive blooms of phytoplankton caused by agricultural run-off can create a perfect environment for starfish larvae to thrive in the plankton, resulting in a bumper crop of adults.

Controlling crown-of-thorns outbreaks on reefs is critical for the ongoing health of these incredible ecosystems. A long-term solution, however, will involve tackling factors such as terrestrial run-off and climate change, which prevent nature from doing its job and cause starfish numbers to get out of hand.

Caribbean reefs under attack: invasion of the lionfish

Lionfish are brightly coloured fish known especially for their covering of highly venomous spines and their seriously big appetites. In their home range, in the Indo-Pacific region, there are many different species of lionfish, and they are both predator and prey – there are animals such as sharks and groupers that enjoy a good feed on a lionfish without worrying about those toxin-filled spines. But unfortunately, lionfish have spread outside their normal range and reached the Caribbean, where they have no natural enemies. No one is exactly sure how they managed to make the journey from eastern Pacific to western Atlantic. Transport of their eggs or larvae in shipping ballast water is the most likely explanation, while escape or release from private home aquariums is another possibility. Either way, lionfish have invaded the Caribbean and are doing incredible damage to the reefs there.

Lionfish don't feed on corals directly. Instead, they move in and around the delicate coral bommies and outcrops, hoovering up all the smaller reef fish hiding in the recesses. Nothing is off the menu for these voracious predators, and they will munch down anything they can fit in their mouth, including smaller lionfish. The real trouble comes when they begin to destroy the population of tangs, surgeonfish and other algal grazers, which are vital for pruning and nibbling the algae that can swamp the coral and take hold during bleaching events. Remove the grazers and the reef has nothing to keep it clear; algae take over and the whole thing starts to crash. The lionfish doesn't care, though – they just move on to the next area of coral and start the process all over again. And it's not just the wildlife that is at risk; as the lionfish spread unchecked, the local economy suffers, as lobster fishermen (for instance) start to see their livelihoods vanish down the throat of the invaders.

We can only hope that the sharks and large predators of the western Atlantic will eventually acquire a taste for lionfish and the natural balance can be restored. However, we have no idea when or if such a diet shift will occur, and by then it could be too late.

Slippery assassin: the moray eel

Moray eels are brilliant residents of the reef: important predators, but awesome for their intelligence and behaviour too. Several species of

The Blowfish goes deep . . .

GREAT BLUE HOLE

Head 70 kilometres off the coast of Belize to the Lighthouse Reef, and you'll find one of the most famous dive spots – indeed, ocean landmarks – on the planet. The Great Blue Hole is a sinkhole that formed over a long period of geological time through glacial erosion of the reef, progressively cut away during several periods of lower sea level. Now stable and filled with seawater, the Great Blue Hole sits near the centre of the reef and has been designated a UNESCO World Heritage Site.

As its name suggests, it really is a great blue hole! Measuring 300 metres across and 125 metres at its deepest point, it is an incredible cave environment filled with ledges and stalactites, as well as a variety of reef fishes and shark species. However, while such a unique space may be alluring to human divers, as far as the fish of the reef are concerned, it is rather dull. Light drops off quickly underwater, even in clear tropical seas, and as there are few large overhangs that block the Sun's rays, corals find it hard to establish in the Great Blue Hole. Patches of coral crop up here and there, along with large sponges and sea fans which are only too happy to forgo light for the rich particles of food that float down from above. To us, visiting this place is like stepping through a wormhole into another world, but to the reef community itself, it's just a big blemish in what would otherwise be perfect coral-growing territory.

varying size and colour are found throughout the world's coral reefs. The largest is the giant moray, which can reach 3 metres in length and weigh in at 30 kilograms or more. Moray eels all share the same body plan, with long dorsal and ventral fins, thick skin and a large mouth (one notable variation is the dragon moray eel, which has very long and elegant tubular nostrils). It's that big mouth that gives the moray such a fearsome appearance – a mass of dagger sharp, spine-like teeth – but its throat is even worse: this has a pharyngeal jaw covered in even more teeth, and just like the Alien of film fame, this jaw can be thrown forward from the back of the throat to grip any prey trapped in the main jaws, which is then pulled down to its doom. Moray eels have a slimy body covered in thick mucus which protects their skin as they move in and out of the rough reef environment. This mucus has the added bonus of containing an anticoagulant, so, if a moray bites you, the wound will not clot and you'll continue to bleed.

A moray on its own is part ambush predator, part nocturnal hunter, but sometimes they join forces with other fish to hunt together. The giant moray and roving coral grouper make a fearsome team when it comes to the hunt. The coral grouper approaches the moray's hole and performs a head-shaking ritual that apparently convinces the eel to come out for a jaunt. Then the team goes to work: the moray dives into crevices in the reef, scaring out smaller fish for the grouper to snatch, while the grouper's presence panics prey fish into staying in the rocks, leaving them vulnerable to the moray. Either way, you don't want to be caught napping when this dangerous duo comes knocking!

The marvellous mantas

The great white shark aside, there can hardly be a more famous ocean inhabitant than the manta ray. Large, graceful and intelligent, I have been privileged enough to dive with these creatures, and I can assure you, they are like nothing else on the planet.

The two species of manta ray – the giant manta and the reef manta – are almost identical apart from their size: the giant manta can grow to a wingspan of 7 metres, while the reef manta's span doesn't get much bigger than 5 metres. Both types have huge mouths, prominent gill slits on the ventral (lower) surface, and horn-shaped tactile flaps (known as cephalic lobes) in front of the mouth. These lobes are usually held curled up but are unfurled when it comes to feeding. The manta ray is an excellent filter-feeder, using its lobes like a shovel to direct as much water as possible into the wide mouth, where zooplankton, tiny shrimps and other edible matter are filtered out. Recent studies have shown that giant mantas get the vast majority of their food in the form of krill at depths of 1,000 metres. It's cold and dark down there, but the ray has an advantage over its quarry: it has a complex system of blood vessels which keep its brain and eyes at a temperature above that of the surrounding water, ensuring that its reactions stay tip-top and are not numbed by the cold.

Manta rays are really intelligent, having the largest brain of any fish. You can see how smart they are just by observing them in the wild and watching the amazing ways they behave and interact. Many scientists believe that mantas have the ability to communicate effectively between themselves, probably exchanging information on food, potential mates, etc. Another benefit of high intelligence is the ability to make long

Manta ray

and complex migrations, returning to a specific place at a specific time. Giant manta rays range over the entire ocean, yet they can still return to hit a tiny patch of reef at just the right time for a really good feast. They like to stay clean too: both giant and reef mantas are regular visitors at cleaning stations, where shoals of fish can be seen cleaning their entire bodies, including working over those large and important gills.

These creatures truly are the most majestic animals you could ever imagine, showing a charm and character beyond anything you'd expect to find in a fish.

How to piss off a starfish: the harlequin shrimp

There can be few creatures on the planet so deceptively cute as the harlequin shrimp. This tiny crustacean grows to no more than 5 centimetres in length, and its ivory-white carapace is covered in beautiful blue or sometimes brown spots; elegant and ornate, it has wide, flat claws and very large and fancy antennae. It looks anything but a cold-bloodied killer, but that is exactly what it is.

Harlequin shrimp feed exclusively on starfish – live starfish – which they hunt over the reefs, usually in pairs. This Bonnie and Clyde duo are tenacious, and once they find a starfish, they work quickly to flip it over to stop it from using its strong sucker-like tube feet to escape. It is quite some effort for two small shrimps to tackle a much larger starfish, which is equipped with so many arms to fight back. Once the hapless victim has finally come unstuck, it is hauled off to a burrow, where the pair of shrimps slowly devour its soft tube feet from the arm tips down to the central mouth. Eventually the starfish is so damaged that the shrimps can rip off its arms and continue feeding on the tissues inside. Now, as you may know, starfish can *regrow* arms, and there are stories that harlequin shrimps actually force-feed their imprisoned dinner guest, waiting for arms to regrow! While this isn't impossible, I can't see it happening myself. These shrimps are voracious killers and are most likely to demolish the starfish entirely, before running off to hijack another one.

Factor 50 snot: coral sliming

Corals live in some wonderful places: Australia, Polynesia, Fiji, Bahamas, the Maldives, to name just a few. Now all these places have one thing in common: a hell of a lot of sun! This, of course, is all well and good – after all, corals need sun to fuel their growth. But the Sun makes things hot, often very hot, and sometimes corals have to bear the brunt of this heat not just underwater but in the air too.

During spring tides, areas of the reef are completely exposed for short periods of time, leaving corals high and dry for up to an hour. To survive exposure to the air and temperatures perhaps reaching 40°C, corals must act fast. And there's only one thing that can save them: snot. Well, mucus, to be more accurate, which the coral tissues start to produce at a fearsome rate of knots. Covering their tissues in slimy mucus gives the coral protection not only from desiccation but from fresh water too. Spring tides occur all year round, and corals exposed on these super-low tides also have to deal with tropical downpours. Their ordeal doesn't last forever, however – the tide quickly turns and before long the coral reef is back under the waves. At this point, the mucus is washed away, exposing the coral polyps to the salt water again. The mucus isn't wasted, though: it is so sticky that it rapidly collects many organic and inorganic floating particles, which in turn attract small microscopic feeders – all of which produces a kind of snot pizza, a delicacy that whets the appetite of hungry fishes and shrimps.

Epaulette shark, hunter of the shallows

Reef sharks are the master hunters of the reef. From tiger sharks patrolling solo to the pack-like feeding of whitetip reef sharks: all fish fear the approach of sharks. However, there is one type of shark that leaves the big boys behind, gaining access to feeding grounds that are denied to others. The epaulette shark is a small shark, only around 1 metre in length, found in the coastal waters around Australia and on other nearby reefs. Its long slender body, small round fins and cute little face will hardly strike fear into humans, but to small molluscs, fish and crustaceans in the shallows, this shark is the Terminator.

When the tide goes out on the reef, small pools of water are trapped between coral heads, and whatever was around those corals at the time the last wave left is trapped too. The oxygen in these tidal pools drops rapidly, creating an anoxic environment that severely reduces the activity of any animal – except, that is, the epaulette shark. This creature has specialized metabolic pathways in its brain and other organs that significantly reduce its oxygen demand, allowing it to function normally in conditions that would otherwise be deadly.

So, this shark can survive in waters where other sharks can't, but that's not the only trick up its sleeve. At low tide, these pools are often shallow and cut off from other pools or channels by stretches of rocky reef. Not a problem for the epaulette shark, which uses its small round fins as feet to crawl and walk over any obstacle in its way, even if that means climbing out of the water and scrabbling over dry land. After all, the shark doesn't need oxygen, so who cares if it's wet or dry? Nothing can stop this hunter in pursuit of its prey ... except, perhaps, the returning tide, when the shark loses its advantage. Oh well, only six hours to wait till the next tide.

Ornamental killer: the cone shell

We all know that the oceans contain some dangerous predators that pose significant risk to humans. However, what is less well known is that you have more to fear from a 15-centimetre-long snail than from a 6-metre-long great white shark. For there is a group of super-deadly molluscs known as cone shells or cone snails, found in all tropical and subtropical seas, whose deadly venom poses a real threat to humans.

In most gastropod molluscs, the specialized feeding structure – the radula – is like a conveyor belt or ribbon covered with tiny teeth. In the cone shell, however, it is highly modified, with the main tooth resembling a large hollow harpoon. This harpoon, infused with some pretty vicious venom, is fired from the snail's tube-like proboscis into prey, which is instantly paralysed or killed. It makes sense for such a slow-moving creature to have such powerful venom, as the snail would have little chance chasing down a fish or other prey, once wounded and flagging, before some other predator got to it first: instant death ensures an instant meal.

But what is good for the snail isn't so good for humans that get on the wrong side of it: the geographic cone shell, for instance, is alarmingly nicknamed the cigarette snail, the idea being that, after you have been stung, you have enough time to smoke a cigarette before you die. It's rather ironic, then, that empty cone shells appear in bathrooms, spas and en-suites in swanky hotels worldwide: not, perhaps, a very fitting end for such a hardcore killer.

Location, location, location: anus

Finding a home these days is hard – after all, there's so much you have to consider before making a commitment. What are the local schools like? Are there good transport links? Is it somebody's anus? Yes, that's right: not at the top of everyone's shopping list, perhaps, but for one ocean inhabitant this is a key concern. Meet your new neighbour: the pearlfish.

Of the many species of pearlfish, a few, such as the silver pearlfish, have unusual tastes in housing: they like to make their home inside the anus of a sea cucumber. Luckily for the sea cucumber, they are not particular long fish – only about 18 centimetres – and they are extremely slender. The juveniles are believed to hunt out suitable 'homes' so that they have a safe place to metamorphose into a full adult. The adults are then quite protective of their homes, and fights have been known to break out between pearlfish at times of a housing shortage. During the night, the pearlfish leaves the safety of its capacious cucumber home and forages in the surrounding area for shrimps, smaller fish and molluscs. It

Above: The mahi-mahi is a prize catch for the seagoing angler. Weighing up to 40 kilograms and reaching 2 metres in length, this beautiful yet brawny fish puts up a fight. Unfortunately, due to commercial longline fishing, too many are being caught up as bycatch.

Left: This eerie yet stunning creature is the comb jelly. Thanks to their photocytes – light-producing cells – they are able to emit a gorgeous glow called bioluminescence. But they're more than just a pretty jelly – combs are master predators of the ocean's microworld.

The leopard seal is a notorious predator of the penguin, baiting and exhausting them until it's time for dinner. However, these half-tonne seals can even pose a threat to humans.

This tropical tube worm extends its feathery crown of feeding tentacles to catch passing edible particles from the current. However, at the first sign of danger, it's ready to pull itself rapidly down into its protective tube.

'Look, but don't touch.' This little guy may appear adorably hypnotic, but one touch from the blue-ringed octopus can cause deadly paralysis of the body and lungs. An antivenom does not exist.

The moray eel is one of the largest reef predators, reaching 3 metres in length. And if you think its mouth is terrifying, that's nothing. Within the moray eel's throat is a pharyngeal jaw covered in even more teeth, which can shoot out and grab its struggling prey, *Alien*-style.

Flying fish can glide for up to 200 metres or more in one swoop. But this isn't just for the fun of it. Flying fish are sought after by many open-sea predators, so they take to the sky to avoid being snapped up.

One of the few 'cute' creatures of the deep sea, the Dumbo octopus embodies its namesake: Dumbo the Disney elephant.

The majestic manta ray is highly intelligent, with the largest brain of any fish. Their acute intelligence allows them to make long and complex migrations, yet still find their way back to the best reefs at prime feeding-time.

The banded sea krait uses its flattened, paddle-shaped tail to power through the water towards its prey. Its highly venomous, convulsion- and-paralysis-inducing bite, allows it to feast on such perilous creatures as the moray eel.

The Portuguese man o' war forms a bulbous gas-filled sac, which floats along, catching the wind like a sail. This allows the man o' war to be blown towards its prey. What you can't see in the image above is its 10-metre-long tentacles, plunging below the water's surface.

At a miniscule 1 centimetre wide, the sand-bubbler crab works tirelessly on the beaches of the Indian and Pacific Oceans, shovelling sand into its mouth, and extracting any tasty nutrients it can.

The crown-of-thorns starfish is one of the most hated members of the reef community. As you can see, this prickly predator latches onto coral, and devours it at an alarmingly high rate. Controlling crown-of-thorns outbreaks on reefs is very important for the ongoing health of these incredible ecosystems.

The tripod fish has developed a very savvy way of catching its prey. The fish is able to perch on the seabed using its fin ray extensions, face the current, and simply wait for its dinner to float by.

You may like to think that this strange looking sea squirt is one of the furthest species from humankind, but this humble tunicate in fact belongs to the phylum Chordata, which contains all animals that have a backbone and dorsal nerve cord at some stage of life – this includes us.

It may seem cute, but the harlequin shrimp is anything but – especially if you're a starfish. In pairs, these 5-centimetre-long shrimps will dislodge a starfish from its sucker-like tube feet, haul it back to their burrow, and devour its legs.

then returns to its preferred cucumber before dawn, assuming it can find it. Certain species of pearlfish are rather troublesome guests, as they are thought to feed on their hosts from the inside, consuming their gonads and other internal structures.

You might not expect a sea cucumber's anus to be an ideal home, but in fact these animals breathe out of their anus, so it is actually a good place for regular water flow. There is, however, a problem with the toxicity of sea cucumbers, which is potent enough to stop most fish from even attempting to eat one. However, the anus-dwelling pearlfish have immunity to these toxins thanks to a thick mucus they excrete onto their skin. The mucus also has the added bonus that it provides useful lubrication if the fish wants to slip out of the house ...

Deadly serpents of the shallows

Banded sea kraits are among the most venomous animals on the planet. This marine serpent is found throughout the tropical waters of the Indo-Pacific, where it makes its home on the abundant reefs and in the coastal shallows. It's shaped like any other snake, except that its tail is flattened from side to side, forming a broad paddle to assist in swimming. The krait has a truly amazing breath-hold and can stay submerged for two hours; it then needs only a 45-second pit stop at the surface before diving down and hunting again. Primarily feeding on small fish and moray eels, it must return to land to rest, digest and breed. Almost unbelievably for such a venomous animal, these snakes are extremely docile and will only attack humans when threatened – which is a good thing too, as their venom attacks the nervous system, causing convulsions and paralysis.

While the banded sea krait is fully capable of hunting on its own, an extraordinary cooperative technique has been observed in which large aggregations of snakes swarm over the reef, closely followed by shoals of giant trevally and goatfish. While the snakes infiltrate small holes and crevices in pursuit of prey, their fellow hunters wait nearby to pounce on creatures fleeing from the reef as the snakes attack. Sadly, this kind of hunting can only occur where reefs are healthy and lush, so it's now only documented in some of the more remote areas of the Indo-Pacific.

The Great Barrier's little brother: Ningaloo Reef

You will all have heard of the Great Barrier Reef, on the eastern coast of Australia, but Down Under boasts another beautiful reef of epic proportions on the western coast. Ningaloo Reef is 260 kilometres long and situated close to the coast, as it is a fringing (not a barrier) reef. Facing out towards the eastern Indian Ocean, Ningaloo is a vital link in the life cycles of many sea creatures, none more so than the whale shark.

The largest fish in the sea, whale sharks are extremely fond of Ningaloo and make annual migrations from all over the world to this special site. Between March and June over 300 whale sharks move from the tropical oceans to visit the reef for the boom in plankton and other tasty offerings that results from the mass spawning events by which reefs spread themselves to new areas. Large ocean wanderers like whale sharks are so widely dispersed in the oceans that for them to congregate in such numbers in one small stretch of coastline is quite an event and probably gives them an opportunity to socialize or even mate. From Ningaloo many of the massive-mouthed fish head north to Christmas Island and feed on the spawning of the Christmas Island crabs there – basically shifting from one all-you-can-eat buffet to another.

Ningaloo isn't all about whale sharks, however. This world heritage site also has manta rays, sea turtles, whales and rare sea snakes, as well as the usual magnificent assortment of coral and reef fish. Pound for pound, it could be argued that Ningaloo plays a role in the ocean's ongoing vitality that is no less important than its bigger eastern brother.

Mind your step: stonefish

When you think about venom, it's probably snakes that first spring to mind, perhaps followed by the odd spider. But in fact, to find some of the worst venom going, you have to get your feet wet. The oceans contain some stone-cold killers, but also some killers that are cold-blooded stones.

Stonefishes are a group of chunky, ugly and highly venomous fish. In fact, the reef stonefish is the most venomous fish on the planet and can kill a human. The venom isn't contained in a stinging tail or needle-like teeth; instead, there's a venom gland beneath the skin, at the base of a hollow dorsal fin spine. To be stung, you basically have to sting yourself. That may sound pretty dumb, but the stonefish is an unbelievable master of camouflage and can completely blend into any rocky or reef environment. So if you are out swimming and put your foot down for a rest, you need to check where you are stepping. If you do get stung, the severity of the sting is proportionate to the amount of force applied to the spine; in other words, you literally squeeze the venom into yourself – it isn't injected into you by muscular contractions of the fish.

Left untreated, a stonefish sting can and does lead to death (stonefish antivenom is the second-most commonly distributed antivenom in Australia). When it's not being stepped on, the stonefish stays motionless on reefs and feeds by ambushing prey. Its jaw can open, snap forward and close on prey faster than you can blink. Stonefish won't even move if the tide recedes around them, and they can survive for twenty-four hours out of the water or in stagnant tidal pools: the ultimate killer – super-deadly, super-lazy.

Blue rings, red alert

The blue-ringed octopus is the living embodiment of 'look, don't touch'. This small cephalopod, growing to no more than 20 centimetres, lives in the tidal pools associated with coral reefs of the western Pacific and eastern Indian Oceans, but they are found in their largest abundance around Australia's southern and western coast. It is rather stunning to behold, with fifty or more vibrant blue rings covering most of its body. Having the amazing cephalopod capacity for colour change and body-morphing, the blue-ringed octopus can camouflage itself superbly, but when threatened and cornered by a predator, it pulses its blue rings violently in a display that firmly suggests: 'Sod off or else!' If the threat is not heeded, the octopus will bite.

All octopuses have specialized saliva that helps break down their food for easy digestion; however, the blue-ringed octopus has taken things much further, making it one of the ocean's deadliest animals. The venom is a neurotoxin and rapidly causes paralysis of the body and lungs – perfect for stopping crabs and shrimps in their tracks, but a bit of a nuisance for humans as there's currently no antivenom! Basically, you are in serious trouble. Since the toxin paralyses the lungs, your only hope of survival is to be put on a respirator and ventilated until your body can fully process the venom and you can breathe again. So: definitely one of those creatures you might want to see in the wild, but a good idea to give it a *very* wide berth.

Open Ocean

The vast blue of the open ocean hides many secrets. In this planet-spanning expanse live some of the greatest nomads and travellers ever to evolve. This is an area where to survive is to keep moving and hope that a life-giving oasis or food source isn't too far away.

The open ocean, in the terms we are using, is immensely broad but not immensely deep. It covers a huge 360 million square kilometres of the planet's surface, encompassing the waters far from shore, past the continental shelf, but still shallow enough to be sunlit. The deep ocean is a dark world apart from the struggles of the waters above, and few specialist species migrate between them.

Surely the world-encircling ocean is teeming with life? In fact, the opposite is the case. The great plankton blooms of the temperate coastal seas don't penetrate far into the wide blue yonder; instead, localized areas seem to explode with life for short periods of time. Huge masses of small baitfish can appear seemingly at random, or a change in the wind can form a productive sea front, packed with plankton. It's then up to the hunters of the sea to track down these flourishes of fauna and exploit them while they can. Speed and stamina are the watchwords of

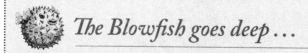

The Blowfish goes deep …

WHY BLUE IS BAD: OLIGOTROPHIC ENVIRONMENTS

Pristine blue waters must surely be perfect for life, right? After all, if *we* love them so much, the animals of the sea presumably love them too. Alas, no. The truth is that clear blue water is pretty crappy for life – after all, it's clear because there's so little in it to eat. The open ocean is considered an oligotrophic environment, one that yields very few nutrients for sustaining life.

There are multiple reasons for this stark truth. One is that any life-giving goodies are rapidly used up by literally anything. Another is the lack of mineralized iron, which is critical if photosynthesizing organisms are to proliferate. As soon as even a tiny speck of the stuff becomes available, either brought up from the depths or blown in as dust from the land, a rapid bloom of life chews it all up and then quickly crashes again. For life in abundance, there needs to be a constant supply of nutrients, but phenomena such as thermoclines and haloclines prevent the mixing of waters and so trap nutrients away from sunlit waters.

The potential for transforming the open ocean, to engineer it so that it will bloom into a hotbed of organic action, has long been debated as a potential method of dealing with climate change. For example, some scientists argue that if we seed the ocean with iron, we will encourage large blooms of carbon dioxide-consuming algae to grow, thereby locking the gas within their bodies and transporting it down to the deep sea when they die. It's not a bad idea, and there have been multiple scientific expeditions to study how it might work. However, the concern is that such a large bloom would generate a huge increase in bacteria feeding on the decaying plankton, and these bacteria would respire the CO_2 back into the atmosphere, consuming a lot of oxygen from the water at the same time. For the moment, then, the open ocean still remains the largest desert on our planet.

any creature looking to make a living in such conditions, and evolution has honed some of the fastest animals on the planet in this watery desert.

Living in such an expanse has produced the greatest migrations you will find on planet Earth: whole schools of fish moving from one side of the world to the other, in search of food or a mate, or a perfect place to spawn. The hunters that follow them do so often in isolation, lone wanderers that have adapted into the most perfect forms for a life constantly on the move. But some hunters travel in groups and use their numbers or their intelligence to outwit and outcompete their prey. And very occasionally, huge masses of predators and prey come together, and then it seems as if the seas, vast as they are, can hardly contain such volume and spectacle.

Science has pondered tinkering with these waters and harnessing the power of photosynthesis to tackle the planet's problems (more on this to come). It would be a drastic and revolutionary step, and thankfully no large-scale experiments have yet disturbed the open ocean. For now, this marine desert retains its combination of emptiness and sporadic life, just as it should. It's a frontier as wild as any of the old Wild West – a place whose inhabitants play out their entire lives on the go, forever striving to be good enough, fast enough and strong enough to make it to the next meal.

The fickleness of fronts

You will know that currents tend to be an unruly bunch. In the ocean, they're constantly interacting with each other, sometimes mixing and becoming one, but often opposing each other in some way, because of certain clashing physical properties. The boundary between two bodies of water is called a front, and in the open ocean they often represent zones of brief activity.

Fronts can be either convergent, where the water masses are moving towards each other, or divergent, where they are doing the opposite. The convergent variety brings together floating particles, plankton and bits of floating debris, and you will often find many fish and jellies feeding on these hard-to-come-by concentrated food sources. With divergent fronts, the opposing movements of the currents draw cooler, deeper water to the surface in an upwelling. The associated increase in nutrients, rising from the deep, can bring on small, localized eruptions of plankton, in turn luring fish from miles around to exploit the boom.

Fronts can be small, forming in great numbers in shallow bays and beaches, while out at sea they can be vast. The Pacific White Line is a front that forms under certain conditions in the southern Pacific, when cold water from Antarctica meets warms water from the tropics, resulting in a convergent 2-kilometre-wide front, many hundreds of kilometres long. In this case, the resultant bloom of plankton can be seen from space.

The problem with fronts – and for those who rely on them – is that they're constantly shifting and changing as the water bodies slowly mix, or as the weather conditions change and currents divert slightly. For many open-ocean species such as flying fish, sardines and tuna, their whole lives are spent chasing these fronts and the brief bonanzas they create.

Have sail, will travel: free-floating zooids

If your life depends on locating plankton blooms in the open ocean, you'd better find the hotspots where it's all happening, which are normally at the fronts. One group of animals, known as siphonophores (relatives of corals, jellyfish and anemones), have a special method of speeding to the best fishing grounds without moving a muscle. The famous Portuguese man o' war and the by-the-wind sailor (*Velella velella*) both rely on the wind to carry them to the ocean's areas of plenty.

Siphonophores aren't actually single animals at all – they are living colonies of small individual organisms, known as zooids, in which each zooid performs a different role. In the by-the-wind sailor, part of the colony forms a buoyant float, filled with air pockets. This keeps it bobbing on the water's surface. But that's not all: it hoists a tall sail, rising from the main disc of the colony, which perfectly catches the wind. The man o' war goes one step further, and members of its zooid community form a bulbous gas-filled sac, which floats on the surface but is large enough to a form of sail, allowing it to catch even the slightest breeze and ensure that its 10-metre-long tentacles can fish freely in the waters below.

The disadvantage of free-floating is that neither of these creatures has any other form of locomotion, so they are completely at the mercy of the wind and current. In bad times, this can lead to mass beach strandings during storms, or being completely blown off course into hostile waters. That's one hell of an ill wind!

Live fast, die young: the rock-star life of anchovies

A dodgy addition to pizza, but potentially the world's most abundant fish species, and certainly one of the greatest diners on the plankton, is the humble yet ultimately brilliant Peruvian anchoveta. Anchovies in general act as primary consumers of the plankton, eating everything from small phytoplankton to larger zooplankton like copepods, or even krill. Feeding at this high-energy stage in the food chain means that anchovies grow and mature quickly until they reach a modest size of around 20 centimetres. They're not very long-lived, making only two or three years at best before they fall to some other predator; nevertheless, that gives them plenty of time to breed.

Anchovies follow what ecologists class as an r reproductive strategy. Put simply, this means grow quick, breed profusely, die soon afterwards. Such biology gives species a great chance to exploit seasonal abundance, but also makes them perfect targets for fisheries. The Peruvian anchoveta is the world's leading example of this pattern and is the most heavily exploited fish in history. In 1971, more than 13 million tonnes of them were landed by the Peruvian fishing fleets. Subsequent overfishing and El Niño events took their toll, however, and now catches are down to between 6 and 8 million tonnes. Despite all that, their no-holds-barred reproductive strategy means that all it takes for a population explosion is one good year. And a good year, for Peruvian anchoveta, is one in which the cold, deep, nutrient-rich upwellings of the Peru Current cause a plankton bloom to spread across the entire west coast of southern South America. In these conditions, multiple shoals of 10 million or more anchoveta are possible. But in El Niño years, when a blanket of warm stagnant water locks the nutrients below, the anchoveta can't form super-shoals and must chase the plankton wherever it may pop up, crossing vast expanses of the Southern Pacific to hunt isolated blooms. And then come the dangers, because seabirds, sharks, tuna and the fishing fleets of Peru all do the same, and with an identical purpose: to tap into that rich anchoveta bounty.

A terminal case: bait balls

When conditions allow it, smaller plankton-feeding fish species such as sardine, herring and anchovy can form huge shoals. Left to their own devices, these shoals are constantly on the move, hiding in the darker waters during the day and moving to the surface to feed as the light fades. Shoaling and schooling provide the fish with protection in numbers, but when cornered, the urge to school becomes their downfall.

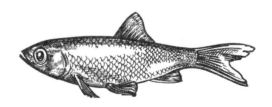

Anchovy

It works like this. If a section of the larger shoal is cut off by the action of predators, then the reaction of the small breakaway group is to form into a tighter group, a bait ball. And in all honesty, once they've done that, they're doomed. Writhing around in a constrained sphere, trying to focus on nothing but survival and too terrified to break away, they are easily driven to the surface by predators, where there is no escape. The killers can strike the ball from all angles, as fish attack from below while diving seabirds strike from above. The trick for the predators is to keep up the pressure on the bait ball and to stop it sinking back down into the depths where it might rejoin the main shoal or escape into the dark. Tuna achieve this by constant high-speed attacks, dolphins and whales use their intellect to trap the fish, whereas sailfish use predatory teamwork to massacre their prey.

The result can be 100 per cent terminal. But it's not all bad. While it may seem a cruel end for every fish in the ball to be wiped out and consumed, it takes a lot of effort from predators to achieve this . . . and while they are hell-bent on finishing off the bait ball, the main mega-shoal can make its escape. The predators will need to try and locate it all over again.

Launch torpedoes: the marlin

Bait balls certainly have little chance against top ocean predators such as marlins, which are the celebrities of the wide blue sea. The species belonging to this famous family all share similar biological characteristics, the most prominent feature of which is a super-long and thin beak or bill, extending from the top jaw of the fish. They have large eyes and gills, a tall dorsal spine, flowing pectoral fins and a beautifully streamlined, torpedo-shaped body that slims right down before reaching a large crescent-shaped tail-fin. They are built for long-term cruising and short-burst speed.

Internally, marlins have those clever *rete mirabile* blood vessels that keep warm blood centred around the core muscles, brain and eyes. This

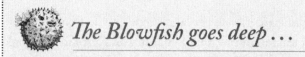

The Blowfish goes deep...

HOW TO ATTRACT FISH

In the featureless expanse of the open ocean, literally anything other than water can be seen as a beacon for life. Such things go by the natty name of 'fish-attracting devices' (FADs), and they are found throughout the ocean in natural and unnatural ways, but however they have appeared, their importance cannot be overlooked. The basic idea is that fish in the open ocean always want to find some cover to counter the constant stress and vulnerability of being completely exposed. Floating debris such as logs, beer crates or man-made rafts protect fish from dangers aloft (seabirds) and provides a hard surface to press against or hide behind if aquatic predators come sniffing around.

It's astonishing just how quickly an entire food chain can develop from something floating in the water. The first fish on site will often be the closest and smallest, usually those that were developing in the plankton. However, it is not long before some species of territorial fish appear, to claim ownership of the FAD. A classic example is the trigger fish, whose bad temper and aggressive attitude scares away most other fish that would otherwise attempt to inhabit the new house. After that, though, it's a free-for-all, and large shoals of baitfish can usually be found skulking in the shadow created by the object. It is the appearance of these fish that can start to bring in the big predators. Tuna spend their whole lives jetting across the oceans looking for balls of baitfish to feed on, so when they find a more stable supply in the form of an FAD, they stay close by to maximize the opportunity.

Fish-attracting devices also turn out to be human-attracting devices. Having taken note of the activity around FADs, many tuna fisheries deploy their own large FADs throughout the oceans. Sometimes these are large rafts that float on the surface, or they can be frames of fabric tethered below the waves. Not all fishing FADs are moored down, and some are allowed to follow the ocean's whims, but they are often equipped with GPS beacons so that the fishing fleets can find them wherever they are.

gives them a significant advantage over prey species which have to match the temperature of the surrounding water and will be slower and more sluggish than any attacking marlin. They used to get big too, with the largest blue marlin ever caught coming in at 5 metres and weighing 818 kilograms. Sadly, those kinds of sizes are the stuff of history, and large marlin of any species are getting ever rarer today.

Like their closely related cousins the tuna, marlins spend their lives chasing bait balls of fish across the open oceans. When a bait ball is cornered at the surface, a feeding frenzy often begins and all the predators present will begin to attack. The marlin relies on its out-and-out speed to smash through prey: its torpedo-like body lives up to its description. But a large blue marlin won't survive just on multiple mouthfuls of baitfish, so squid, tuna and even other smaller marlin species have all been found in the gut contents of big specimens.

Sea mount: underwater metropolis . . .

Fish don't have to completely rely on fish-attracting devices for something solid to swim in, under or around, for there are the very contours of the undersea world itself. Rising up from the ocean floor are the undersea mountains or sea mounts, usually formed from extinct volcanoes: these are the peaks that tried, but failed, to escape the big blue to become islands. They are widespread across all oceans, especially in areas of tectonic shift, where the Earth's crust is constantly moving.

The Pacific Ocean has many sea mounts, some of which have actually peeped through the surface and become the myriad tiny, wonderful islands in the areas around Indonesia and Micronesia. Sea mounts that were once land but have been eroded back below the waves are called guyots. Currently, the largest sea mount we know of is the Davidson Sea Mount, at 42 kilometres long, 13 kilometres wide, rising nearly 2,300 metres from the seabed.

Underwater peaks might not be much use to a mountaineer, but they form critical areas of biodiversity in open-ocean environments. Not only are they a landmark for navigation, or for aggregation before breeding, but their large physical presence disrupts the water flowing around them. Many organisms take advantage of this, and filter-feeding worms, corals, sponges and anemones all colonize the sides of a mountain. They are now perfectly placed in the path of constant currents that bring a supply of nutrients and food as they break and twist around the rocks in their path. This biodiversity then brings more life in the form of fish and invertebrates, whose larvae are deposited there by the disrupted currents and which now make the sea mount their home. In fact, the life around sea mounts is *so* rich in what would otherwise be barren ocean, that they are heavily targeted by fisheries around the world. Thankfully, because of their prime ecological importance, many sea mounts are now marine reserves, allowing these islands-that-never-were to becomes oases of the open sea.

. . . and ecological niche

If you're a wanderer of the open ocean, it can be hard to find, well, anything, from food to a mate. So anywhere that life congregates becomes a vital habitat, and for some of the world's largest predators, their brief visits to dedicated sea mounts become the most crucial times of their lives. While many fish may never leave their sea mounts, taking advantage of all that comes from the nutrients swirling around them, larger predators like sharks tend to be more transitory. We still don't know a huge amount about the behaviour of ocean-dwelling sharks such as the 3-metre-long long silky shark, but we know they use certain sea mounts as focal points for migrations, or as safe havens between hunts.

Data from tagging has shown that during the day, sharks will mill around sea mounts, waiting for night to fall. Then, once the light starts to fade, the sharks leave the sea mount and head out to well-known feeding grounds, or follow their senses for opportunistic hunting on passing prey. When they are done feeding, they follow a direct line straight back to the sea mount. Scientists aren't exactly sure how they do this, but they believe the sharks follow the geomagnetic fields of the Earth to make the shortest journey possible. Nearer the coast, some sea mounts become breeding grounds for huge swarms of hammerhead sharks, and there is nothing to suggest that this kind of behaviour doesn't occur at many more, as yet unexplored, areas throughout the open ocean.

Looks like a bus, but still beautiful: mahi-mahi

A fan of FADs is the stunningly beautiful mahi-mahi. This fish, which can reach 2 metres in length and weigh 40 kilograms, is highly prized for its meat, but it's also a sportsman's challenge, putting up a good fight for the seagoing angler.

The main body of a mahi-mahi is a deep golden yellow moving to emerald green around the dorsal surface and fin, but it can be highly variable, with spots of blue, purple and even red marking its body. The adult males have a large square forehead that makes the front of this fish look strangely like a London bus. Travelling in shoals, mahi-mahi seem to be obsessed with any kind of floating debris. The younger among them certainly mature and develop here, but large shoals of adult fish will seek out and stay with whatever flotsam and jetsam they find. This lust for floating objects was even noted by ancient Greek and Roman fishermen, who would deploy rafts for the purposes: the first known examples of FADs, and the way many local fishermen still catch mahi-mahi. It's as simple as setting out the floating object to attract the fish, waiting for them to establish themselves, and setting out your nets. Bish, bash, bosh.

Mahi-mahi are one of the fastest-growing fish in the ocean, and can develop from a floating egg to a 16-kilogram fish in just eight months. That kind of growth rate means that these fish don't live very long, and it's almost unheard of for any adult to last more than four years. But their accelerated growth makes them great prey for both larger predators and, of course, fishermen. Unfortunately, too many are being accidentally caught up in commercial longline fishing (as bycatch): the technique of pole and line is a far better and more ethical option.

Captain Cook's surprise: the oceanic puffer

More commonly seen lurking around reefs and pecking at anything that looks even slightly edible, pufferfish may not be the first type of fish you'd expect to see loose in the open ocean. The oceanic puffer grows to a decent length of 60 centimetres and weighs 3 kilograms. Unlike its coastal relatives, its fins have developed for a more active lifestyle of being constantly on the move, so it has a wide caudal (tail) fin and much sturdier pectoral, dorsal and anal fins. Its coloration also reflects its open-ocean existence, as it is counter-shaded with a silver belly and flanks, leading up to a deep blue back.

Like all puffers, the oceanic has a large, constantly growing beak, which it uses to tackle cephalopods and crustaceans. Also, its flesh is just as toxic as that of the rest of its family; consumption of the liver could be especially deadly. There is a report that the famous eighteenth-century explorer James Cook once spent three days in delirium after eating the flesh of what was most likely an oceanic puffer. He was lucky to survive. Of course, you'd be adventurous to eat a puffer in the first place, as when threatened they rapidly gulp water into their highly extendable stomachs, doubling their size and making them a lot less appetizing. When it comes to breeding time, large shoals of puffers mass together at island sites such as the Canaries, spawning in great numbers before heading back out into the wider blue beyond.

Tuned-up tuna: aquatic supercar

Tuna just might be the world's most famous fish. Whether tinned or sandwiched, grilled or tossed in a niçoise salad, they have earned their place in the culinary repertoire. Perhaps less well known is that they are key players in the open-ocean environment.

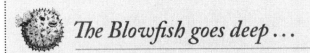

The Blowfish goes deep . . .

THE FORMULA ONE OF FISH

There have always been tall tales and big fish stories, but there also seem to have been some fast fish stories too: tales of marlin and tuna reaching 110 kilometres an hour and the like. Well, while they certainly have the bodies for it, I'm not sure they can bend the laws of physics.

A significant hitch is that if you start to travel at more than 50 kilometres an hour underwater, tiny microbubbles form through a process known as cavitation. Basically, you start to pull water apart, and water doesn't like that, so when the microbubbles burst they release energy, and that would certainly damage soft tissues. True, there have been reports of fish stripping line from fishing reels at 130 kilometres an hour, and of sharks following boats with baited hooks travelling at 74 kilometres an hour. The problem here is the method and accuracy of calculation in the open ocean, and distinguishing how fast the fish is travelling from the speed of the surrounding water. After all, a fish swimming at 5 kilometres an hour in a 10-kilometres-an-hour current would have a total speed of 15 kilometres an hour.

Maths and myths aside, that doesn't mean there aren't some seriously fast fish out there, and launching into burst speed, not to mention cruising through the ocean your whole life, requires some well-modified kit. Fast predatory fish like tuna and marlin have greatly enlarged hearts and gills to ensure an adequate oxygen supply to the thick internal muscles. This is not so critical during the actual chase, where anaerobic respiration takes over, allowing for faster metabolic response, but is vital after the fish has slowed back down and there's a serious oxygen debt to repay. Added touches like *rete mirabile* blood vessels, ramjet ventilation, fusiform body shapes and even stiff yet stabilizing finlets allow some of the fastest fish to happily cruise around at 8 kilometres an hour and jet at up to 29 kilometres an hour (while the shortfin mako shark is in a league of its own – more on that to come). If you're thinking that this doesn't sound very impressive, remember that the fastest human swimmer can only just touch 8 kilometres an hour in very short bursts and would normally average only 4.5 kilometres an hour.

Tuna belong to the mackerel family and range in size from half a metre to 5 metres, and they can weigh more than 500 kilograms, depending on the species. They live in large schools and smaller shoals, spending their entire lives on the move, roaming the ocean looking for food in the form of schooling fish, squid, jellyfish and even smaller tuna. They have evolved perfectly to be constantly in transit. In order to breathe, they rely on ramjet ventilation, whereby their continuous movement pushes water into the mouth and over their gills, giving them a steady and vital oxygen supply.

As with other closely related species, such as billfish, tuna have some central heating via the *rete mirabile* network surrounding their core muscles. In this mechanism, heat generated by the biochemical reactions of the internal muscles is not lost to the cold ocean water. As blood vessels carry cold blood from the fish's exterior, they pass within a few cells of vessels carrying hot blood from the fish's interior, and in this bloody cross-current heat is retained as it is transferred from the outgoing to the incoming vessels. In some cases, this will allow the fish to stay a decent 10°C warmer than the surrounding water.

The tuna's ability to break into short and incredibly fast bursts of speed owes something to this temperature control; but the real power comes from the incredible weave of muscles that wrap around the strong rudder-like caudal peduncle – that part of the body from which the tail-fin emerges. Essentially, all the force the fish generates with its body gets focused on either the right or left side of the tail, so that nothing is wasted on anything other than thrust.

Jellyfish: built to last

Before all the sharks and tuna, there was an unstoppable force in the ocean. Unchanged for countless eons, jellyfish have covered every inch of the planet's seas, and the open ocean is the perfect place for them to live.

True jellyfish of the class Scyphozoa have existed for 550 million years and have quite an intricate biology, albeit run on very simple systems. A nerve net spans the whole creature, sending waves of electrical impulses to the muscles in the 'bell' to pulse and keep the jellyfish moving. In the case of the highly developed box jellyfish, that can be at a speed of nearly 8 kilometres an hour. Structures called rhopalia, arrayed around the edges of the bell, can act as eyes and give the animal a sense of orientation. Then, of course, you have the stinging cells, the cnidocytes, which coat the feeding tentacles and internal digestive structures.

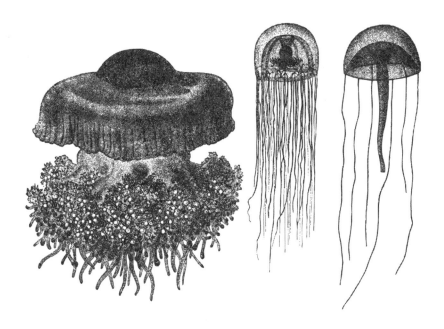

Jellyfish

Jellies primarily feed on plankton, both zoo- and phyto-, with the barbed stinging cells making short work of anything else they may touch, such as small fish, invertebrate larvae and other smaller jellies. While some jellyfish are actually good swimmers, currents and weather patterns tend to bunch jellies together in large aggregations – all good, *if* they find themselves concentrated on the plankton and not washed up on a beach. When times get harder, jellies' low metabolic rates mean they can survive on very little food, and that doesn't inhibit their astonishing, even out-of-control, reproductive powers, which in turn means that any open-ocean bloom in plankton is quickly exploited. So jellyfish have done all right. Floating around the oceans, they were the first complex life on Earth, and if we humans keep going as we are, they could be the last!

Sea turtle secrets – jelly for pudding!

One thing we have discovered about sea turtles, though only recently, is that they are partial to a bit of jellyfish. But that's one of rather few things we know: even though there are just seven sea turtle species and they've been around for 110 million years, we still know very little about their behaviour and lives in the open ocean.

Related to tortoises and terrapins, sea turtles have the characteristic hard shell that provides near-unbeatable protection. It is actually the highly modified ribcage of the animal, which grows skin and protective plates called scutes. Sea turtles can't draw their bodies into the cover of their shell, so in this respect they differ from their land-dwelling cousins; but then they don't need to, as they're super-fast swimmers. Most turtles can cruise happily at around 5–8 kilometres an hour but can switch on a turbo-boost if avoiding predators. The largest sea turtle, the leatherback, has been clocked at more than 30 kilometres an hour, making it the fastest reptile on the planet.

Sea turtles are designed for a life constantly moving through the oceans. Some species spend a large amount of time around coastal areas, feeding on seagrass meadows, but larger species such as leatherbacks and loggerheads only come close to the coast to breed. Most species of turtle are omnivorous, eating whatever they can find in the open ocean, including those jellyfish. But it seems that the massive leatherback *only* eats jellyfish. Some other exciting secrets are beginning to be revealed about sea turtles, such as the startling nature of the hitchhiking animals (epiphytes) that grow on their bodies. It turns out there are species of barnacle unique to the shells of sea turtles, and there's even one that is found nowhere else but in the throats of loggerheads!

Stupendous size, dodgy diet: the ocean sunfish

Another jellyfish muncher is also the heaviest bony fish on the planet: the frankly freakish-looking *Mola mola*, or ocean sunfish. This deep-sea open-ocean relative of the pufferfish is one strange animal. As high as it is long, thanks to highly overdeveloped dorsal and anal fins, the sunfish has a significantly reduced tail, giving its body a round or slightly oval shape. With most adults weighing in at a tonne, and measuring 2 metres (head to tail, and fin to fin), it's a huge barn door of a fish. And that's just average dimensions – the largest individual recorded stands at 3.3 metres long, 4.2 metres high, and weighing an estimated 2.2 tonnes.

With all this weight, length and girth, you might suppose that the sunfish is one hell of a predator, and I suppose you would be half right. It spends most of its time feeding at a depth of around 200 metres or more, and very likely it never stops, because its primary prey is jellyfish. That's a nutritionally poor choice for such a giant, as jellyfish are mainly seawater. To try and compensate, sunfish seek out the energy-rich gonads and easily digestible arms of jellies, rather than the chewy and watery bell.

So why are we discussing this fish here, if it spends its time way down deep? Because living and feeding at such cold depths is metabolically tiring, and this is where the sunfish gets its name. They rise to the surface, lie flat on one side, and bask in the warmer waters and the heat of the Sun. Not only does this spot of sunbathing allow them to warm up for yet more deep diving, it also gives them a chance for ablutions to smarten themselves up. Sunfish carry a huge variety of parasites on their skin, and by reclining in the surface waters, especially near floating debris where other fish and seabirds might be present, they can solicit for some spa treatment. Wrasses, parrotfish and even gulls will peck at the skin of the sunfish, scoring a free meal, and in the process the vast fish gets spruced up.

A miscellany of monsters

Sailing out into the open ocean always gives me a moment of pause. Watching the land finally disappear behind you and knowing you are truly out on your own is always a slightly daunting prospect; but for the early seafarers and fishermen, it must have been terrifying. Stories of the horrors of the deep have, accordingly, always been part of the history and lore of the sea, and while some are definitely tall tales spun by old seadogs to entrance the gullible, others are most certainly based on fact.

The infamous Kraken is a mythical sea monster, a truly giant squid, able to pull down entire ships to the depths below. There is little doubt that this story is based on the real giant squid, which, although 15 metres long, is hardly something to worry the average sea captain. Sea serpents made for other good tales, appearing, for example, in the Norse myths of the Viking era. The stories featuring giant sea serpents with the heads of dragons, which attack sailors and wreck boats, might have been based on the super-long oarfish, or even the very snake-like and fearsome-looking frilled shark: these may have something of the monstrous about them, but they're not serpents. On the other hand, there are *true* sea serpents, the banded sea krait for one, but they're usually less than a metre long (they happen to be the most venomous snakes on the planet, which might be regarded as pretty monstrous in itself).

It's tempting to hope that mermaids exist. Perhaps sailors spotted the submerging mammal tails of manatees or dugongs, the sea cows, and got a little excited. It's possible also that a marine animal, the narwhal, may have helped fuel the long-held belief in unicorns.

While all these mythical creatures are rooted in fact, it cannot be denied that early cultures saw real sea creatures of sizes we no longer witness: exceptionally large blue whales, sperm whales, whale sharks and basking sharks would need no storytelling elaboration to make them seem monstrous, and they remain awe-inspiring even at the reduced sizes we see in modern times.

The king of the herring

Since we've mentioned it, let's say a bit more about the oarfish – it is, after all, royalty. The giant oarfish is also known as 'king of the herring', and it is the longest bony fish on the planet, the current record-holder coming in at a whopping 11 metres long. There have been stories of even bigger specimens, with one ranging to a scarcely credible 17 metres, though these could be *really* big fish stories. Nevertheless, the documented lengths are enough to give the giant oarfish a whiff of the monstrous.

Oarfish

It is normally found somewhat deeper down in the ocean, between around 200 and 1,000 metres, where it feeds on zooplankton, small shrimp and squid. Why so big? No one really knows, but it isn't a strong swimmer. You don't need much muscle mass down in the deep ocean just waiting for prey to swim by, so perhaps its length allows it to maximize the lateral line on its body, giving it an edge when it comes to hunting in the dark.

Widespread in the world's oceans, even at higher latitudes, the giant oarfish managed to get its kingly title thanks to its overdeveloped dorsal spines, which crown its head. But in other respects it's a bit of a misnomer, for it is not closely related to herrings at all. Another derivation of the name has it that one was landed with a catch of herring, and the fishermen assumed the giant beast had to be their ruler.

In Japan, it was believed that if a close relative of the giant oarfish, the slender oarfish, washed up on beaches, an earthquake was imminent. This seemingly fanciful idea just might have some scientific basis. Tectonic shifts in the Earth's plates would certainly disturb the ocean-dwellers above, perhaps sending the oarfish towards the surface, where its long and weak body could easily be dragged by strong surface currents to nearby land.

Down and dirty with the red devil

Squid are famous denizens of the deep waters, where they are rather weird and slow, save for the occasional giant. In surface waters, however, squid tend to be quick and small, dashing around looking for blooms of food in the big blue. But there is one species of squid that fills a role you would normally expect of a shark or tuna.

The Humboldt squid is a serious nocturnal predator, which hunts shoals of schooling fish in the open ocean, rising each night from the safety of the deep to attack. It's even been called a man-eater, after stories of it dragging down and consuming unlucky fishermen who have fallen overboard in rough seas. This might be a bit of a tall tale, but they are extremely intelligent and have certainly been recorded attacking the masks and regulators of scuba divers. Moreover, the beak of the Humboldt squid is razor-sharp and can pierce through Kevlar. Combine all this with an animal nearly 2 metres long and weighing 50 kilograms and you have a real beast on your hands; but it doesn't stop there.

Humboldts hunt in large shoals, termed 'squads', of fifty or more individuals. They organize attacking runs on unfortunate fish by communicating in flashing colours, created by the chromatophores in their skin. They're distinctly unsentimental about it. Any squid damaged, weakened or just not paying sufficient attention is likely to be cannibalized by the rest of the hunting pack; no wonder, then, that one of the common names for this squid is *diablo rojo*, the red devil.

To be fair, the squid play an important role in the open-ocean ecosystem of the southern Pacific, rising and feeding during the night and then taking themselves and whatever they have eaten back to the depths, where they may then become prey themselves. They form an important part of the diet for large sharks, tuna and cetaceans. However, because of the rapid growth rates of the Humboldt and overfishing of its natural predators, this squid is starting to spread out of its native range, where its insatiable hunting practices have the potential to impact negatively on other species or commercially important fisheries.

Hungry and dangerous: the oceanic whitetip

Many sharks travel great distances across the open ocean, but none are more widespread and dangerous than the oceanic whitetip. Like other sharks, the whitetip uses its extraordinary array of senses to hunt and navigate across the vast expanses of the world's oceans. These sharks are found worldwide in tropical seas, hunting down schools of smaller fish, or following predators such as tuna while always on the look-out for distressed or wounded animals to finish off. It is thought that the electroreceptive cells of the elasmobranchs (the subclass which includes sharks and rays) are sensitive enough to pick up the geomagnetic fields of the Earth. This certainly would explain how sharks like the oceanic whitetip never get lost in the featureless waters. To aid its constant nomadic lifestyle, the oceanic whitetip has evolved large, rounded, paddle-like pectoral fins, allowing it to waste as little energy as possible when swimming, an ability that is crucial when six weeks or more may elapse between feeds.

It is the infrequency of eating that makes the oceanic whitetip a far more dangerous prospect to humans than any great white or tiger shark. When an oceanic comes across a potential dinner, it has to take all the chances it can get – who knows when the next meal will come along? When the USS *Indianapolis* was sunk in 1945 by a Japanese torpedo, 880 men entered the water, but only 321 were recovered. Exposure, shock and dehydration killed most of them, but the oceanic whitetip took its toll too, as large numbers of the sharks circled and attacked the floating survivors. In reality, it was only the dead or dying men the sharks actually took, but it must have been truly terrifying to watch a 4-metre-long shark carry off the body of your shipmate and imagine you would be next.

Marine matador: the sailfish

Closely related to the marlins and swordfish, sailfish share many of their characteristics, such as that long bill, the missile-shaped body and a tendency for high-speed strikes. Not as large as the marlin, sailfish reach around 3 metres and can weigh 100 kilograms. There are two known species, found in the tropical Atlantic and Pacific Oceans.

There's still much debate about precisely where sailfish sit in the Top Trumps of fish speed, and while some stories have recorded them zooming at the best part of 110 kilometres an hour, maybe 40 kilometres an hour is a more honest estimate (allowing for the effects of favourable currents, etc.). But that's still a hell of a speed.

Sailfish enjoy the same schooling baitfish and squid as their larger cousins, but have developed a slightly different method of feeding. Their unique characteristic is their 'sail' – a large and long dorsal fin that extends down the back of the animal. By raising or lowering the dorsal spines, this sail can be unfurled, making the fish appear almost twice as deep. Sailfish use it to herd baitfish together into tight balls, almost like a matador uses a cape – or a farmer using a pig board to shift his prize sow (well, I am from Yorkshire). Once some hunting sailfish have cornered their prey, they circle the ball like wolves, flicking up the sail and flashing different colours to confuse the fish. This colour change is also important for communication, since two sailfish striking simultaneously could lead to a nasty injury. So, a sailfish will flash a colour code to its fellow hunters to let it know it is about to make an attacking strike.

Drugged-up slasher of the seas: the swordfish

Looking very similar to the marlin and sailfish, the swordfish is another big predator of the open-ocean environment, and with a wider range than its warmer-water cousins. Swordfish can be found throughout tropical waters, but they also like temperate conditions, being able to survive in temperatures as low as 5°C if pushed.

Let's immediately dispel a myth: swordfish do *not* use their greatly enlarged bill to spear fish to death. They are not living kebab-skewers. After all, it wouldn't be much use to have a dead fish stuck on your nose, far away from your mouth. However, swordfish do use that weapon to slash and wound their prey, making darting runs towards large prey and striking with a rapid sideways shift of the head. In other words, in operation the sword is more a swishing cutlass than a piercing rapier. Marlin and sailfish display this swashbuckling behaviour too, and in fact the sailfish is considered the true master of the swish-and-kill. Smaller prey items are gobbled up whole, however, and the swordfish will really eat anything it can squeeze into its mouth: from baitfish to krill, herring to hake, they are truly ferocious predators.

To find their prey in the oceans, especially at the depths they sometimes visit, swordfish have huge well-developed eyes, and, like their billfish brethren, they also have the *rete mirabile* blood vessels to keep them warm. This adaptation makes their eyesight even keener than it would otherwise be in colder waters, where they can respond much more quickly to flashes of light that could indicate prey.

So we've established that they like to eat – but we like to eat them too, and swordfish is on many a menu in the modern restaurant scene. But a word of caution: think twice. Being such wide-roaming and wide-feeding predators, fish like swordfish have the propensity to accumulate toxins in their tissues. Chemicals like mercury and other heavy metals persist for a long time in the oceans, and swordfish act as accumulators by simply swimming through areas of pollution as well as through the prey they consume. Either way, a slice of swordfish just might contain more mercury than a rectal thermometer . . . and that should be enough to put anyone off their dinner.

Supersonic jetsetter: the shortfin mako

When it comes to speed among open-ocean predators, there's little doubt about who is king of the fish. In a sentence, there's the shortfin mako shark – and there's the rest. No other fish comes close when compared with this supersonic jet of the seas.

This shark is essentially a stripped-down and quicker version of the great white shark, to which it is very closely related. Shortfin makos typically reach around 4 metres in length and can weigh more than half a tonne. Like other mackerel sharks, they are equipped with the wondrous counter-current blood vessel system (*rete mirabile*) to centrally heat their core muscles and vital organs when in colder seas, meaning they're happy hunting in cooler temperate seas: some makos have even been found visiting the coasts of Scandinavia. The shortfin mako preys on fish, squid, jellyfish and smaller sharks, striking from below and behind, much in the manner of their great white cousins.

The real magic of the mako, however, is that incredible speed, helped by a torpedo-shaped body and those uniquely sharky streamlining scales. Makos have been recorded travelling at very nearly 50 kilometres an hour, and there are suggestions that they can reach up to 80 kilometres an hour at burst speed – though the jury is out here, because, as previously discussed, that seems more than physics would tolerate. It's that power that also turns the mako into not just a jet but a record-breaking jump-jet: this shark can propel itself 6 metres out of the water, the highest leap known for any animal. At whatever speed, mako sharks are always on the hunt, by night or day. They tend to stick below the thermocline during the day in tropical open oceans, where the cooler water can provide their bodies with more oxygen and potentially the chance to find something to eat. Their fearsome appetite supports an incredible growth rate, and mako sharks can slam on as much as 70 kilograms in their first few years of life. It all makes sense: the faster you grow, the faster you swim, the more you can eat . . . and the less likely you are to get eaten first!

Who's top predator? Us, alas

While many of us may still think of the open ocean as the last great frontier on Earth, it is slowly and methodically being exploited. Mining, drilling, pollution and aquaculture all have their impact; but it is fishing, or rather *over*fishing, that has had the biggest impact – as many a shark would know.

This happened only relatively recently, beginning with the introduction of steam-powered ships in the industrial revolution. Before that, most fishing boats plied their trade in local, coastal waters. Later, in the 1960s, the introduction of sonar became the death knell for many fish stocks, as large shoals could now be located and accurately targeted. Since then, destructive fishing practices like deep-sea dredging, longline fishing and the advent of super-trawlers have had catastrophic impacts on the inhabitants of the open ocean. The result? It's believed, for example, that over the last fifty years oceanic whitetip populations have decreased by a catastrophic 99 per cent. Hammerhead sharks in the

Atlantic have seen a similar crash, with 89 per cent of the population disappearing in just fifteen years, between 1990 and 2005.

Losing top predators causes major problems for any food chain, especially ones so very delicate as those found in the open ocean. We are already seeing fast-growing, short-lived species like the Humboldt squid stretching far out of their natural range as their predators disappear. And as fish stocks decline, we are travelling further and further to attempt to land catches. Using super-trawlers, a country such as China can fish in the waters around Ireland or venture deep into the Atlantic for weeks, or sometimes months, of fishing. With fleets so widespread, and the vast ocean so hard to police and protect, our fishing practices are threatening the delicate balance of the largest habitat on the planet. A change is needed to prevent the big blue become some planet-spanning empty water-feature.

Is it a bird, is it a plane? It's a fish!

If the wide open seas are threatening, you might think about taking to the air instead, which is exactly what the extraordinary flying fish do. There are many different species of these amazing creatures, all distributed across the tropical and subtropical areas of the world's oceans. Like many open-ocean fish, they feed on the plankton blooms that spring up seemingly at random; and like so many other smaller plankton-feeding fish, they're the target of many predators. Tuna, dolphin, marlin, shark – you name it, all will more than likely try to snack on a flying fish or two. But they'd have to catch one first, and so to avoid this sticky end the fish have taken to the skies.

Take-off, if you're a fish, requires swimming up to the water's surface at speed, after which hugely overdeveloped pectoral, and in some cases pelvic, fins unfurl and enable you to glide for distances of 200 metres or more. The ventral lobe on your tail is larger and longer than the dorsal lobe, which means that you can still touch the very surface of the water with 'wings' outstretched and gliding.

Flying fish

When not feeding or avoiding predators, schools of flying fish are always on the look-out for a chance to breed. Rather than spawning their eggs freely into the ocean, they actually lay their eggs, and to do this they require a hard surface. Anything from an old fishing net to a floating log can prompt spawning behaviour in flying fish, if the time is right. The female fish lay long strands of sticky eggs onto whatever is available, and the males follow behind to fertilize them. Indeed, given enough time, so many eggs can be laid on a floating structure as to sink it. A disaster? Actually, no. This is a critically important stage in the life cycle of the flying fish, for the deeper and cooler water provides better conditions for the eggs to develop and hatch.

It's a bird, it's a plane, it's ... er, a jet-propelled squid?

Anxious not to be left out of all the fun, some squid also take their chances with flight. Pacific flying squid populate the western reaches of the northern Pacific, and while they can be found all the way up to Russia, they seem to be most common around the islands of Japan. This isn't a big squid, measuring a meagre 40–50 centimetres when fully grown, which only takes a year. In fact, everything about flying squid seems totally normal and squiddy ... until you factor in the whole launching-into-the-air scenario.

The fins on the upper mantle of the flying squid are quite large and placed about as far up the body as possible. When flying, the mantle fins stretch wide, and the eight arms and two feeding tentacles are flattened, held in a tight fan shape, at the opposite end of the animal. There is a thin membrane between the arms and tentacles, so that the whole thing acts like the aerofoil of a kite. This may not seem much in the way of aerodynamic kit, especially when compared with the wing fins of the flying fish, but Pacific flying squid can actually control their glide and will form into a streamlined bullet again for re-entering the ocean.

They are quick, too. To launch into the air requires the squid to use its siphon to jet water out at high speed and break the surface. Once in the air, squid have been recorded travelling 30 metres or more at a rate of 11 metres a second, which is seriously fast. Usain Bolt can't do the 100 metres that quickly. This escape response mimics that of the flying fish, and it is true that everything is trying to eat the squid too. Incredible to think, though, that evolution has twice created a flying marine creature; and even more incredible to think that one of them is an invertebrate!

Is it a bird? Yep

While we're on the subject of oceanic animals that have taken to the skies, there's one seabird – the albatross – that really should make the cut, for in its own way it's a full-time inhabitant of the high seas. Birds of this family spend almost their entire lives on the wing, circling the waters of the globe. Found in the North Pacific and all around the southern oceans, albatrosses only return to land to mate and rear their chicks. Like many an underwater ocean wanderer, they spend their lives chasing schools of fish, squid and krill, always on the look-out for seasonal blooms and opportunistic feeds.

Flying around the world's waters is demanding, and we already know food can be in short supply, so the albatross has evolved a range of different attributes that allow it to live with minimal exertion. For

Albatross

starters, they can have huge wingspans: the great albatross, reaching 3.5 metres tip to tip, has the longest wingspan of any bird now living. Being equipped this way allows gliding over enormous distances, thanks to the large aerodynamic surface area that can catch and ride the thermals rising from the ocean, as well as manipulate the winds driven by the fearsome weather at higher latitudes.

An albatross has a razor-sharp beak on its bill, adapted to deal with almost any fish; but more impressive still are the well-developed nostrils, which can sniff out food over countless kilometres of ocean. These nostrils also play a role in determining air speed, allowing the birds to accurately gauge currents and exploit them for soaring and gliding.

It's a great shame that every species of albatross is in some way threatened, some even critically endangered. These winged travellers of the great blue could soon be lost from the skies and the oceans altogether.

The Blowfish goes deep ...

CLOCKING UP THE WATER MILES

The benefit of living in the open ocean is that you really can go wherever you want, whenever you want. The drawback is that you may have to travel an awfully long way for a meal or to spawn. Pacific salmon begin their lives in North American rivers before swapping fresh water for the salty sea as they mature, roam the open ocean to feed, and eventually make the long return journey to spawn in those same rivers. Chinook salmon, the largest salmon species, are known to complete migrations of 4,000 kilometres before returning to spawn, essentially swimming across the entire Pacific to the islands of Japan and back again. The now critically endangered European eel, which was once common in UK rivers, makes the opposite journey, leaving its freshwater home to spawn in the ocean. They travel across the Atlantic, using favourable currents to aid their journey, and spawn in the Sargasso Sea near the Bahamas. The eggs then drift back across the ocean, where they develop into young 'glass eels', which, all being well, re-enter the rivers and streams. All in all, this total journey is getting on for 5,000 kilometres.

For other larger species, journeys in the tens of thousands of kilometres are common. Humpback whales calve in warm tropical waters before travelling half the planet to feed in the productive polar seas, then returning and doing it all over again. Some migrations are not just long but incredibly specific. Leatherback turtles can travel across the Pacific and Atlantic Oceans to feed before navigating back to one strip of beach only a few hundred metres long. While these distances and navigational skills seem impossible feats to us, for the animals of the open ocean they're just the daily commute to work.

Long-haul glider: the blue shark

There's one shark that could challenge the oceanic whitetip for the title of most widely spread shark in the planet's seas. Ranging from Greenland to the waters off the coast of South America, this inveterate traveller is the blue shark – he just might be the *true* lone wolf of the sea.

This large 4-metre-long beast is an excellent predator, specializing in fast-moving fish and squid, but it will not say no to jellies, swimming crabs and floating whale carcasses. Indeed, blue sharks have even been witnessed feeding on krill aggregations in a crude but effective way: swimming open-mouthed through the swarms and effectively straining the krill out with their gill-rakers. With their lithe, streamlined bodies and long crescent-like pectoral fins, blue sharks waste very little energy swimming, as they glide through the water after each fin stroke. They're commonly sighted, and fished for, around the UK, but blue sharks don't just spend time in the surface waters – they've been recorded diving down as deep as 1,000 metres for hunting expeditions.

Blue sharks' migrations are truly mammoth. The current confirmed record is from an individual who was tagged off New York and then travelled about 6,000 kilometres south to the coast of Brazil. But this is probably just part of a much greater story, and recent studies have shown that while male blue sharks tend to stay in a wide but roughly similar area, the females are the true long-haul travellers, heading to safe pupping grounds in warm waters. Mating off the US east coast and then swimming across the Atlantic to pup in the Azores, followed by the return journey, would send a female blue on a trek of more than 15,000 kilometres.

Madame Whiplash: the common thresher

There's one more species of open-ocean shark that definitely deserves a mention because of its truly unique method of feeding. Thresher sharks possess the entire battery of senses that other sharks have, and of course they have a jaw filled with lethal teeth, but what sets them apart is the way they hunt their quarry. In a nutshell, they whip them to death with their super-long tails. Strange, a little kinky maybe, but effective.

If you look at a thresher, it's much the same design as any other basic shark; but let your eyes wander down to the tail and you get a big surprise. The upper lobe of the shark's tail has been greatly elongated to the point where it can be as long as the animal itself. So a large 5-metre common thresher will be 2.5 metres of shark body and another 2.5 metres of tail. When feeding, threshers target shoals of fish like herring or anchovy, and are often found working in pairs or small groups to separate off manageable balls of fish. Once a bait ball has formed, the shark will swim rapidly at the school and then flick its head down, stick out its pectorals and whip its long tail over. It's almost like riding a bike and slamming the front brakes on, so that the back tyre rears up. The long flexible tail will kill, injure or stun any fish it touches, which the shark can then consume at leisure.

The thresher's unique tail can sometimes land it in trouble because it is so long, getting caught up in fishing gear. Also, like many other open-ocean species, the common thresher is at risk from longline fishing. In this scenario, its whiplash becomes its downfall when its tail, striking at the fishing bait, itself gets caught on the hook.

Shark-friendly dental floss: the pilot fish

If you've an interest in the seas, you might have already come upon the curious little pilot fish species. These small, black-and-white banded fish are members of the jack family; but unlike their fast, predatory reef-dwelling cousins, pilot fish live out on the open seas. More than that, they head towards the sort of big predators that most other fish are desperate to flee from.

In fact, pilot fish have a great fondness for larger animals, particularly predators like sharks, and are often to be seen swimming in great numbers around them. Why? It's all about mutual back-scratching. These stripy hangers-on perform a useful role in keeping the larger animals clean. The level of trust is so great between pilot fish and their host that sharks will allow them to enter their mouths to perform cleaning duties *without* gobbling them up. The pilot fish get to feed on parasites and the scraps the host leaves behind. In addition, they gain protection from proximity to such predators: who would be dumb enough to try and snatch a pilot fish from under a shark's nose? Pilot fish can be fickle, though. If there's a better predator around, or if they've grown too large to benefit from their host's protective abilities, they can jump ship.

It's believed that pilot fish got their name from their habit of following large ships in the age of sail. Sailors would see these fish riding in the bow wave of their vessel, seemingly guiding them to their destination.

Deep Ocean

I t is the largest environment on our planet, but the chances are you'll never see it, let alone visit it. Statistically, you are more likely to make a trip into space than you are to get a glimpse of the Earth's most expansive yet remotest realm: the deep ocean. The conditions within this strange, uncharted world are about as hostile as you could possibly imagine, but its influence on the oceans, and on our planet as a whole, is immense. It is time to stare into the abyss and see what stares back.

The shift from surface waters to deep ocean occurs at around 200 metres, where the light begins to fade and photosynthesis is no longer a reliable method of sustaining life. The deepest depths of the ocean are a staggering 11 kilometres down, but the average depth is still an impressive 3.7 kilometres. This vast body of water comprising the deep ocean provides 95 per cent of all the potential living space on planet Earth.

The sunlit surface waters and the inky depths are, literally, worlds apart, separated by an invisible but powerful barrier. Warmed by the Sun, the water on the light side may be 15 or 20°C, but on the dark side the temperature plummets to 6°C or lower. Crossing from the warmth into the cold, dark waters is a serious biological undertaking.

This vast ecosystem, hidden beneath the light, is in fact remarkably stable. While the surface waters are whipped into a frenzy by wind and rain, the deep ocean remains untroubled, insulated from these savage forces. Temperature and salinity remain nearly constant once you start to descend into the blackness, so animals can happily move great distances without suffering physiological stress. At 1,000 metres no light at all penetrates – it is completely dark, ensuring a uniform environment all the way to the bottom. The one factor that does change with depth is pressure, and this is certainly a significant issue for any lifeform – including humans – that wishes to explore the depths. But the effects of pressure build up more slowly the deeper you go, so the deeper waters still provide a relatively stable and predictable environment.

It is thanks to this stability and calm that the creatures of the deep sea have been allowed to live on, undisturbed, for millions of years. While new niches and opportunities for life were appearing in the shallows, the bottom hardly changed. This otherworldly world remained largely unnoticed by humankind until the last half-century – it is only now that we have really begun the task of exploring, understanding and learning from it. So far we have managed to explore less than 5 per cent of the deep sea. Yet the changes that are afflicting our planet and an intense interest in exploiting the riches of the ocean have suddenly put this mysterious world right into the spotlight!

Gulper eel: all jaw and no body

The deep ocean is not only huge, it can be a barren place. There's not much about, so if you are a predator trying to make a living down there, you'd better be ready to take any meal you can get. And to do that, a few clever (not to say scary) adaptations won't go amiss.

Living at depths between 500 and 3,000 metres, the gulper eel doesn't bother to actively hunt prey – instead, it goes fishing. It has a super-long tail which accounts for most of its two-metre-long body, and at the tip of this there is a bioluminescent organ that glows in the inky darkness.

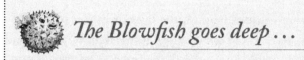

The Blowfish goes deep …

THE FOUR ZONES

The deep ocean is roughly split into four layers or zones, each of which has slightly different conditions and so creates unique environments for organisms to exploit.

The mesopelagic is the shallowest zone, starting at the 200-metre mark, the point where light begins to fade rapidly, and extending down to 1,000 metres. This is the twilight zone of the ocean, where many animals have developed highly modified eyes to make best use of the remaining light. It is a very rich zone with many predators living here, either hunting in the semi-dark or travelling daily into the shallower waters to feed. It is estimated that 90 per cent of the ocean's fish biomass is found within this region.

Next, from 1,000 to 4,000 metres, there is the bathypelagic zone, which is completely dark, cold and sparsely populated. Here animals show increasing adaptations to harsh physical conditions, and bioluminescence plays a major role in nearly every creature's life, be they predator or prey.

From 4,000 metres to the ocean floor at 6,000 metres, there is the abyssopelagic zone, where nutrients are rare – most have already been consumed in the water column above – and so life is rarer still. This is the zone of the really deep dwellers, animals such as the Dumbo octopus, tripod fish and giant squid. Most of the animals within this zone are so highly evolved for survival in these brutal conditions that they would die instantly if removed from them.

Finally, there is the hadopelagic zone, which extends from 6,000 metres to the very bottom of the world, at 11,000 metres. The hadopelagic includes the deep ocean trenches like the Mariana, and such is the extreme pressure at these depths that it is the least explored area on Earth. Nobody knows for certain what may yet be awaiting discovery in this remote and alien world.

This acts as a lure to bring unwary prey within snapping range. And when it comes to snapping, this guy really takes some beating. The part of the body that isn't tail is mostly made up of a massive mouth and jaws. Incorporated into the lower jaw is an expandable pouch – hence the fish's other name, pelican eel – and like a pelican, the gulper eats whatever it can stuff into its capacious mouth and then shove down into its highly stretchy stomach. Still, it's not only large fishes that make up the diet of this big-mouthed muncher. In fact, big fishes are so rare in the deep ocean that it usually sets its sights on deep-sea squid and swarms of small shrimp-like crustaceans, which it 'nets' in great mouthfuls with its giant jaw.

Hatchetfish: masters of stealth

At first sight, marine hatchetfish might not seem that impressive. Small creatures, laterally compressed – fish-shaped, in fact – they live in the shallower parts of the deep ocean, usually in areas where light still *just* manages to penetrate. So, across the Atlantic, Pacific and Indian Oceans, anywhere between 200 and 500 metres below the surface, there's a good chance you'll run into some kind of hatchetfish. So far, so ordinary. But take a look at those big bug eyes …

The hatchetfish's eyes are works of art, large and incredibly sensitive. Staring upwards allows the hatchets to detect the faintest silhouettes of small fish and shrimps feeding or swimming above them. Once they spot something, they lunge from the darkness, striking the unfortunate victim from below.

Such a trick wouldn't be much good if the hatchetfish fell for it itself, getting gobbled up by a predator stalking beneath it. So, to avoid being hoisted by its own petard, this canny fish has an array of light-producing organs (photophores) set on its belly. Facing downwards, these emit light that is the same intensity and from the same part of the spectrum as the light falling from the surface, allowing the small fish to enter 'stealth mode', seemingly disappearing into the surrounding gloom.

Squid and the art of parenting

Most fish aren't exactly model parents – no sooner have they laid their eggs than they abandon them to the whims of the ocean currents. By this standard, at least, cephalopods – the group that includes squid, octopuses and cuttlefish – are pretty decent parents for the most part. The giant Pacific octopus, for example, lays its eggs in a burrow, protecting and nurturing them until they hatch, while cuttlefish lay clumps of grape-like eggs in secluded rocks and reefs.

But what about in the deep ocean, where there are no hard surfaces to lay eggs on? Well, deep-sea squid still don't abandon their offspring to the dark waters – instead, they carry their eggs with them until hatching. We don't really know that much about the breeding behaviour of deep-sea squid, but a small species called *Gonatus onyx* – the clawed armhook squid – has recently been observed carrying its eggs around in a large sack, containing up to 3,000 eggs, held firmly by talon-like hooks on four of its eight arms. By gently pulsing its arms, as if playing a very delicate accordion, the squid can aerate its eggs by swooshing water through the sack (which is actually more of a hollow tube than a sack). While grasping its precious cargo, the female squid cannot feed, so it slowly deteriorates as the eggs develop. Because of the very cold water temperatures and reduced levels of oxygen, the eggs may take up to nine months to develop and hatch. Once they do, the new mother – like many of her kind – dies, leaving her brood to carry on her legacy.

Size isn't everything – but it helps

Think of a woodlouse: a small arthropod, perhaps 1 centimetre in length, often found with tens or hundreds of others, scurrying about in the soil beneath rocks or rotting trunks. Now make it fifty times bigger, and you've got the giant isopod *Bathynomus*. This deep-sea cousin of the land-dwelling woodlouse – and of many other isopods found commonly in fresh and salt water – is similar in appearance to its relatives, with one

BIG difference: *Bathynomus* is *much* bigger, approaching half a metre in length (the largest one recorded clocked in at a scale-busting 76 centimetres).

The giant isopod is an example of a phenomenon known as abyssal gigantism: the tendency of deep-sea species – many invertebrates and some fish species – to grow much, much bigger than their shallow-water relatives. Probably the most famous case is the giant squid (for more on that, see below). No one knows for certain why this happens, and there are lots of rival theories out there that try to explain it. One part of the reason is likely to be that the deep ocean is not only vast but also incredibly stable: the environment is little changed from the way it was many millions of years ago, allowing species to develop – and grow – in relatively uniform conditions. The constant low temperature is thought to lead to larger and longer-lived cells, and this allows animals to grow bigger and mature later. Another theory is that food in the deep ocean is so scarce that the animals living there have slower growth rates, which again, over long periods of time, lead to larger animals. But, for now, this remains speculation, and a BIG question mark hangs over the whole issue.

Giant monsters of the abyss

Many of us fear the dark – and it's natural enough if that inky darkness is thousands of metres of seawater stretching into an abyss beneath us. Such fears have spawned many horrors and not all of them are myths. One such monster of the deep – sometimes identified with the Kraken of legend – is the giant squid.

This astonishing creature remains shrouded in mystery, but what we do know is wondrous enough. First, there's the size. The largest giant squid ever recorded was a female, 13 metres long and weighing in at nearly a tonne. This species also holds the record for the largest eye in the animal kingdom: at 30 centimetres across, this truly massive peeper is able to detect even the faintest light emitted by biological sources or

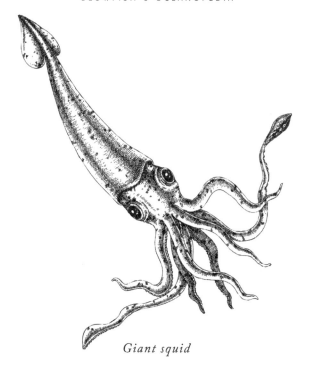

Giant squid

trickling down from the surface. Sharp vision is really handy in the deep
ocean not just for spotting prey but also for avoiding predators. While
humans have had a hell of a job trying to find giant squid, this isn't a
problem that has troubled another ocean-dweller – the sperm whale.
These deep-sea divers feed on giant squid and seem to excel in finding
them – so much so that scientists study the behaviour of the whales
in the hope of learning more about the squid. What we do know is
that these squid are vicious hunters, using their two feeding tentacles
to grab prey at a distance. These tentacles can be twice the length of the
squid's body, reaching up to 10 metres in some cases. Once the tentacles'
hooked suckers are firmly attached, they hold fast to the prey, which
is then hauled back and completely immobilized in a tangle of arms
before being ripped apart by a razor-sharp beak.

It is testament to the vastness of the oceans that we still know so little
about this enormous creature. We still don't know for certain if it is a
single species – though recent genetic tests suggest that it probably is.

Most of what we do know comes from the dead bodies of washed-up squid. Indeed, it wasn't until 2006 that the first ever giant squid was caught on camera, when Japanese researchers managed to haul a live individual to the surface. Then, in 2012, the same researchers managed the seemingly impossible and filmed a giant squid in its natural habitat, deep down in the Pacific Ocean.

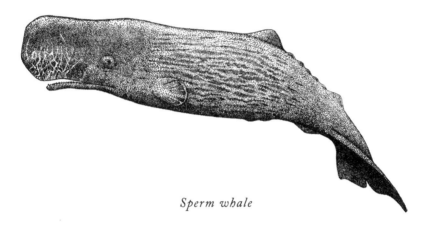

Sperm whale

Dracula of the deep

There couldn't be a better poster child for the deep sea than the vampire squid. This bizarre creature's scientific name says it all: *Vampyroteuthis infernalis*, literally 'vampire squid from hell'. It isn't a big squid, growing to just 30 centimetres in length, but as befits this pocket-sized Dracula, it comes with its very own cloak: its eight arms are connected by a fleshy webbing, and each arm is lined with soft but intimidating spines.

This cloak is very handy when it comes to dinnertime. The squid extends long, thin filaments down into the water column, and when any potential meal comes into contact with these, it swoops, engulfing the food in its web of arms. Favourite items on the menu are the remains of large jellies and salps, and the squid may round off its meal with some tasty planktonic crustaceans.

The squid's outer body is covered in light-producing organs known as photophores, with especially large and well-developed ones at the tip of each arm. The animal has incredible control over these, allowing it to create an astonishing array of flashing lights in virtually any combination – a phantasmagoric light show put on to confuse would-be predators. If this doesn't do the trick and further defence is needed, the squid is able to launch glowing balls of mucus from its arm tips, before, as a last resort, folding its webbed arms back around its body and becoming a floating ball of spines.

The origin of life on Earth?

Down at the ocean's deepest depths, near the ridges of tectonic plates, lie unique pockets of life which may well be the origin of all life on planet Earth. These hydrothermal vents are formed when water is drawn down into the newly forming crust, where it becomes superheated and loaded with dissolved chemicals, before emerging from the rocks as large mineral towers, known as black smokers. The water that pours out of these towers is over 300°C and is laced with dissolved heavy metals; as the water cools, the metals crystallize out of the seawater and the tower grows taller. This may not seem like a place where *any* life could live, but there is a special group of organisms that make a living here and are found nowhere else on Earth. And the star among these creatures is the giant tube worm.

It might be related to the tube worms you find elsewhere, but really the only characteristic the giant tube worm shares with some of its wriggling cousins is that it builds a limestone tube to protect its soft body: everything else is modded to the max. The worm's most recogniz-able feature is its large, highly vasculated gills. These deep-red furry frills are Stage 1 in the story of the animal's success, creating a huge surface area for exchange not only of respiratory gases but also of hydrogen sulphide. The worm has no mouth, no anus and no complete gut: all these got lost as it developed from larva to adult, all so it could accommodate its long-term lodger – and food source. In a modified part of its gut, called the trophosome, the giant tube worm hosts chemosynthetic bacteria which consume hydrogen sulphide as their source of energy. This is Stage 2 in the worm's success story, as the resident bacteria, fed with a steady supply of dissolved gases and hydrogen sulphide, provide the worm with all the nutrients it needs to grow. And boy, does it grow: the giant tube worm has the fastest growth rate of any known marine invertebrate. It's a good thing too, as hydrothermal vents don't remain active forever and the mineral-rich water supplying the worm eventually runs out. The worms at a dying site perish, but their offspring colonize a new vent and grow to full maturity in just two years!

So, in the weird world of the deep-sea vents, we find complex life thriving in the total absence of the sun's energy – and perhaps the origin of all life on Earth. Conditions here, unchanged for millennia, would have allowed simple creatures to establish themselves, before making a push to claim the turbulent sunlit waters above.

The bacteria-juiced yeti

It isn't just worms that can harness the power of bacteria at deep-ocean vents. It's too good an opportunity to pass up, so there are crustaceans down there which have also struck up a friendship with chemosynthetic – chemical-munching – bacteria.

The yeti crab is actually a type of squat lobster – it has the body of a crab but the long legs and claws of a lobster. If you just look at the main part of this crab's body, you might think there isn't much to write home about: it lacks pigment so appears white, and there are no eyes. But you are missing the best bit, for this crab has really hairy arms: both claws and limbs are thickly covered in long hair-like extensions called setae. In some shallow-water crustaceans, these setae serve as anchor points for encrusting growths and seaweeds, which provide the animal with camouflage. In the case of the yeti crab, the setae are used to house colonies of those ever-present and invaluable chemosynthetic bacteria.

The crab is still a carnivore, catching prey and scavenging food in much the same way that any of its crabby cousins would, but scientists believe that the yeti crab also harvests and feeds on the colonies of bacteria growing on its hairy limbs. By waving its arms over vents spewing out water rich in methane and other nutritional chemicals, the crab ensures its bacteria are well fed, before using its specialized mouthparts to scrape its arms and enjoy a meal itself.

Small, but mighty!

Ostracods are generally small and unassuming creatures – technically, they are crustaceans, like crabs and lobsters – but they provide a window into the distant history of the marine world and may offer vital clues as to how marine environments may be preserved in future.

Most ostracods are tiny – 1 millimetre long or less – and live in a hinged shell, like mussels and cockles. The shell is very thin and light, and the animal inside extends its various limbs and appendages out of the shell to move and feed. This gives them the appearance of a pea with fluffy hairy bits sticking out of one end, and they are commonly known as seed shrimp. Ostracods are found free-swimming in the plankton and living in or on the sediment of the seafloor; they fill many niches, ranging from herbivores and filter-feeders to out-and-out predators. The largest ostracod, called *Gigantocypris*, grows to some 30 millimetres and, thanks to its huge eyes, is able to actively seek prey in the darkness of the deep ocean, where it feeds on copepods and even small fish. Certain species of seed shrimp can produce bioluminescence, which is great for disturbing predators or even attracting mates. The blue glow of Pacific sand-dwelling ostracods didn't go unnoticed in the Second World War, when Japanese soldiers would collect the animals in jars to use their light for their night work.

Ostracods have been around for many millions of years, and thanks to their hard shell, they leave a brilliant imprint in the fossil record. Studying the remains of these tiny animals has allowed scientists to reconstruct and understand the ancient marine environments that once were, in the hope of helping marine environments that yet may be.

Teeth to make a dentist weep

If you want to find a genuine, top-of-the-range, all-singing, all-dancing monster of the deep, the Pacific viperfish ticks all the boxes. While it's impressively ghoulish from head to toe (OK, so it hasn't got toes), what makes this fearsome predator stand out from the crowd is its massive and super-scary teeth. As with many deep-sea hunters, the viperfish cannot let the opportunity of a good square meal pass it by, and to this end it has developed a set of gnashers that would put a toothy 1980s Bond villain to shame. Normal dining etiquette is not observed: the long and extremely sharp teeth are used to impale prey and stop it escaping, and once it has been subdued, it is swallowed whole – the lower jaw is specially hinged to allow the widest possible gape. The viperfish is scarcely a fussy eater, taking anything from large shrimp to fish and squid. This grisly gourmand does, however, have to be careful not to get *too* greedy. It's an ironic way to go – starving to death with your mouth full – but large prey can get immovably lodged in the massive teeth, making it impossible for the fish to feed.

The viperfish's other cunning feature is a light-producing organ placed at the very tip of its greatly elongated primary dorsal fin ray. Hanging motionless in the water, it waves this fishing lure around, waiting for something tasty to come and investigate the glow: not a good idea if you happen to be on the menu.

When it pays to see red: the stoplight loosejaw

In a pitch-black world, light naturally has little role to play. Right? Wrong! Strange as it may seem, light is a matter of life and death to pretty much all of the deep-ocean inhabitants, and producing and detecting light has driven these animals along some ingenious and often weird evolutionary paths. Many fishes use light to hunt, usually as a lure to attract prey (it's a risky move, though, as they may attract predators too). There's one type of fish, however, that uses an 'invisible' light to hunt its prey, like a pair of night-vision goggles. Meet the snappily named stoplight loosejaw, aka the rat-trap fish.

Loosejaws have light-producing organs (photophores) below the eyes to shine light out into the darkness. But it's not just any light: it's red light (hence 'stoplight'), which is the first wavelength to be eliminated when sunlight penetrates water, so many deep-sea creatures cannot see it – to them, it appears black. It's for just this reason that many smaller deep-water species are deep red in colour: if predators can't see red, they have no way of detecting red-coloured prey, which simply vanishes into the blackness. The stoplight loosejaw *can* see red, though, so the red torch beam from its photophores enables it to see while remaining invisible to others. These others include future dinner, and it is when a tasty morsel is spotted that the 'loosejaw' bit comes into play. These fishes have extensively hinged jaws that are not connected by flesh to the rest of the fish: this gives them one of the widest gapes of any animal, but the downside is that any prey snapped up could swim straight out through the gaps between the bones. The loosejaw gets around this by using its dagger-sharp teeth to impale its prey and stop it from escaping.

It's a pig . . . it's a cucumber . . . it's a . . .

Sea pigs aren't really pigs: they are cucumbers. Actually, they aren't really cucumbers either. What they are is *sea* cucumbers – and they are also among the weirdest of the many weird animals that inhabit the deep ocean. Just how bizarre they are is hard to say, because they live down at the very bottom of the ocean, as much as 5 kilometres below the surface, and studying them at such depths is about as hard as firing someone into space.

Growing to a modest 10 centimetres in length, sea pigs have the fat oval body of other sea cucumbers, but they have between five and seven pairs of feet, which are quite long and make the animal look like it is walking across the seabed on stilts. On the animal's back, there are 'horns', usually arranged in three pairs, with long extensions that project out into the surrounding water; these are probably sensory papillae, used to collect information in the pitch dark of the deep ocean. At the mouth, there are ten feeding tentacles, which are used to pick up clumps of silt and stuff it into the sea pig's mouth. Moving in great herds, hundreds strong, they spend their entire lives systematically scouring the seabed, shovelling up anything that might vaguely be called food: a particular favourite is the rich organic matter found around the rotting carcasses of whales.

A slippery customer

Hagfish are a perfect example of one of the main principles of evolution: 'if it ain't broke, don't fix it'. These slippery eel-like animals are said to be 'primitive' – basically, they have remained unchanged for some 300 million years – but the fact is that they are extremely successful scavengers and ruthless hunters.

One of the weird features of hagfish is their jaws – or rather, the lack of them. Instead, they have two horizontal rasping plates, covered in backward-facing teeth, which they use to grip flesh – they cannot chew or grind their food. Once they have a firm hold of some flesh, the animal forms its elongated body into a coil or knot, which it uses to bear down on the corpse and tear a lump of meat clear from the body. Because of their jawless nature and primitive development, hagfish remain a mystery to scientists, who still argue just where they stand in the giant tree of life.

The hagfish's most spectacular trick is its ability to produce copious quantities of mucus when threatened – for this reason it is also known as the slime eel. This mucus provides a terrific defence against predators as it can be produced in such quantities as to rapidly clog the gills of any animal attempting to eat it. And the slime isn't only good for defence – it is also a great weapon for catching prey. Scientists have only recently discovered that hagfish can chase fish down into their burrows and seize them with their clamp-like jaws. Preventing the fish from leaving the burrow, the hagfish then proceeds to create a huge mass of slime, which pours down its body, filling the burrow and suffocating the hapless fish. The slime-drowned fish is then removed from the sediment, allowing the hagfish to feed upon it at leisure.

A glimpse into the world of early sharks

Sharks have been around for quite a while – about 450 million years, in fact: they made their first appearance on planet Earth before there were even trees or flowers. Over that huge span of time, the basic form and function of sharks haven't changed much. But that's not to say that today's sharks are fossilized remnants, identical in every way to their ancient ancestors. There are a few relatively 'primitive' representatives around today that provide a glimpse of what early sharks may have been like. Most modern sharks have five gill slits, but survivors of a lost family (well, a nearly lost family) of ancient species have six or seven gill slits. The best-known representatives, the bluntnose sixgill shark and the broadnose sevengill, are similar in appearance, with a distinctive single dorsal fin set far down the back, close to the tail, and a similar arrangement of teeth. While both are found in the deep ocean, they make feeding and breeding trips into shallower waters as needed. Apart from the extra gill slit, the major difference between the two is size: while sevengills are only around 2.5 metres in length, mature sixgills rival the great white shark in body size and can reach up to 8 metres.

The truth is we know very little about these granddaddies of the deep. One thing we do know is that they age and mature slowly, which means that they are especially at risk from overfishing. As the deep sea becomes more and more heavily exploited, there's a danger that the ancient lineage of these sharks may finally be coming to an end.

The seriously strange sex life of the hairy angler

Of the many weird creatures of the deep that have captured the popular imagination, perhaps the oddest of the lot is the hairy anglerfish. This bizarre-looking fish has many of the modifications that make for a successful life in the pitch darkness 1 kilometre or more below the surface. First, it has a massive set of jaws, filled with long spine-like teeth; it also has lots of long, thin antennae sprouting from its body (hence 'hairy'), which allow it to sense movement in its inky-black surroundings. Where food is very hard to find, you may need special gear to catch it: the angler has a special lure – a fleshy extension sprouting from the top of the head, with a glowing bioluminescent tip – which it waves around in the water to attract prey. And the angler can't afford to be too choosy about prey, big or small, so it has a highly expandable stomach which allows it to eat fish many times its own size. But it's when it comes to sex that the angler *really* stands out …

The female of the species is a real beauty: she's about the size of a football and sports all the delightful features, described above, that make anglers so angelic. The male, on the other hand, is a sorry specimen: he looks positively deformed and malnourished and is only one-tenth of the female's size. His only purpose is to sniff out a female in the darkness (he has a highly developed 'nose' for the job) and, once located, to bite her on the bum. The reason for this rather forward mating tactic is that the male is in fact parasitic on the female: he binds bodily with her, her blood starts to circulate through his body, his organs all but disappear except for the all-important testes, and before long, he appears as nothing more than a small fleshy bag attached to the female's flank. In fact, when the first anglers were pulled to the surface, scientists had no idea what they were looking at. It was only after a good deal of head-scratching that they worked out that a single angler could actually be a large host female with five or more parasitic males attached. Now that's the kind of relationship even Oprah wouldn't want to deal with.

Lured into the jaws of death

Even by the standards of anglerfishes, wolftrap anglers are pretty bizarre-looking creatures. Their distinctive feature – and the origin of their name – is a weird set-up of the jaws: think a fishy version of a Venus fly-trap. The bones at the tip of the massively extended upper jaw are highly manoeuvrable and lined with long, thin teeth. When the angler makes a strike, these teeth extend outwards and then down and around the tip of the lower jaw, which is smaller and shorter. Interlocked upper and lower jaws thus form a cage-like trap, ensuring that no prey caught within can escape.

Like other anglers, wolftrap anglerfishes have lures to entice their prey to within snaffling range. The pelagic species (those that live in the open water) have an extremely long 'fishing rod' (illicium); at the end of this there is a bioluminescent pod, which is sometimes barbed and emits a bright glow. By contrast, the benthic species (those living at or near the bottom) have their lure in the roof of the mouth, just behind the fearsome teeth, the idea being to entice prey directly into the jaws before snapping shut behind them.

The diminutive wolf of the sea

Most deep-sea fish are content to sit and wait for their food to deliver itself, but that's not to say that there aren't some serious predators who constantly roam the depths in search of their dinner. The common fangtooth is the wolf of the sea ... Well, it would be if it were a *tiny* bit bigger. At just 15 centimetres in length this pocket-sized predator presents no immediate danger to human life – but you still wouldn't want to mess with it. The greater part of the fangtooth's body is made up of its massive head, which is deeply grooved with lateral lines – special organs that provide the fish with information about the water movement of its surroundings and therefore potential prey. The fish's eyes are relatively small and probably don't help much except when it migrates towards

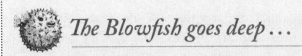

The Blowfish goes deep ...

SAVE YOUR BREATH!

The deep ocean isn't a place we can visit on a whim ... Actually, it's hardly a place we can visit at all: diving down into the deepest and blackest parts of the ocean is about as tough as flying to the Moon. To spend any time underwater, we humans need a vast array of hi-tech equipment and training, not to mention plenty of pure stamina, but there are some other air-breathing mammals that are much better at diving and do it regularly as part of their daily lives.

The biology of diving mammals is pretty complex, but probably the most interesting bit of it is dealing with the need for air. At depth, pressure changes affect the behaviour of gases in our bodies and start to interfere with the biochemical reactions of our nerves. If human divers rise too quickly in the water, they get the bends: a nasty condition that occurs when pockets of nitrogen gas form in the joints of the body (or even in the lungs, heart and brain) – a bad case can cause a horrible death. For this reason, humans don't often scuba-dive deeper than 100 metres, and they have to take great care to surface slowly, decompressing as they do so. The deepest dive ever was over 300 metres and took twelve minutes on the way down and fourteen hours – allowing for proper decompression – to get back to the surface. Yet marine mammals make similar descents daily without suffering any adverse effects. The deepest-diving mammal on the planet – Cuvier's beaked whale – can dive down to around 3,000 metres and hold its breath for over two hours during the dive. And that's only the deepest dive recorded: there's no reason to suppose that these animals don't go deeper still.

the surface waters at night to feed. The really impressive bit of gear is the mouth, which boasts the largest teeth in the ocean, relative to body size. These super-long fangs are so large that the fangtooth can't fully close its mouth – there are deep sockets on either side of the brain which house the tips of large teeth of the lower jaw when they are not snapping shut on prey.

Fangtooth are widespread throughout the world's oceans and are found at a huge range of depths, from 200 to 5,000 metres, where they hunt anything – fish, squid, crustaceans – that they can get their dagger-sharp fangs into. But being so small makes predator potential prey: sharks, tuna and albacore are all known to feed on fangtooth. So these pint-sized predators provide a vital link between the deep-ocean food chain and some of the larger and more familiar predators of the sunlit waters.

Brainless but beautiful

Comb jellies show that you can be brainless and still succeed: sometimes a decentralized nerve net is good enough. These simple animals are master predators of the microworld, found ocean-wide from the deepest depths to the sunlit shallows, where they use long tentacles covered in sticky threads or stolen stinging cells (cnidocytes) to capture prey. Even more surprisingly, it seems comb jellies have developed one hell of a wardrobe when it comes to body pigments.

While the comb jellies you find at the surface are usually transparent, some deeper-living species have developed an array of colours. Under the lights of a submersible, the bright colours of these animals shine out – most often purples and reds, which appear black at depth, thus making their owners invisible. Some have red stomachs, allowing them to eat bioluminescent animals, which would otherwise give away the jelly's location with bursts of light emitted in their death throes. Then you get spectacular rainbow effects from the animals' combs – the tiny paddles they use to propel themselves in the water. As they beat and move, the tiny hairs that make up the combs cause light hitting them to refract, producing a spectrum of colour; covered from top to bottom in these brilliant pulsating structures, the jellies appear to fizz like electricity. Finally, there's the light the jellies produce themselves – bioluminescence. Their photocytes – light-producing cells – are dispersed at regular intervals across the body, revealing a complete outline of the animal in eerie blue or green.

Pompeii worms and the joys of a fireproof bottom

The hydrothermal vents of the deep ocean, belching forth super-hot water, would seem to present some of the most hostile conditions for any life to thrive. Yet this inhospitable realm is inhabited and exploited by specialized pioneers. And none is more unique to the vent ecosystem than the Pompeii worm.

Most life at the vents steers well clear of the hottest superheated water, filled with deadly dissolved heavy metals. But not the intrepid Pompeii worm, one of the world's most heat-tolerant animals, surviving temperatures of 80°C as if it were nothing! Living in large colonies at the vents in the Pacific Ocean, the Pompeii worm inhabits a thin paper-like tube. Its tail lies closest to the hottest outpourings from the vent, while its head – distinguished by huge bright red gills – pokes out into the cooler water, around 20°C, where it breathes and feeds. This is a staggering temperature gradient for an animal measuring just 13 centimetres long. How does it survive? One theory points to the worm's 'hairy' back – which isn't actually hairy at all: it is covered in a thick coat of filamentous bacteria. It appears that the worm 'feeds' these bacteria with mucus secreted from glands on its back; as a result, they grow so thick (up to 1 centimetre deep) that they offer some sort of protection against the heat. Furthermore, the bacteria are chemosynthetic – they happily consume the deadly chemicals in the vent water, thereby 'cleaning' the toxic brew and allowing the worm to survive.

A chilled life in the cold seeps

For every yin, there is a yang; and so for the heat and fury of the hydrothermal vents, there is an altogether calmer opposite: a cooler deep-sea environment, with a much gentler pace of life, but still fuelled by energy-rich chemicals creeping up from below the Earth's crust.

Hydrocarbons, such as methane and oil, can find their way to the surface of the crust without the need for superheated water. They gently seep up through gaps in the rocks and slowly diffuse out over a large area of the seabed. There is plenty of food to be had in the rich hydrocarbons and hydrogen sulphide that often accompanies the oily seeps. Bacterial mats form wherever they can get a meal and start to feed on the rich chemical soup flowing beneath. The cold seeps are home to more complex life too – there is a vast array of filter-feeders, from tube worms to large bottom-dwelling mussels. These filter-feeders play host to chemosynthesizing bacteria, which feed on methane and other dissolved chemicals in the water and produce carbohydrates that are then harvested by their hosts. In the relatively cold conditions of the seeps, growth rates are slow (some tube worms grow less than a centimetre a year), but animals may be extremely long-lived: a mature colony of worms can be well over 100 years old, while some hydrogen sulphide-specializing species can live in excess of 250 years.

An alien world deep beneath us

Near the island of Guam in the western Pacific, hidden far beneath the waves, lies the Mariana Trench – the deepest point of all the oceans and as alien to us as the surface of Mars. The trench itself is a deep scar in the Earth's crust which runs for about 2,500 kilometres and is around 70 kilometres across. The depth of the trench is truly staggering: you have to descend roughly 11 kilometres to hit the bottom at its lowest point, in a small valley called the Challenger Deep, and the pressure down there is 1,000 times greater than at the surface. The trench is so deep that Mount Everest could be completely submerged and its peak would still be 2,000 metres below the surface.

Attempting to visit the Challenger Deep is an awesome task and has only been achieved on four occasions in history. The first trip was made in 1960, when a manned bathyscaphe called *Trieste* made the downward journey in nearly five hours and then took three hours to return to the surface. In 2012 the film director James Cameron took a submersible called *Deepsea Challenger* down to the Challenger Deep, making the journey down in 2.5 hours and returning in a super-rapid time of just over an hour. Cameron spotted life in abundance – fishes, sea cucumbers and giant crustaceans all being caught on camera, mostly for the first time. Sadly, humanity has already left its mark on the Earth's deepest point: high levels of PCBs (polychlorinated biphenyls) – nasty toxic chemicals that were banned in the 1970s – have recently been detected both in the animals living in the trench and in the sediments they live on. It is another stark reminder that our whole planet, from highest peak to deepest depth, is connected: a fact we ignore at our peril.

Living life in the current: the tripod fish

Sometimes it's good just to relax and let the world go by, and see what life brings. In the case of the tripod fish, it's usually a meal, and all it has to do is sit and wait. A relatively large fish at 30 centimetres or more, the tripod fish gets its name from the super-long fin ray extensions which sprout from its lower caudal (tail) fin and both pectoral and pelvic fins. The rays pointing down from the pelvic and caudal fins allow the fish to rest, perched on mud or ooze, raised off the seabed. The upper and lower extensions of the pectoral fins, meanwhile, fan out widely from either side of the fish's head, with the two longest rays projected forward way in front of the mouth. The fish then points its body towards the current and simply sits and waits for food to float by. The pectoral fins clearly have a sensory role, alerting the fish to any movement in the water or chemical trace that signifies prey, but they are also used to bat food towards the mouth. By doing this, the fish manages to cover a much wider area of the current than if it simply sat open-mouthed and waited for something to swim in.

Tripod fish are also hermaphrodites – they have both male and female reproductive organs, which is very handy if you live in the often barren depths of the ocean. So, *if* two tripod fish meet, there's no danger that they'll have nothing to do but talk about the weather: they can get it on regardless!

Growing to extraordinary lengths: the giant siphonophore

In the vast expanse of the deep ocean, where food is always thin on the ground (and in the water), it is smart to spread your net wide and use as little fuel as possible. That's why jellyfishes and comb jellies both flourish in the depths: drifting with the current, they don't use much energy, and their long tentacles can gather food as they go. But a different kind of animal has taken this trick to extreme lengths – literally. Living up to a kilometre below the surface, the giant siphonophore (*Praya dubia*) may hold the title of the world's longest animal. This super-slim but enormously long creature can reach 50 metres in length, allowing its feeding and stinging organs to access large swathes of ocean.

Siphonophore

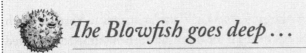

The Blowfish goes deep ...

CELLS UNDER PRESSURE

When it comes to water, humans are like fish ... out of water. The world's finest swimmers might seem to us like speedboats, but they are nothing but pedalos when compared to just about any fish. And things aren't much better when it comes to staying underwater. The record for humans holding their breath underwater is twenty-four minutes, but that was a static breath-hold, and being static isn't much use in the ocean – it's a good idea to move around a bit. Still, perhaps we shouldn't feel too bad about it: the deep ocean, in particular, is so hostile to life that many animals can only live there because of major biological and physiological adaptations. These are often so extreme that the animals concerned are completely unable to leave their high-pressure world and cannot cope at all if placed in the shallows.

Pressure is the major concern for all creatures of the deep ocean. High pressure causes air pockets to become compressed and changes the way cellular membranes function. To combat this, the great majority of deep-sea fish have lost their swim bladder, instead relying on wax esters in the body to help maintain neutral buoyancy, having very fatty livers, or decreasing the density of bones in the body to stop them being crushed under pressure. Deep-sea fishes maintain cell membrane function by having a much higher lipid content in the membranes themselves and a higher level of trimethylamine oxide (TMAO) in the body. Scientists don't yet know exactly how this compound helps protect and maintain cell membrane function, but that's what it does (it is also the chemical that gives fish their fishy smell), and its concentration within the tissues of deep-sea fishes is directly related to depth: the deeper the fish lives, the more TMAO it has.

Siphonophores – the group to which *Praya dubia* belongs – are extraordinary creatures. Some of them are often confused with jellyfishes: they share a lot of characteristics, including the 'jelly' of which they are made and the stinging cells they use to catch, kill and digest prey. But there's one really BIG difference. A jellyfish is one individual creature, but a siphonophore is a living colony of creatures: it is composed of a whole host of individual organisms called zooids – small biological building blocks, each doing a specialized job. There are zooids that act as stingers and collect food, while others play a role in propulsion or – in the case of the famous Portuguese man o' war – serve as a gas-filled float. Whatever their role, the zooids are connected to each other, looking and acting like a single animal.

Deadfall: a bounty from above

The deep-sea floor can be an extremely barren place – a layer of deep, fine silt littered only with the odd rock here and there. Usually, anything falling from the ocean's productive sunlit waters is rapidly consumed, very rarely reaching the dark zones beneath. However, the bigger the creature, the more chance it will make it to the bottom, and there is one kind of animal in the oceans that always finds a way down: whales. On these occasions, an oasis of life can suddenly spring up and flourish in the black depths, attracting a huge variety of creatures.

A whale carcass is an essential source of food for the animals of the deep ocean, bringing in a huge array of scavengers large and small. Conger eels and sleeper sharks can rip the flesh, tearing huge chunks from the body. This allows small animals like hagfish to delve into the corpse and start to strip the meat from inside. Not a single scrap is wasted: as the larger animals take their fill and move on, starfish and urchins set to work on the connective tissues and ligaments, while the bones provide a cornucopia of nutrients for specialist bacteria.

Scientists have found many unique species on whale carcasses, raising the question whether these creatures are endemic, only to be found on the sites of large deadfall. If this turns out to be true, then the impact of large marine animals on the oceanic ecosystem is even more important that previously realized.

The deep-sea Dumbo

A lot of the creatures of the deepest part of the ocean aren't exactly what you'd call cute and cuddly. The idea of deep-sea conservation becomes a hard sell if your poster child displays more teeth than a politician on the campaign trail. But there is one small group of animals that might just about fall under the 'cute' banner: the Dumbo octopuses.

The members of this group belong to a larger family known as the umbrella octopuses, which get their name from a webbing of skin that connects their eight arms, giving them the appearance of an umbrella when their arms are spread. The Dumbo octopuses also have two large fins that project out on either side of their mantle, which are wide and rounded, resembling the ears of Disney's famous cartoon elephant. Gently flapping these 'ears', the octopuses glide through the deep ocean hunting for prey – a more energy-efficient means of getting about than the jet propulsion used by other cephalopods. Although they can be found in open water, it is believed that most of their hunting is done on the seabed, where they pounce on small invertebrates such as shrimps, crabs, snails and worms. That is almost all we know about this appealing group of octopuses – and given the challenges of studying deep-sea life, they are likely to remain mysterious for some time to come.

Getting a different perspective: the cock-eyed squid

Most squid look pretty similar. Generally, the biggest difference between different kinds is size. But there are some nifty adaptations in the squid world, and none niftier than those of the cock-eyed squid.

 *The Blowfish goes deep …*

AN ALIEN WORLD

It has been said that it is easier to visit outer space than travel a mile down into the ocean. Just think that 60 per cent of the Earth's surface is covered in water more than a mile deep, and you realize just how much of our own planet is alien to us.

Huge problems face humans wishing to visit the deep places of the world. The most obvious issue is that we need to breathe air, but there are a host of others, including the effects of cold water on the human body, problems of buoyancy and the need for an effective means of propulsion down to the depths. All these factors must be taken into account before you even get your toes wet. At the bottom of the Challenger Deep in the Mariana Trench, you would experience pressure 1,000 times stronger than that at the surface – something that would kill you instantly. So any equipment used at these depths must be immune to the crushing effects of miles and miles of water above it. For this reason, submersibles designed to explore the deep sea are very heavily armoured, with drastically reduced viewing ports compared to shallow-water subs. To achieve some degree of interaction in the pitch-black depths, deep-sea submersibles are equipped with a wide array of specialized gear, from large powerful lamps to illuminate the waters, to highly manoeuvrable robotic arms for collection of rocks, minerals and other samples. Because using a robotic arm to catch a fish or other biological specimen is extremely difficult, special 'slurp' guns are often used: basically, modified tubes that gently suck in passing creatures for capture and return to the surface for study.

All this high-tech gear comes at a price. To explore the deep ocean, you don't just need the submersible: you need the boat that acts as its hub, fuel and other consumables, and a crew and team of engineers to run the sub and the mothership. Hiring *Alvin*, probably the most famous deep-sea submersible, costs about $45,000 a day.

The film director James Cameron's famous dive to the bottom of the Challenger Deep was said to have cost $8 million. Given the inherent difficulties of deep-sea exploration, combined with massive overheads and crippling underfunding, humanity's real final frontier is set to remain largely unexplored and unprotected.

These squid live in the twilight zone, somewhere between 200 and 1,000 metres, where scant light makes its way from the surface, creating the faintest silhouettes and shadows visible only to animals with eyes sharp enough to see them: enter the cock-eyed squid. These predators have the most astonishing (and ill-matched) eyes: one is small, round and appears blue; the other is much larger, tubular and shines with a yellow tinge. The squid sits vertically in the water column with each eye at a 45-degree angle, the smaller blue eye pointing down and the larger yellow one pointing up. This unusual arrangement allows the squid to spot the tiniest glimmers of blue bioluminescence arising from the darkness below and to discern the outlines of fishes and other prey silhouetted from above. Many animals that live in the twilight zone use counter-illumination to make themselves invisible to predators hunting from below. The marine hatchetfish, for example, has light-producing cells (photophores) on its belly which closely mimic the light filtering down from above, making it blend imperceptibly with the background. Imperceptible, that is, to most predators, but not to the cock-eyed squid, whose big yellow eye acts as a polarized filter that allows it to distinguish between natural and biological light and so to see through its prey's clever camouflage.

Flying buttocks

It is unfortunate to be called a pigbutt worm; worse still if your variant name is flying buttocks; and if your scientific name is *Chaetopterus pugaporcinus* – basically, 'resembling a pig's arse' – you really must have been born under a bad star. But the greatest stroke of ill fortune is if your various names are entirely apt. And so they are in the case of a particularly strange member of the deep-ocean community.

The pigbutt worm belongs to the group known as the polychaetes, or bristle worms, but it doesn't look like any other member of the group – and it doesn't have bristles. The only similarity is that its body is segmented, and it is the middle segments that are inflated to give the appearance of a plump, rounded pair of buttocks. Measuring barely 20 millimetres in size, this curious creature lives in the oxygen minimum zone, an area of the deep ocean where the water becomes trapped by the currents, making it stagnant and a hard place for life to survive. The worm seems to be neutrally buoyant, but it has no method of locomotion and probably relies on its inflated 'cheeks' to prevent it from sinking. It feeds with its head down in the water column, filtering marine snow – the shower of organic detritus falling from above – and other particles that drift by. To assist its feeding, the worm produces a mucous 'net', which collects yet more marine snow and particulate matter.

At this point, details about the pigbutt worm become sketchy – not least because only ten have ever been found. One theory is that it isn't actually an adult at all, but rather the floating juvenile larva of some bottom-dwelling worm whose relationship with the pigbutt has not yet been recognized. Certainly, other members of the group to which this animal belongs are all known to be bottom-dwelling tube-dwellers, so perhaps this comical-looking creature is simply ... going through a phase.

The greatest migration

Where is the world's greatest migration? The mass movement of wildebeest across the Serengeti plains of Africa, perhaps? Or the huge herds of caribou sweeping across the North American continent? In fact, these events – which happen only once a year – are *dwarfed* by a synchronized movement of animals that occurs every night in the ocean. In the so-called diel (daily) vertical migration (DVM), vast numbers of animals living in the first kilometre or so of water move towards the surface at night to feed. The movement is initiated by zooplankton, which are at greater risk of predation in shallow waters during the day, and their night-time ascension draws many other animals up with them, as they all take advantage of the darkness to feed.

You'd think that the daily movement of millions of tonnes of living matter – by far the largest migration on planet Earth in terms of sheer biomass – would hardly go unnoticed. But, amazingly, until the development of sonar technology during the Second World War, the DVM was largely unknown. While scientists had noted the movement of plankton towards the surface at night, they had never realized what came in its wake. Sonar readings revealed a deep scattering layer (DSL) – a false (or second) bottom, above the true bottom (seabed), and it was soon noticed that the DSL moved towards the surface at night, before sinking again during the day. What the sonar was actually detecting was the DVM, consisting of countless millions of fish, together with squid, siphonophores, jellies, shrimps and other marine organisms.

The DVM is incredibly important in feeding the deep ocean and transporting carbon away from the surface. Animals that feed in the productive shallow waters at night return to the deep, where they become food themselves for other, deeper predators, or their faeces becomes part of the marine snow which is so vital for many deep-ocean ecosystems. Without the massive daily movement of biomass, much of the food and faeces created in the sunlit waters of the world's oceans would not make it down to the seabed miles below, and a huge swathe of biological diversity would be lost.

Alien eviction: the pram bug

There's a story that the inspiration for the terrifying alien in Ridley Scott's 1979 film *Alien* came from the amphipod crustacean *Phronima*, aka the pram bug. Whatever the truth of this, it is certainly the case that the pram bug has all the hallmarks of some deadly extraterrestrial butcher.

For ocean-dwelling animals, adequate protection is a matter of life or death, whether they live in the sunlit shallows or the deep ocean. And if you can't build suitable protection for yourself, you can always steal it from somebody else. The pram bug attacks a living salp (a planktonic filter-feeder) with its fearsome set of front claws and mandibles, eating or removing all the internal structure but leaving the barrel-shaped gelatinous body in one piece. It then makes its home inside the hollowed-out barrel, gripping tight with its front claws and propelling itself through the oceans, feeding on food that passes by. Once a female has taken charge of a new home, she lays her eggs inside the salp body – hence 'pram bug' – where they stay until they are fully developed and can leave to find a home/barrel of their own. Living inside the salp body may cost the pram bug slightly more in terms of energy – after all, it has to push a corpse around wherever it goes – but it is worth it to gain protection for its offspring and itself.

Ancient sweepers of the ocean floor

Vent communities aside, the deep-ocean seabed is an extremely bleak environment. There is almost no life growing independently down here, so organisms trying to survive have to rely on food falling from above. So-called marine snow, consisting of dead microscopic animals, mucous chains, faecal pellets and other detritus, slowly accumulates as a fine ooze-like silt on the ocean floor. But at this point on its long journey from the surface waters most of the organic matter has been stripped from the marine snow by other filter-feeders higher up the water column. What remains is extremely low in nutriment.

Even so, there are creatures that spend their entire lives shifting and sifting through this meagre gruel, looking for any scraps or particles of food. Areas of the deep-ocean floor can become carpeted with sea urchins that form into massive swarms as they slowly sweep up whatever they can find. Gut analysis suggests that these animals feed mainly on bacteria coating the fine particles of sediment. This certainly isn't much in the way of fuel, though it evidently suits echinothurioid sea urchins, the group most commonly found in the deep sea. These are very ancient animals, so it's likely they have been acting as caretakers of the ocean floor since the time of the dinosaurs.

An ancient shark shoveller

The chimaeras are a very ancient group of fishes, perhaps even pre-dating their closest relatives, the sharks. Like sharks, their skeletons are made not of bone but cartilage. Though they once dominated the oceans, most now live in the very deep sea, where conditions are little changed from what their ancestors knew 450 million years ago, and some are even found down in the Mariana Trench itself. Others, however, are found in shallower waters, and one such shallow-water dweller – it is usually found at around 200 metres, if you can call that shallow – is the extraordinary elephant shark.

This chimaera didn't get its name for nothing, and sure enough, it has a long, flexible, fleshy snout which extends out from the top jaw and terminates in a peculiar plough-shaped growth. This unique protuberance is used to shovel through the sediment in search of bivalves and other tasty molluscs. The snout is covered in ampullae of Lorenzini (the same electroreceptive organs found in sharks), so the whole thing acts like a mine-sweeper – well, a mollusc-sweeper that is specially tuned to minute bioelectric signals given out by such things as mussels and snails. By swinging this piece of gear across the surface of the bottom and digging down, the elephant shark can gain access to unseen morsels that are out of reach to less well-endowed hunters.

Frozen Seas

There are few places on Earth that witness greater change and convulsion than the polar ice caps. Situated at opposite ends of the planet, seemingly forever on the verge of succumbing to the Sun's warming rays, the polar regions of the Arctic and the Antarctic have always posed the ultimate test of the resourcefulness of life on Earth. More than just giant and remote chunks of frozen water, the polar seas and the massive sheets of ice that cover them are drivers of our planet's climate and a key factor in determining the quality of human life and even our chances of survival.

At first glance, you could be forgiven for thinking that the two poles are pretty much the same. It is true that these regions have much in common, and it is only recently that we have started to appreciate quite how unique and different the Arctic and Antarctic environments are. The Arctic is essentially an ocean, with just scattered fragments of land and the occasional island here and there; the pack ice in the north forms completely from the seas beneath and hence can shift with great freedom. The Antarctic, by contrast, is a continent – a large landmass twice the size of Australia; the ice here forms on top of the land and stretches out into the Southern Ocean in large expansive sheets.

The animals and plants you find in these regions differ too. The Arctic ice expansion during winter allows bridges to form between the landmasses of the northern continents, so land animals can range freely, exploring their frozen world. In the south, the fierce and forbidding Southern Ocean ensures that, no matter how extensive the ice coverage, Antarctica remains isolated from the rest of the world. Swimming or flying are the only means of access, providing a barrier that has effectively shaped the southern flora and fauna.

However, both poles are extremely hostile to life, so the animals and plants that make their home there show extraordinary levels of adaptation. While humans have barely managed to make a dent in the extreme north, resourceful creatures have found a way to colonize and exploit every possible nook and cranny. In adapting to the harsh polar conditions, many animals have become reliant on predictable ice patterns that change with the shifting climate: the big question is whether they can adapt quickly enough to survive the rapid changes we are currently seeing.

The polar regions play a hugely significant role in determining our climate and hence how – and even where – we humans can live on this planet. Ice acts as a vast store of fresh water, so the extent of its coverage and rising sea levels are intrinsically linked, but it goes much further than that. The mere presence of ice – creating an enormous expanse of white – helps reflect heat back into space. The animals that thrive in these zones play a vital role in the amount of carbon entering our atmosphere, while a huge and vitally important global food chain relies on the seasonal shifts in both northern and southern ice coverage.

The ice caps were once objects of respect and awe: places that were shunned by human settlers and avoided by their ships. Then, gradually and tentatively, explorers made inroads. Today, their future lies in the balance, as they are assaulted by the huge impact of global warming and increasingly exploited for the commercial riches they promise. However you want to look at it, the ice caps are shrinking. What that means for humans – and indeed for all other life on planet Earth – only time will tell.

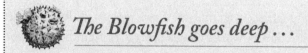 *The Blowfish goes deep ...*

THE FORMATION OF ICE SHEETS

We might think we know about ice and how it forms – after all, we all have those little cubes in our freezers, don't we? But how does an entire sea freeze? That turns out to be an altogether more interesting and complicated business.

As the temperature drops and strong winds blow over the sea, the first stage is that tiny ice crystals called frazil ice start to form and float to the surface. These crystals get pushed around by currents and winds, clumping together and forming into floating masses, or slicks; these are known as grease ice, because of their remarkable resemblance to an oil slick. At this point, two different things can happen. If the sea is rough, the grease ice forms into discs known as ice pancakes, which grow and grow as more frazil ice crystals join them and can reach several metres in diameter. If the waters are calm, the frazil ice crystals have a chance to align themselves properly, and nilas ice forms – this is flat, clean and clear, exactly like the ice you get on the surface of a pond or lake. As the temperature continues to drop, pancake ice and nilas ice start to consolidate and thicken into a complete ice covering. Now the ice begins to grow from beneath the covering sheets; this is known as columnar ice and forms in long, regular crystals, giving the ice sheet depth and strength.

Snow falling on top of the sea ice helps to reflect what little light there is away from the ice and may prevent it from melting. However, snow is also a very good insulator, so areas of sea ice with dense snow layers tend to grow more slowly. There is more snowfall at the South Pole than at the North Pole, so Arctic ice tends to be thicker than Antarctic ice: sea ice in the Arctic is around 2 metres deep, on average, but only about 1 metre in the Antarctic. In theory, sea ice could continue to grow and grow as long as the water stayed below freezing, but changing conditions ensure that this does not happen, and with the return of the Sun, ice always melts back into the sea.

Furry flurry beneath the ice

Beneath the frozen surface, the sea below is still extremely cold, so while ice sheets continue to grow down, ice can also form in the water and float up. This results in the formation of platelet ice, which often occurs where there are large ice shelves and immobile landfast sea ice (ice that cannot move because it is attached to the land or bottom). Here, the movement of the tides and currents beneath the ice causes the seawater to supercool and form, essentially, massive snowflakes. These thin, round plates then float up and stick to the bottom of the ice above, making it appear furry or fluffy.

The habitat formed by thousands of small, thin pieces of ice provides a great place for organisms to exploit. The water spaces between ice platelets tend to be stable and conditions stay above freezing, allowing for blooms of plankton that then attract grazers and predators. If you dive beneath areas of ice floe where platelet ice has formed, you'll see a deep green forest attached to the bottom of the ice. If the overlying ice sheet then splits or cracks, the cloud of platelets floats up into the gap, further increasing the amount of light for photosynthesis and resulting in even more productivity. The only problem with this undersea ice formation is that it can happen anywhere in the water column, so ice crystals can suddenly form in, on or around animals such as sponges, benthic crustaceans and sea urchins. This may damage or kill the creature outright, or lift it up into the fuzzy freezing cloud above.

Cracks in the ice

While the sea ice may seem static and frozen in place, in reality it is always on the move. Constant stresses and strains from the water below and the weather above test the ice and weaknesses can appear. As the ice is pushed around or broken apart by wind, the water beneath may be exposed, producing an open area known as a lead. Leads can be small or stretch for hundreds of kilometres, but they usually freeze over quickly, or the wind shifts and the ice closes in once more. If they persist, however, they are termed polynyas. These are areas where the weather and current keep the sea free of ice throughout the winter regardless of temperature; either newly formed ice is blown away, keeping the water clear, or warmer water rises up to keep the sea above from freezing.

Leads and polynyas are critical in the survival of certain polar species during the winter months. They give unrestricted access to the water for hunting, act as pathways for animals to travel through the ice, and provide areas where whales and seals can breathe. They are also important to native hunters: Inuit communities know exactly where the annual polynyas are and when best to hunt from them. The North Water Polynya between Canada and Greenland opens every year and covers an area of 50,000 square kilometres. The Weddell Sea Polynya, which opened from 1974 to 1976, covered an area of 350,000 square kilometres. Effectively, these are seas within the ice, providing an essential oasis for life during the bitter winters.

Icebergs on the move

Icebergs may be most famous for their starring role in the sinking of the *Titanic* in 1912, but in fact there is much more to them than just getting in the way of shipping. We might only see the tip of an iceberg – 90 per cent remains below the water line – but they are still truly imposing structures. The largest iceberg reliably recorded (in 2000), named B-15, measured 295 kilometres long and 37 kilometres wide: that's pretty much the same size as Qatar or the Bahamas. Icebergs break off (calve) from floating sea ice sheets or from coastal glaciers; this is most common during the spring and summer months, when temperatures rise and the ice weakens. And when bergs break and move off, it's not only ships that may get hurt. The keel of an iceberg can scrape along the seabed for miles and miles, creating an ice scour that can do tremendous damage to everything in its path; it can be as destructive to the polar seabed as any forest fire or hurricane would be on land.

Icebergs are not all bad, though, and they can bring productivity with them too. Depending on the conditions under which the ice originally formed, they can be packed full of organic material and rich sediments. Layers of diatoms and other photosynthetic algae can live in the ice layers of an iceberg, and when they are finally released by melting, they drop to the seafloor and are consumed. Melting icebergs and the rapid deposition of the materials they carry can also help to lock up carbon and transport it to the deep ocean floor.

Manna from heaven: feeding the seabed communities

The seabed (benthic) communities of the Arctic and Antarctic are filled with surprisingly active forms of life – certainly surprising considering the rather chilly conditions. Living under a ceiling of ice can be hard, though, and waiting for food to drop from above is often the best policy. Diatoms and other photosynthetic life form the basis of the polar food chains. During the winter months, these microscopic algae are often found trapped deep within the sea ice, where they cannot be grazed and their waste products cannot drop to the ocean floor below. It is not until spring and the melt that the real bonanza starts. As the ice edge melts, the change in salinity can trap plankton near the surface, keeping them in the optimal position for photosynthesis, and an ice-edge bloom occurs. Just like any other planktonic bloom, it is quickly exploited by zooplankton grazers and filter-feeding fish, and a food chain develops. The organic matter that is now produced and consumed can fall directly to the seafloor below and fuel the communities waiting there. Filter-feeders like sponges and bryozoans are eager to collect the riches falling from above, but others, such as anemones and soft corals, also get in on the act. It is not just fish poo and dead diatoms that sink to the floor, but dead bodies too. Half-eaten fish, mortally wounded seals and even dead whales provide the mobile members of the seabed community with a much-needed feed, and there are large numbers of scavenging sea stars, sea urchins, flatworms, crustaceans and isopods to gorge themselves on the fallen carcasses.

Freezing channels of death

As you'll know if you have ever gritted your drive, ice and salt do not mix. Simply put, the sodium chloride (salt) ions interrupt the formation of ice crystals by getting in the way of the bonds that try to form between the hydrogen and oxygen parts of water molecules as the temperature drops. Basically, for ice to form in the presence of salt, it has to be extremely cold. When this happens, the salt is actually forced out of the ice as it forms, away from the molecular bonds. So, when you get a significant chunk of an ocean freezing, there's a lot of salt to force away.

When pack ice forms, brine channels appear within the structure. Brine is super-concentrated salt water, and as it is heavier than the ice and seawater around it, it starts to flow in channels towards the bottom of the forming ice pack. Several brine channels then come together, forming larger and larger channels and becoming increasingly more concentrated. This high salt concentration in the (still liquid) brine means the temperature in the brine channel is considerably lower than the water around it. So, once the super-chilled, super-salty brine hits the stable seawater beneath the ice pack, a strange and beautiful ice drainpipe called a brinicle forms. Inside the brinicle, the super-cooled brine continues to sink and the salt water around it freezes on contact, causing the ice pipe to continue growing. When the heavy brine reaches the ocean floor, it flows along the seabed, bringing devastation to slow-moving invertebrates and other animals that cannot get out of its path – these hapless creatures are instantly frozen and entombed.

Living within ice

Just as there are animals that live their lives between the sand grains on a beach, so there are creatures that make their homes *within* ice. The ecosystems that build up within the sea ice are vital components at the base of all food chains within the polar seas.

Within the matrix structure of sea ice, there are many microscopic channels through which brine travels on its way back to the ocean after it has been expelled from ice crystals as they form. These brine channels vary in size and therefore determine what can live in them. The smallest channels tend to be the deepest into the ice, where it first formed, and therefore the closest to the surface and the Sun's rays. This makes them the perfect place for photosynthesizing diatoms, whose hard silica cell wall (frustule) prevents them from being crushed by the ice. As the brine channels increase in size and frequency towards the bottom of the ice sheet, grazers begin to appear – small copepods, crustacean larvae and nematode worms that feed on the trapped assemblages of photosynthetic organisms. Living within the ice during winter has some major advantages. Most importantly, these tiny grazers are not only close to their food supply but also safe from larger predators that cannot access the sea-ice matrix. And when the melt comes, these creatures of the ice become accessible to all, so supporting all life throughout the polar year.

The longest-living animals: glass sponges

Delicate and fragile, glass sponges appear as ghostly white tubes, with skeletons of star-shaped spicules of silica to which the animal's cells are anchored. While most species are found in the deeper parts of the ocean, they are relatively common in shallower depths under the protection of the Antarctic sea ice. It is here, in these special conditions, that these sponges have become the longest-living animals on the planet. Cell metabolism is greatly reduced in low and stable temperatures, so cells are not damaged so rapidly by the usual wear and tear of their internal chemistry, allowing organisms to live longer and grow bigger. The glass sponge *Rosella nuda* can grow to a height of 2 metres and weigh 500 kilograms. Its growth rate, calculated on the basis of its metabolism, indicates that it might be some 10,000 years old. This is

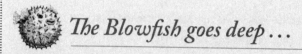
The Blowfish goes deep…

THE GIANT SIEVES OF THE SEA

The baleen whales are a truly unique group of mammals that range from big to seriously big, and among them is the largest animal to have ever lived: the blue whale. Though widely dispersed over the ocean, most species are associated with the polar regions, especially during the productive summer months, and they undertake long migrations to reach the best feeding grounds.

As their name suggests, the defining characteristic of these whales is baleen, a unique biological structure that allows them to hoover up a vast tonnage of their favourite food – plankton, and especially krill, small shrimp-like crustaceans that form into mega-swarms numbering trillions of individuals. Baleen grows from the whale's upper jaw in long plates formed of bristles; these bristles are strengthened and stiffened with keratin (the same substance found in human fingernails), and in some species they are calcified too, to give extra strength. The whale feeds by taking a massive mouthful of water and closing the jaw to leave a small gap through which the baleen is exposed. The tongue is then raised to the roof of the mouth, forcing the water out through the baleen, which acts like a sieve to filter anything edible; this is licked up by the tongue and sent to the back of the throat to be swallowed.

Different whales use different tactics to get their grub. Some rush at the target shoals, mouths gaping at almost 90 degrees, and take in truly enormous mouthfuls thanks to highly extendable skin around their lower jaws. Others feed on the seabed, sieving sand for molluscs and crustaceans. Whatever the method, though, it's the baleen that has made these whales the dominant filter-feeders of the oceans.

only an estimate, of course, but even so, there is little doubt that glass sponges are older than any other animal on Earth.

And the planet's most important creatures are ...

...krill. Arguably: for a world without krill really would be a very different place. These small shrimp-like crustaceans – most species just 10 to 20 millimetres long – feed mainly on phytoplankton, the tiny plant-like organisms that float in the sunlit upper waters, producing organic matter through photosynthesis; and krill, in turn, provide food for countless larger animals, including some of the largest animals ever to have lived.

Whatever krill lack in size they certainly make up for in sheer tonnage. In the Southern Ocean, Antarctic krill can reach densities of up to 30,000–60,000 individuals per cubic metre; some estimates put their population at around 6 billion tonnes – and given that a single krill weighs no more than a couple of grams, that's a LOT of krill. Gathering to feast on planktonic blooms, this vast army of minuscule filter-feeders strain their food from the water by rapid beats of their forelegs (thoracopods), which are covered in fine hair-like projections (setae). Such numbers don't go unnoticed, and nearly every predator in the Southern Ocean – including penguins, seals, seabirds, tuna, sharks and baleen whales – feeds on Antarctic krill.

As well as providing a vital link between the smallest and largest life in the ocean, krill also allow their predators access to the life found on ice. Krill graze on the green algal films growing on the underside of fringing pack ice, where light can still penetrate and photosynthesis is possible. This under-ice larder is essential for long-term krill stocks, as this is where they feed and mature during the leaner winter months, ensuring they are ready to mate and proliferate rapidly when the spring returns. In years of reduced ice, there is a smaller area to offer krill protection and sustenance and thus a smaller population of krill in the springtime – and the big knock-on effect is felt by nearly every food chain in the Southern Ocean.

All baleen and blubber: the bowhead whale

A lot of whales are fair-weather visitors to the Arctic, only showing up when times are good and food is plentiful. Not so the bowhead whale, which is a true Arctic resident, spending its entire life in the northern polar waters. Ranging from 15 to 18 metres in length and weighing in at up to 100 tonnes, this stocky beast is built not for long-distance travel but for brute survival.

Of all the baleen whales, the bowhead has the longest known baleen plates, reaching up to 3 metres in length. To house such massive sheets of baleen, you need a pretty massive head, and the bowhead almost looks like a mouth with a fin attached to the back. This enormous bonce comes in handy when the water freezes over during the long, dark polar winter: the bowhead needs to surface to breathe, so it uses its head to hammer through the sea ice to create breathing holes. It's risky behaviour, as extreme weather can thicken the ice to a point where even the toughest skull can't crack it, but it's worth it in the long run as the whale can exploit the richness of the Arctic seas all year round.

Bowhead whale

In the cold you want a nice, thick overcoat, and the bowhead's is second to none: it has the thickest layer of blubber – up to half a metre thick – of any animal. In fact, it is so well insulated that it risks overheating during periods of extreme activity. In order to keep cool, the bowhead has a mesh of sponge-like tissue running along the roof of its mouth (biologically, it's identical to the sponge-like tissue in the human penis). When the whale gets too hot, this organ fills with blood and greatly expands. All the whale has to do now is open its mouth and allow cold water to flow in, thus cooling the blood and stopping it from having a hot flush in near-freezing conditions.

The unicorn of the sea

Narwhals are impressive creatures – related to killer whales, they can reach around 5 or 6 metres in length and weigh over a tonne. But their fame depends on a single incredible feature: a long, spiral tusk that extends from the whale's face. In days gone by, these tusks were sometimes said to be the horns of the fabled unicorn. So narwhals, the 'unicorns of the north', became the stuff of legend, giving rise to many a tall tale among the sailors of former times. The narwhal's tusk is in fact a modified canine tooth originating from the upper left part of the animal's jaw. The tooth can grow anywhere up to 3 metres in length and grows throughout the animal's life, only stopping with the death of the whale.

You might think that having a huge tusk on the front of your face would be a significant disadvantage, but the opposite is true. Densely packed with nerve endings, the tusk is an incredible sense organ, able to transmit information about the surrounding seawater direct to the whale's brain. It is likely that narwhals use their tusks to communicate with each other, to establish dominance, to share information or perhaps just to socialize. Being hollow, the tusk is quite light, and the animal uses it to probe sediments as it hunts for prey in the dark beneath the ice. Males also use their tusks to 'fence' with one another, but these encounters are ritualized and no serious violence or extreme jousting has ever been recorded. Narwhals spend most of their lives near or under the Arctic ice, actively hunting energy-rich species such as halibut and cod. Having a large tusk has changed the arrangement of the animal's teeth, so rather than bite their prey, they chase it down and slurp it up in one big gulp.

The Arctic chatterbox

The white whale of the north, the beluga is an Arctic specialist, closely related to the narwhal but lacking the fancy tusk. Unlike their long-toothed cousins, beluga whales can be found deep within the pack ice itself, using open stretches of water (leads and polynyas) to move up to 80 kilometres a day. Living so deep within the pack ice is dangerous, so pods of belugas can be seen actively swimming at the surface to keep breathing holes open; they do not have a dorsal fin, which allows them to swim right up against the ice and even break thin ice layers with their back. This behaviour can lead to trouble, though, as polar bears watch, wait and pounce on unsuspecting whales when they make their regular breathing stops at the surface. Lithe and streamlined, belugas are relatively small whales, at 6 metres in length, so they do not have the great metabolic demands of larger whales. They dive down to 500 metres or more in search of fish, squid and pretty much anything else they can catch.

Like other whales and dolphins, belugas hunt and communicate by means of echolocation, emitting a range of clicks and pulses through the melon, an organ containing fatty tissue located in the forehead. The beluga seems to be a very chatty little whale. The melon bulges in its huge forehead and appears to be extremely malleable: as the whale takes in gulps of air and moves them around sinus cavities in its head, the melon becomes deformed, allowing a wide range of different sounds to be produced. Belugas have even been recorded mimicking human speech. It is likely that this sophisticated use of sound has allowed these whales to exploit the ever-changing terrain of the frozen seas, producing 'soundscapes' to map the ice from below.

Whaling stations: unlikely sanctuaries of wildlife

The rise and fall (thank God!) of industrial whaling has left its mark on the polar regions. Not only are we a couple of million whales short, but physical relics of that once-booming industry are still to be found. When large industrial whaling ships first started to hunt in the Antarctic, shore-based whaling stations were established to give support to the fleets. These stations had to be in the most extreme locations to best serve the boats operating in the Southern Ocean, so inhospitable islands such as South Georgia in the South Atlantic suddenly became home to many men – up to 2,000 during the high season. These stations didn't just act as safe harbours where ships could refuel and refit; they also provided spaces where whale carcasses could be butchered and processed. Huge factories sprang up, with rendering plants, steam-powered saws and flensing platforms, all designed to use every bit of the whale as quickly and efficiently as possible.

When the whaling industry ceased, so did the stations, and they were quickly abandoned, with the last station, Leigh Harbour on South Georgia, closing in 1965. There is, however, one positive legacy of these stations that now stand rusting and empty in some of the furthest-flung corners of the world. Many of them are off-limits to the public (not that there is much public to be kept away) – ever opportunistic, nature has taken hold, establishing havens of wildlife in these monuments to past barbarity.

Underpaid and under the ice: whale oceanographers

Learning about life under the ice is hard work for scientists. Drilling, coring, diving – all are labour-intensive, expensive, and only give a tiny glimpse of all that is to be discovered. The use of ROVs (remotely operated vehicles) and submarines is always an option, but again, very expensive. There have been many military subs under the Arctic ice, but they don't necessarily want to share the information they get. What you need is a non-partisan third party, who loves to spend time swimming around under the ice ... and preferably doesn't want to get paid. Bring on the whales!

In recent years, scientists have been using these marine mammals as underwater oceanographers as they can get to areas of the ice that are otherwise beyond reach. By attaching measuring devices to the back of, say, a beluga whale, we can record information on salinity, temperature, depth, or whatever else we might want, all while the whale goes about its normal business. A nice thing, too, is that whenever the whale comes to the surface to breathe, the transmitter is exposed, giving a real-time update on data obtained in the course of the latest dive.

There are, admittedly, some drawbacks to this method. For one thing, whales don't exactly volunteer for this kind of work, so nets must be set to catch them. These nets are monitored 24/7 until a whale is caught; the measuring gear is then attached and the whale sent on its way. And that's when the next problem occurs: you might want to study a particular ice shelf or patch of ocean floor, but what you end up studying is always exactly what the *whale* wants to study. Finally, there is an issue with the device itself. In contrast to sharks, whose fins are made of flexible cartilage and perfect for drilling holes to attach trackers, whales are altogether more delicate. So trackers need to be stuck to the back of the animal, and it takes just one decent bash against the ice and the tracker is gone.

Green-eyed monster: the Greenland shark

The Greenland shark is arguably the second-largest predatory shark, after the great white, growing to 6 metres in length and weighing over a tonne. Found in the cold coastal waters surrounding the Arctic, at depths down to 2,000 metres, Greenland sharks like to take things *really* slow and easy. They have one of the slowest tail beats of any fish of their size, and since no one has ever seen one hunting, it is assumed that they must sneak up on sleeping animals. They must certainly have some special trick up their sleeve, as a wide range of different prey items have been found in their stomach – everything from smaller sharks to cod, seals, and even moose and polar bears. However, in these latter cases it is likely that the shark merely scavenged the meat off an already-dead animal.

It would be pretty scary to think of these sharks actively hunting and subduing a full-sized polar bear . . . What really is scary is that 90 per cent of all observed Greenland sharks have a copepod parasite living directly on their eye. This tiny crustacean burrows into the centre of the lens, probably blinding the shark in the process. The shark doesn't seem that bothered though, and sight is doubtless the least useful sense for hunting prey in the deep dark under the ice. In a weird twist, currently unexplained, the parasite is bioluminescent, and it has been suggested that this faint green glow might attract prey close to those deadly jaws.

As for many other animals that live in the deep, cold waters of the polar regions, longevity seems to be a key issue for the Greenland shark, and there has been much speculation on just how long they might be able to live. A recent study of radioactive isotopes in the eye of a large Greenland shark suggested that her age could have been anywhere between 272 and 512 years, with a reasonable estimate putting her at about 400. This would make the Greenland shark the longest-living vertebrate currently known to science.

Fin-footed fatties: seals, sea lions, walruses

Seals, sea lions, walruses . . . all majestic, all graceful, all fat! These marine mammals, which together make up a group called the pinnipeds ('fin-feet'), dominate the temperate and polar shores of the world. Generally large and capable predators, these animals have some truly superb adaptations for moving and surviving in freezing waters. All pinnipeds are wonderfully streamlined, with limbs modified into fins and flippers. Some have a dense coat of fur, others no fur at all, but all

Elephant seal

have a protective layer of blubber beneath the skin to protect them from the cold and provide an energy source when times are hard. The layer of blubber is so important that in some species, such as the walrus and elephant seal, it can be as much as 15 centimetres thick.

But you don't get fat unless you bring home the bacon, and pinnipeds are superbly equipped as predators. Acute hearing plays a very important part in the life of these animals (external ears are clearly visible in sea lions) – this allows them to listen for the sounds of schooling fish, while keeping an ear out for predators that may be hunting them. Seals can also be extremely vocal, with males of many species vocalizing underwater to attract mates and communicate over great distances. And when it comes to diving, there are some serious records held by these flippered fiends. The largest pinniped, the southern elephant seal, has been recorded diving for over an hour and tracked down to a depth of 2 kilometres. It takes some fancy physiological adaptations to achieve such incredible feats, including the capacity to slow the heart rate and to restrict blood flow to vital organs in order to save oxygen. But the cleverest trick lies in pinniped flesh: the muscle contains a large quantity of myoglobin, a substance that can 'store' oxygen within cells and release it as needed during those super-long dives.

The 'tache-tastic tusker of the north

Think of a creature that is fat, toothy, moustachioed, and sits around all day scratching itself. You might be thinking of me, but more likely it's a walrus. These well-loved animals are pinnipeds, like seals and sea lions, but they have one feature that really stands out – literally: those super-long tusks.

Male walruses grow to a tonne on average, females to half a tonne (depending on the subspecies), so don't be deceived by the lovable looks: these fellas aren't to be messed with. Of the pinnipeds, they are surpassed in size only by the enormous elephant seals. Such massive bulk is critical to surviving the freezing-cold temperatures of their northern polar home. The enormous tusk can reach up to a metre in males, but females have some pretty decent dentition too. Males use their tusks for display (showing off, basically) and fighting, but both sexes use them to help maintain breathing holes in sea ice during the winter. Being a bit of a fatty can make it hard to haul yourself onto ice floes, so walruses also use their tusks like ice picks to gain purchase when beaching themselves. It was once thought that the tusks were used to dig up the walrus's favourite food – clams and crustaceans – from the seabed, but this is actually done by the strong and powerful snout, guided by the super-sensitive moustache, each whisker of which has a dedicated nerve bundle and blood vessel. This highly developed structure means that the walrus can 'see' the surface it brushes its whiskers (vibrissae) over and can tell the difference between a smooth rock and an edible shell without the need for visual confirmation. Now *that's* what I call a proper moustache!

Masters of the ice dive

Living around ice – on it, under it, near it – is fraught with all sorts of danger. As well as the freezing temperatures and the effects of continual freezing and thawing, there are problems posed by a constantly shifting environment: a world that literally moves under your feet – or over your

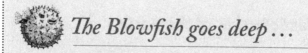 *The Blowfish goes deep…*

DIVING UNDER THE ICE

Diving under the ice is a real privilege – I'd recommend anyone who enjoys scuba-diving gives it a go. You enter a world like no other, enclosed beneath a roof of ice: it's quite intimidating … and bloody cold too.

To dive under the ice, you need to ensure you have all the right kit; most of it has to be specially designed for near-freezing conditions or subsequently modified to fit the bill. For example, a standard regulator – the part that goes in your mouth to deliver air – can freeze in an open position when at extreme temperatures, causing all your vital air to come rushing out: not something you want 20 metres below the surface. The cold doesn't just affect your kit, it has a big effect on you too. A decent dry suit with multiple underlayers is essential – and even then, you'll still be freezing when you get out. Commercial divers use suits with hot-water feeds that allow for increased bottom time.

The biggest concern when diving under ice is that you'll get lost. You enter via a very small opening and you must leave by the very same opening, so divers are attached to a lifeline that is held by someone at the surface. Not only is this a way for you to find your way back, but the surface team can also haul you in if necessary. If you lose your line while diving, you must stop and slowly rise to the surface, where you wait underneath the ice for rescue, or you could attempt to find your own way back to the hole: neither prospect sounds very appealing.

Recreational divers normally use open-circuit systems in which exhaled air is vented to the sea. However, scientists working under sea ice much prefer rebreathers or surface-fed systems where there are no lost bubbles. Bubbles rise and get trapped beneath the ice sheet, and in sufficient quantity they can disturb and damage the delicate ecosystems that thrive there.

head. If you want to make a living *under* the ice – and if you don't have the fish's advantage of being able to breathe underwater – you had better make sure you have a route back to the surface. Diving under ice is a truly incredible experience, but it is an extremely unforgiving habitat and you are immediately aware that, in an emergency, there is no easy rising to the surface and safety. Many marine mammals living at the poles face this problem all the time. While it is not such an issue for animals that live on the edge of the ice shelf, any air-breathing creature that ventures further to exploit the rich environment under the ice must, at all costs, have a strategy to get back to the surface.

The Weddell seal has the most southerly distribution of all marine mammals, and as it spends its whole life in the waters surrounding Antarctica, it has become a master of the ice dive. In the winter, when the ice cover is at its greatest, these seals continue to hunt beneath the deadly floes. They seek out cracks where they can haul themselves out, to rest and to pup, or – if a blizzard strikes – dive back into the relative safety of the sea. But these cracks often open, close and freeze over in the blink of an eye, so they cannot be trusted as a reliable safety exit. To get around this, Weddell seals use their strong teeth to grind away at the ice as it forms, thus maintaining their vital air holes. The grinding action wears down their teeth and causes problems for some older seals when hunting, but, crucially, it allows them to take advantage of the stable feeding grounds under the Antarctic ice all year round.

The cuddly killer

It looks kind of cute and cuddly, chubby with a dog-like face and big doe eyes. Well, sorry to disappoint, but the leopard seal didn't get its name for nothing: it is a bloody (good) hunter. It is also a bit big to cuddle, growing to 3.5 metres in length and weighing half a tonne or more: the third-largest seal on the planet. Like many other animals living in the Southern Ocean, the leopard seal feeds on the mega-swarms of krill, using special rear molars that lock together in such a way as to allow the tiny crustaceans to be sieved out. Krill make up around 40 per cent of the seal's diet. But it's probably the other 60 per cent you should worry about . . .

The leopard seal performs a particularly memorable dance of death with penguins. The seal patrols the ice edge where the birds enter and exit the water. Now, penguins aren't stupid, so they wait until they think the coast is clear before jumping in en masse. Sadly for them, leopard seals are no fools either: they hide behind nearby ice floes, then dash out, seize a penguin and thrash it to death in the water. These seals have even been observed toying with their prey: they chase a penguin to and fro, constantly denying it access to the safety of the ice – the performance only ends when the penguin slips through and escapes, or when it is just too knackered to carry on and is finished off by the seal's very large and well-developed canines.

Leopard seals are so big and powerful that they may even present a danger to humans, with at least one fatality attributed to the animal. In 2003, a marine biologist working in Antarctic research was snorkelling when she was dragged down 60 metres by a leopard seal. Although it is true that the seal never wanted to kill and eat this person, it just goes to show how dangerous this 'cuddly' animal can be.

Penguin

All for the love of a good cow (or forty)

The southern elephant seal – the largest of all seals and the heaviest of all carnivorous mammals – isn't exactly a looker … The male, in particular, has a face like a bag of spanners: hideous on land, though deadly underwater. And bulls are not only hard on the eye, they are hard on the kitchen scales: in good condition, a male can weigh 4 tonnes and reach up to 6 metres in length (the females, on the other hand, are positively petite, at 2.5 metres and a mere 1 tonne). You might think that their massive size explains the 'elephant' bit of the name, but actually there's another reason …

Elephant seals got their common name because of the massive schnoz the males develop as they mature. This large trunk is a dual-purpose instrument that is especially handy when it comes to breeding. In the mating season, bull seals occupy an area of beach and refuse to budge unless defeated by a larger, stronger male. In fact, most fights are avoided by shouting matches as rival males use their stupendous honkers to exchange extremely loud roaring noises. It is only when evenly matched animals square off against one another that blood gets spilled – and then there's plenty of it. However tough they are, though, holding down a harem of forty-odd females takes utter dedication, and this means that the big males can't afford to return to the water to feed or drink. This is where that wonderful nose comes into play again. It is estimated that, by using their extensive nasal passages and some clever counter-current blood vessels, adult males can recover some 70 per cent of the water vapour in the air they breathe out. And this water conservation is the difference between life and death, because it means that bulls do not die of thirst during their three-month-long vigil at the centre of the beach.

The perils of pupping

You might think that for seals living around the poles, swimming about in a larder with more food than they can eat, every day is Christmas day. There is *one* day, though, that isn't quite so special: their birthday.

In the Antarctic, where large land predators are absent, female seals give birth to their pups directly on the freezing-cold ice and in full blast of the biting polar winds. In just a few squeezes, a pup is yanked from a cosy 37°C to a freezing –20°C or lower. Luckily, the pups have a thick coat of hair which protects them against the worst of the weather. On the Arctic ice, where predators like polar bears are an ever-present danger, some pupping seals are much more cautious. They give birth to their young in specially built lairs under thick snow, with a bolthole that gives access to the ocean beneath. Here, the pup is far better protected from the elements than any seal born on the open ice.

Wherever a pup is born, it is always a race against time to grow up and get fishing! Number 1 priority is to stack on those critical layers of blubber which give protection against the freezing temperatures, so to ensure a healthy youngster, seal milk is extremely fatty. Weddell seal milk is nearly 60 per cent fat – that compares with human milk at around 4 per cent. Pups grow quickly, and they need to, as their mothers are keen to get feeding and breeding again: as the ice floes begin to break up, rich fishing grounds are exposed, but at the same time resting space for pups is shrinking. Depending on species, weaning can occur anywhere between two and four weeks, but for the hooded seal it lasts just four days! That's the shortest weaning period for any mammal.

Polar bear: seal terminator

The polar bear is the undisputed pin-up of the frozen north. Indeed, so beloved of cartoonists is the magnificent beast that it is often shown diving and splashing around with another favourite – penguins – but it is actually found only in the (strictly penguin-free) Arctic and the outlying polar regions of the northern hemisphere.

The polar bear's preferred prey is in fact seals, and this ace hunter shows an amazing array of adaptations that help it catch them. Staying in areas of thin and broken pack ice – the top spot to bag a seal – means constant travelling over ice and snow and through freezing waters.

These bears have amazing stamina – they can walk for 30 kilometres a day for several days in a row, and they have been known to swim more than 100 kilometres if they need to. Their wide feet and paws not only act as excellent paddles while swimming, but ensure the weight of the animal is distributed evenly when it is moving over snow and ice. To protect itself from the freezing cold, the polar bear has a dense layer of fatty tissue beneath its thick coat of hair. This coat must be kept in tip-top condition to ensure the bear does not freeze, so after each swim it spends time rubbing itself in the snow and ice to remove excess water. The hair itself isn't actually white but transparent, but the overall effect is that the bear has the perfect camouflage for its ice-white environment. Like all bears, the polar bear has a superb sense of smell – so good, in fact, that it can detect the breath of a surfacing seal at an ice hole or sniff out hollowed-out dens containing seal pups under thick snow. Once the bear has its prey, it makes short work of it – and the ice splattered with blood and gore tells its tale.

Seals under threat

Seals have faced the same kind of persecution as whales and dolphins, but they haven't received the same share of the conservation limelight. Still, seal-hunting has stirred a lot of controversy, and it continues to have a considerable impact on polar ecosystems.

Originally, it would have only been Inuit groups that hunted seals, surviving on their meat and using their skins to make clothing and other such things. These communities would have taken only what they needed – their survival depended on the seals' survival, and their culture ensured that the animals were treated with the utmost respect. The trouble began in the modern era, when ships started to visit the furthest reaches of the world and the sealing industry boomed. Seals were now killed in their hundreds of thousands and taken back to America and Europe, where they were sold for their meat, pelts and blubber (which was rendered into lamp oil). As with other kinds of early 'fishing', sealing got way out of hand, and northern seal populations crashed. Particularly damaged was the northern fur seal – its populations have not fully recovered to this day, and it is currently classified as vulnerable by the International Union for Conservation of Nature.

During the twentieth century various laws and regulations were introduced that progressively curtailed the activities of the sealing industry. Certainly, the modern-day rejection of wearing fur has kept many animals safe on the ice as demand for seal pelts has dropped. Today, there are only nine countries that still practise any form of large-scale seal-hunting, with the largest annual hunts in Canada and Greenland. Sadly, though, seal populations are still at threat, and many culls are carried out under the pretext of protecting commercial fish stocks.

The p-p-perfect predators: penguins

The world's most famous flightless birds, a wide range of penguins – varying in size and appearance, but snappy dressers one and all – are found along the coastlines of the southern hemisphere. They extend all the way up to the Galápagos Islands on the Equator, although the great majority of species are found much further south, with the emperor penguin even overwintering in the heart of the Antarctic itself.

While each different kind of penguin has its own way of surviving on land, they all share some great biological features that make them so incredible in water. First, their body shape is perfectly evolved to allow them to 'fly' underwater: the stout wings are flippers, the short muscular tail serves as a rudder, and the feathers knit together into a dense waterproof coat, keeping the penguin warm during its deep dives. At the front end, there's a strong beak, perfect for skewering prey, while inside the mouth, coating the tongue, there are long, keratinized bristles that sprout out like a mohawk haircut – these all point backwards towards the penguin's throat, preventing prey from fighting its way out of the bird's mouth. Penguins have a highly salty diet of squid, fish, krill and the like, so you might well wonder how they can survive without access to fresh water. Well, penguins have a supraorbital gland – i.e., just above the eye socket – that acts like a kidney to remove salt from the bloodstream. This gland has a network of capillaries through which salty blood passes and where salts are excreted. These are then drained via a duct to the penguin's nasal passages, where they either drip off or are sneezed away.

The Napoleon of the Antarctic

The largest penguin on the planet is also the biggest celebrity, mainly thanks to its hardcore breeding behaviour. The subject of many films and documentaries, the emperor penguin is as close to natural-world royalty as you can get. Growing to 1.2 metres and 50 kilograms, this big bird is a serious marine predator, able to swim down to depths of 200 metres, where it feeds on schools of fish and squid, as well as taking big mouthfuls of krill when available. Feeding in the rich Southern Ocean means there is always a decent meal to be had, and thanks to the emperor's sheer size and speed, very little can threaten it in its natural habitat. Sadly, though, these avian giants cannot spend their whole lives in the water: they have to lay their eggs on dry land – and that's when the fun really *doesn't* start.

While many other penguin species nest around the landmasses of the southern hemisphere, the emperor is the only bird to overwinter at the very heart of the Antarctic continent. There is a bonus to breeding at the centre of the coldest place on Earth: no predators. But that's about where the good news ends. To reach their breeding grounds, emperors have to trek up to 120 kilometres from where the ocean meets the ice. Once at the breeding site, males and females pair off and mate; the female then lays one massive egg before buzzing off back to the ocean to feed. The male picks up the egg and carries it on the tops of his feet, sheltering it within a special brood pouch to keep it warm. These expectant fathers, each now carrying his own egg, withstand temperatures as low as −40°C and winds up to 150 kilometres an hour, as they huddle together in huge crowds and wait out the Antarctic winter. No penguin can constantly withstand the extreme weather, so the cluster regularly budges, giving each bird a turn in the middle and a turn on the edge. When the winter finally ends, the male gives his newly hatched chick its first meal: a fatty protein 'milkshake' produced by a gland in his throat. The female, now fat from a good winter's fishing, returns to the colony, where she takes over from her mate, allowing him to make the journey to the sea, to feed and recover from his harsh ordeal. As the chick develops, the parents take it in turns to look after it and to forage in the now-super-productive spring conditions. Before long the nipper is big enough to be left alone by both parents, and by summertime it is completely abandoned to get on with its own life. And some life it is that awaits the youngster, as within three years – just like its parents – it will be back in this hellish freezer to breed.

The tireless migrant: Arctic tern

There are few animals found in both the Arctic and the Antarctic – after all, they are literally poles apart ... But there is one little fella who spends his entire life moving from north to south and back again. The Arctic tern completes the longest migration of any animal, breeding during the Arctic summer in the extreme north and polar regions, before flying the entire length of the globe to overwinter in the summer of the rich and fertile Southern Ocean. Completing this journey, one tracked tern covered 96,000 kilometres, which is equivalent to circling the Equator . .. twice.

Now, at this point you may wonder: why bother? Rather a long trek, isn't it? Well, yes, it is – but that is testimony to the staggering productivity of the Arctic and Antarctic summers. Breeding in the north during the summer is a good option: after all, there are plenty of landmasses in northern Eurasia and North America to lay your eggs; plus, there are giant schools of herring that arrive to feed on the krill swarms sparked by the planktonic bloom. The terns make good use of this time of plenty to raise their chicks. Then, when the weather starts to break, they travel to the next most happening spot – which just happens to be on the other side of the planet – reaching the Antarctic seas just in time for the krill mega-swarms to bloom and feed an entire ocean. It's certainly a long way to go for an all-you-can-eat buffet, though – especially when you consider that, by the age of thirty, these long-lived birds may have covered about 2.4 million kilometres, which is like travelling to the Moon and back three times!

The northern chunderer

The northern fulmar is quite an impressive seabird. It looks pretty much like a gull, weighing up to 1 kilo and having a 1-metre wingspan. They are found throughout the Arctic and Subarctic seas in the northern hemisphere (as you might have guessed from the name – just as unsurprisingly, there is a southern fulmar in the southern hemisphere). These birds belong to a group called the petrels and shearwaters, making them relations of albatrosses, with which they share a similar ecological niche. Fulmars feed in large flocks on shoals of fish, squid, krill and jellyfish; they also feed on carrion if they get the chance. Now, the only time you will see these birds on land is when they come together to breed. They tend to choose high cliffs with strong winds and updrafts, as this is very useful for getting airborne again after landing, and it allows them to make rapid swoops straight into the sea – they sometimes dive down several metres into the water in search of fish.

So far, so (fairly) interesting. But why have I singled out fulmars here? Because they are excellent chunderers. These birds produce a rich oily substance in a special part of their throat, which is really useful for feeding chicks and for consuming themselves when energy is needed on long flights. But it is also perfect for puking on predators. When nesting, fulmars may be attacked by vicious skuas and other seabirds, which try to get at their eggs or chicks. The vomit from a defending fulmar is so thick and oily that if the attacking bird gets a good face full, its feathers can become clogged and cease to function: one decent barf in the right direction and a fulmar can cause a predator to plunge to its doom. Now that really is sick ...

The flying penguin of the north

It's probably not going to come as a big surprise to you that there are no penguins at the North Pole. But there *are* black-and-white birds that dive underwater for their food – *and* (any penguins listening, cover your ears) they can fly ...

Little auks are very small seabirds, only about the size of a starling. They are fearsome predators, though, using powerful wing beats and webbed feet to dive to 30 metres in pursuit of small fish, crustaceans and other invertebrates. They feed in large flocks (or is that shoals?), swimming down to forage on the bottom or striking up at prey from beneath. Not content with being wizards in water, these birds are swift flyers too, beating their wings like crazy to achieve straight-line speeds of up to 65 kilometres an hour. Though they spend most of their lives at sea, they are very social, coming together in large colonies on far-northern landmasses once a year to breed. When they get together, they really know how to throw a party, with some breeding colonies numbering in the millions. All these birds provide a bonanza for Arctic foxes and other land-based predators – even polar bears have been known to eat auk eggs. Once the chicks have hatched, the parents make numerous fishing trips to keep them healthy, using their special extendable throat pouches to carry food back to base. And whatever these diminutive birds are doing is clearly working, for their global population stands at an estimated 30 million.

A vast lake, forever hidden from view

Life under the ice is hard, but at least living under the Arctic or Antarctic sea ice comes with plenty of benefits – and you can always swim off

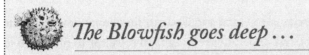

The Blowfish goes deep ...

LIFE IN THE DEEP-FREEZE: BLOOD ANTIFREEZE

Living under the ice might seem a good option for fish: it may be cold, but at least it's not freezing, right? Well ... no, not exactly. Salt water freezes at around −2°C, but fresh water freezes at 0°C: fresh water, that is, like the stuff found in the cells and tissues of fish. So it's perfectly possible for a fish to turn into a swimming ice cube if it's not properly adapted to deal with the severe temperatures. The actual freezing point of fish blood is around 1°C, so to survive in sub-zero waters they produce special antifreeze proteins. These substances work by binding to the edges of internally forming ice crystal molecules, thereby stopping them from growing to dangerous proportions and damaging tissues.

It sounds crazy, but some fish that produce antifreeze proteins actually *encourage* ice to form by providing nuclei for the crystals to grow from. This may seem strange, but it means the growth of ice is more under the animal's control and can be localized in non-essential areas. These methods of controlling ice growth are so effective that ice crystals sometimes persist in the fish even when the water temperature rises, as the crystals are so well protected by the proteins.

to warmer waters. Not so if you are trapped between the landmass of Antarctica and the many glaciers that cover it. Nothing could live there, right? Well, we don't know, but we may soon find out ...

Lake Vostok lies 4,000 metres below the ice and snow of Antarctica; measuring 250 kilometres long by 50 kilometres wide, it is one of the world's largest freshwater lakes. It was cut off from the rest of the world around 25 million years ago by the encroaching ice and has remained isolated ever since. It is believed that the water of the lake continually freezes and is carried away by movement of the glaciers above, and is replenished by meltwater; estimates suggest that the whole volume of water is renewed in this way every 13,000 years or so. Lake Vostok, then, is a massive time capsule, containing water, sediments and (possibly) life that existed many eons ago. Studying its secrets might even allow scientists to get an idea of how, or if, life is present on some of the ice-covered moons of Jupiter and Saturn. There's just one snag . . .

Sampling a lake through 4 kilometres of rock-hard ice is not an easy task. Drilling down to such depths – and not immediately losing your gear as the borehole freezes over – means using a lot of chemicals as antifreeze, and these could easily contaminate a sample or even pollute the lake. Contamination was the problem when, in 2013, the first core was drilled and Lake Vostok finally reached, casting doubt on the findings that followed. Russian scientists have reported that a clean, uncontaminated sample was taken in 2015, but it will be some time yet before their findings are released and subjected to wider scientific scrutiny. For now, nobody really knows what we might find and where on earth (or in space) it might lead.

Melting ice and rising seas

Thanks to the wonderful weirdness of water, ice takes up more space than the water from which it is made (basically, it's due to the way bonds form between water molecules). Take a glass, fill it three-quarters full with water, mark the water line, then freeze it. When you get it out of the freezer, the ice will now be higher than the line you marked before freezing. But you haven't suddenly got more water, even if it looks like it. Let that ice melt and the water level returns to the original mark. So what's the problem? You had ice – lots of it. It melted, but you did not see any increase in the water level. So, when people talk about the ice caps melting and the sea level rising, they cannot be referring to the ice which forms yearly from the ocean,

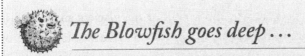
The Blowfish goes deep...

ICE-CORE SAMPLING

Ice doesn't always melt and re-form every year. Sea ice tends to last only a single season in the Antarctic, but often it remains for several years in the Arctic. The ice that forms on the landmass of Antarctica, on the other hand, is very stable and does not melt away. Using large coring drills, samples of ice can be taken from many metres down in these glacial stacks. These long cylinders of ice act as a timeline of the past, allowing us to see the conditions under which the ice was formed and opening a window into what the environment was like many years ago.

Gases such as carbon dioxide (CO_2) are trapped in the ice, along with chemicals such as methanesulfonic acid (MSA). Measuring CO_2 levels obviously helps inform us in our constant battle with global warming, but the presence of MSA is just as important as an indicator of the amount of sea ice that was formed in a given year. MSA is formed from gases given off by sea-ice algae, so a lower level of MSA indicates a drop in these algae, and this in turn indicates that there was less sea ice available for the algae to colonize. A fall in the quantity of algae would have a huge knock-on effect on all the food chains of the Southern Ocean.

Core-sampling sea ice can also give excellent results. Although it can't tell us much about what happened in the distant past, it offers a fascinating insight into how various lifeforms find a way to live *within* the ice itself: diatoms, rotifers, bacteria, viruses and other small microscopic organisms are found thriving in the brine channels in between the matrix of ice crystals.

because – just like the glass you had in the freezer – whatever ice formed from the sea is returned to the sea, without any appreciable sea-level change. However, there is a core of sea ice at the centre of the Arctic that formed many years ago and has not shifted in our lifetime. If this melts, the 10 per cent of it that is *not* currently being displaced will affect global sea levels. Even so, none of this will be anything like as bad as if the South Pole starts to go.

The real issue is the ice-cap melt around Antarctica – or rather, the melt *of* Antarctica. The permanent ice sheet covering the continent of Antarctica contains 90 per cent of all the world's fresh water, and if all that were to melt, sea levels wouldn't rise just a few centimetres – they'd soar up by around 80 metres. The reason for this is that unlike the Arctic – where the sea ice is floating in the water, formed from the water, and already displacing 90 per cent of its own volume – the ice in Antarctica is situated on a landmass, which means any melted water isn't replacing ice but adding to the overall oceanic volume. This is like adding ice cubes to your glass after you've poured the water in and marked the level. This is the real concern for mankind: if we melt the ice at the South Pole, we are going to be in really deep water ... around 80 metres of deep water.

If the ice caps melt . . .

As more and more attention has focused on global warming, the polar ice has become the barometer to gauge just how much trouble we are in. Antarctica is a landmass: the ice coverage grows out into the sea, but the land itself doesn't change. The Arctic, on the other hand, is just floating sea ice: there is no landmass, so it could – theoretically, at least – melt away to give a clear passage of water over the top of the world.

Now, it has to be said that if *all* the ice at the North Pole were to melt, we'd be in trouble as a planet, let alone as a species. It is likely that there will always be *some* ice there as long as there are humans to see it. The real problem is how far this ice reaches. During a 'normal' healthy winter, the Arctic sea ice should encroach onto Canada, Russia and Greenland, and cover an area around 16 million square kilometres, shrinking down to about 7 million square kilometres in the summer. Now, while winter coverage has dropped, it remains reasonably stable. Summer coverage, however, is getting smaller and smaller, and scientists fear that we are heading towards an 'ice-free summer'. This doesn't mean there will be no sea ice at all, but that it will cover an area less than 1 million square kilometres.

While this might not seem all bad – for instance, it might sound like a good idea to have shipping lanes running over the top of the planet – having so little ice would have a very serious impact on both climate and wildlife. Animals such as polar bears, seals and walruses which need ice to hunt and rest would be in deep trouble, having to travel further to find prey or just a place to sleep. Meanwhile, the greater volume of fresh water entering the oceanic systems as a result of melting ice would have a major impact on ocean currents and circulations, and this would have a direct effect on global climate. Finally, the shrinking area of white ice reflecting heat back into space, and the growing expanse of dark water absorbing heat, would further warm the atmosphere and drive yet more ice-cap melt. It's a vicious cycle, but one that would stabilize if we could only control emissions of greenhouse gases.

The Arctic land grab

Many countries are showing a lot of interest in the Arctic, but mostly it's for the wrong reasons. The Arctic has been targeted as an area of untapped resources, with the US, Russia and others all itching to get their hands on the oil, gas and mineral riches. It is estimated that many billions of tonnes of oil and gas lie undiscovered within the Arctic Circle, so it's no surprise that there's a mad scramble to get a slice of the pie.

In the seventeenth century, most countries accepted a 'freedom of the seas' doctrine, according to which you could lay claim to the areas off your immediate shoreline, but otherwise the sea was open to all. This changed around the end of the Second World War, when the US started to claim exclusive access to pretty much anything on its own continental shelf. This started a chaotic rush as other countries followed suit, so in 1982 the United Nations introduced the Convention on the Law of the Sea (UNCLOS), which gave countries exclusive rights to resources within 200 nautical miles (370 kilometres) of their own coast-line. However, this hasn't led to complete peace and tranquillity, and if you look at a map of the claims made by various countries over the Arctic, it would make your head spin! Different countries come up with different calculations to show where their continental shelf ends – all with a view to extending their boundaries and grabbing a bigger share of the action.

True masters of ice and snow

If any one people could really lay claim to the Arctic, it would be the Inuit, the aboriginal people who have become masters of snow and ice. The term 'Inuit' covers eight main groups found across northern Canada, Alaska and Greenland. There have been people living within the Arctic Circle for around 4,000 years, and the modern-day Inuit established themselves around 1,000 years ago. Over that time, the aboriginal people have developed a truly mind-blowing set of skills to survive some of the harshest conditions the Earth has to offer.

The inhospitable conditions to be found in the extreme north meant that the Inuit never became farmers, so fruits, berries and vegetables had to be gathered at opportune times and stored throughout the year. To survive in the Arctic, the Inuit had to become extremely efficient hunters, and they have hunted nearly every animal they encounter, including whales, polar bears, seabirds, sharks, fishes and seals. Nothing is wasted in Inuit culture, and the furs and skins of polar bears and seals are used to make clothes for the community. Living across vast expanses of frozen ocean has led the Inuit to develop an extraordinary rapport with the natural world. They are able to predict the movements of ice, knowing when and where leads (ice-free areas) might open up, and they can look at an ice formation and judge its suitability for hunting or crossing. Inuit culture has an array of precise technical terms for different ice formations and aggregations, such as *uiguaq*, which means thin ice attached to the edge of an ice floe, and *ivuniraarjuruluk*, the word for an ice structure that can be used to collect fresh water and to navigate by.

Living in the Arctic is like living on a knife edge; conditions can change quickly and hunts can fail, leading to lean times or death. As their lives are always in the balance, the Inuit have a deep respect for the animals and the land they live off. For example, after a seal is killed, fresh water is dripped into its mouth, because – as it is a saltwater animal – it is supposed that it must be thirsty. This care and respect appeases the goddess of the seas and ensure that there will be seals, whales, walruses and fish to hunt for many years to come.

Ice-breaking ships

You don't have to be a salty old sea-dog to figure out that ice is hard and that boats are going to have a hard time getting through it. Sea ice has been a barrier to ships since the early days of exploration. The first explorers and travellers of the polar seas simply waited for fair conditions before setting out. Travelling in summer meant less ice, and leads and polynyas (open areas of water within the ice) made navigation possible. Even then, the chances of getting caught out were high, so attempts were made to design boats that could withstand the pinching and crushing of the ice. Wooden vessels could have reinforced hulls, or even steel plates on the bow and keel. Even so, such measures hardly made a true icebreaker, and Ernest Shackleton's ship *Endurance* (to name but one) still had its hull crushed by ice in the Weddell Sea in 1915.

Fast forward some years, and heavy steam-powered vessels started to make an appearance, and now gas-powered turbines or even nuclear reactors drive the largest ice-breaking vessels. The Russian nuclear-powered icebreaker *Arktika*, launched in 2016, is currently the largest ship smashing its way through the polar ice. This vessel weighs in at 33,540 tonnes and is 173 metres long. It is doubled-hulled and even has powerful air jets situated below the water line, which assist in breaking up ice floes. An icebreaker works, essentially, by beaching its bow on the targeted ice floe and then powering forward until enough of its weight is stacked on the ice to cause it to crack. For this reason, icebreakers have rounded hulls with reduced keels – this doesn't make for a smooth journey – although when smashing through ice 3 metres thick, you barely exceed 5 kilometres an hour anyway.

Polar exploration: Amundsen, Scott and Shackleton

So fiercely inhospitable are the poles that they remained inaccessible to humans until the early decades of the twentieth century. Then, a single man – the Norwegian explorer Roald Amundsen – became the first (undisputed) person to visit both ends of the world. In December 1911, at a time when the best cold-weather gear was made from skins and furs, Amundsen and his team used sleds, dogs and skis to complete the journey to the South Pole in just under two months. In this race to the bottom of the world, he arrived five weeks earlier than a team led by British explorer Robert Falcon Scott, who died with his men on the return journey from the pole, through lack of supplies and exposure to −40°C temperatures. Another well-known polar explorer was Ernest Shackleton, who attempted to become the first person to cross the entire Antarctic continent via the South Pole. Once again, the harsh nature of the polar regions scuppered his plans, and his ship, *Endurance*, became locked in sea ice before being crushed and sinking. He and his men were forced to camp out on the ice shelf for months before setting off in lifeboats to an uninhabited island nearby. The party was eventually saved by some daring seafaring from Shackleton and a small group of brave men, who travelled a further 1,300 kilometres to South Georgia to get help. Shackleton's attempt is considered the last great expedition of what became known as the Heroic Age of Antarctic Exploration. Today, it is mainly just scientists who make these once-deadly trips in the (relative) comfort of an aeroplane seat.

Threat to the poles: commercial fishing

The rich polar seas don't just attract the world's largest mammals to feed, but also one of the most widespread: humans. Both the North and South Poles are areas of great abundance during their spring and summer seasons, and every year many fleets head out into these waters to bring home a mammoth catch.

In the north, Arctic cod, pollack and herring are all sought-after species, with species like snow crab and king crab also fetching very high prices. In recent years, there has been growing concern over the northern fishing fleets, as greater shrinkage of ice during the Arctic summer means that vessels could fish higher and higher in the Arctic Circle. Few studies have been conducted into fish stocks in this area, so we have very little idea how the environment might react to such a rapid increase in fishing pressure. Thankfully, there is currently legislation in place to protect the high seas of the Arctic from unregulated commercial fishing.

In the south, the Southern Ocean is much larger and rougher than its equivalent in the north, so it presents a much more difficult challenge to commercial fishing. Even so, large fleets use benthic longlines to fish for Patagonian toothfish, a species which is slow-growing and long-lived, and so does not cope well with extensive fishing pressure (only the Falklands toothfish industry has managed to gain recognition for sustainable management). Antarctic krill, which provide the base diet of nearly everything in the Southern Ocean, are also netted. These are in decline in any case, and their distribution is patchy at best; where there is a lot of krill, there are a lot of predators, so fishing fleets pose a significant risk of bycatch, and there is even a danger of boat strike on hunting whales.

Managing polar seas is a huge task, especially when illegal fishing is rife and many countries don't want to play by the rules. But without protection we could see a complete crash not only in polar flora and fauna, but also in the vast array of non-polar animals which rely on the great seasonal production of these frozen seas.

Threats to the Oceans

O ut of sight, out of mind. Not many of us have the privilege of living within walking distance of the coast, let alone viewing the sea every morning as we wake up. It's perhaps no wonder that a large slice of the global population has little idea of just how important the planet's salty waters are to their daily comings and goings. This disconnection has in turn put great strain on our relationship with the seas, which have come to be seen as dumping grounds, gold mines to be exploited, or places to be feared.

The first really big hit that the oceans took was not that long ago. Before the industrial revolution, when fishing boats were powered by oars or sail, even a large vessel rarely ventured any further than a day's journey from the coast. Wet and heavy fishing nets had to be deployed and collected by hand, and in an era when most fishing boats were small, these constraints limited the impact that fishing could have on the seas. Things began to change with the advent of steam boilers: ships grew larger, travelled further and used bigger nets, hauled in by machines. Fishing expanded around the globe and started to access fishing grounds that had previously been untouched. Large, slow-growing marine mammals took the brunt of this industrializing of fishing, and they have not yet recovered.

The development of better ships and fishing gear, improved storage, and an ever-increasing human population pushed the fishing industry on and on. Nevertheless, it was only as recently as the 1960s when things truly got bad. It was then that sonar technology gave fishing fleets pinpoint accuracy. As a result, worldwide fish stocks began to crash as fishing vessels were always able to locate the large shoals they desired, and many mature breeding fish were lost. And fishing was not the only line of attack, for deforestation, mining, shipping, coastal development, litter and terrestrial industry were all combining to cause huge environmental changes in the oceans – the largest habitat on Earth.

The effects weren't only observable in the decline of large oceanic species and fish stocks, but also in the unforeseen consequences for unique and delicate areas of the world that were only just being explored. It became clear that something had to be done, yet the state of the oceans still did not get the attention it deserved. Which is remarkable, because if the oceans were to fail, it would not just mean an end to fish and chips, but huge climate shift, massive species deterioration and extinction, the desolation of once-rich coastal regions, an increase in the impact of natural disasters, and even the threat of a new ice age.

It's not all doom and gloom. Areas that have been protected by science and legislation have shown a scarcely believable ability to recover in terms of species richness and density, in very short periods of time. We know what needs to be done to repair the damage, and we still have time to do it. The real battle is to get us, the human race, to mobilize in time; and the real fear is what will happen if we don't.

Turning up the temperature

Although global warming has been talked about and studied for many years, it is only recently that ocean warming has become the focus of research. The oceans *are* the climate of this planet; the rains that fall, the storms that form, the currents that heat or cool entire continents – all are dependent on a stable sea. So what changes if the oceans grow warmer?

First and most worrying, hotter seas mean less polar ice formation in the Arctic and Antarctic. It doesn't take a genius to know that ice melts in warm water, and the more meltwater we see, the higher the rise in sea level and the warmer the planet will get. As temperatures continue to increase, rainfall and tropical storms will become heavier and more frequent in places, as more water evaporates from the surface of the ocean, leading to more erosion and damage to the land, especially in areas where mangroves or coastal forests have been cut down. The hot, warmer water also acts like a thick blanket, smothering the colder, nutrient-rich water beneath.

In tropical regions, life may already be used to higher temperatures, but that doesn't mean it can get hotter without consequences. Tropical fish species are already starting to migrate away to cooler waters away from their traditional habitats in the tropics, but for marine life that can't swim away, it's a different story. Coral reefs are extremely delicate ecosystems, and during prolonged periods of abnormally increased water temperature the coral can become stressed and bleach. During bleaching, the host coral ejects its symbiotic zooxanthellae, which become overactive at higher temperatures and would otherwise damage coral tissues. This wouldn't normally be a great problem, when such hot temperatures are experienced for just a few days a year. Now, however, you can find the water temperature in some areas staying at dangerously high levels for weeks or even months, causing mass catastrophic bleaching that is wiping out entire reefs.

By how much have the oceans warmed? The global average may seem small at 0.5°C, but even this seemingly trivial amount is enough to lead to enormous and worrying change. Scientists can only speculate what will happen as the heat increases.

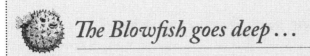

The Blowfish goes deep ...

THE NEW ATLANTIS: THE STORY OF KIRIBATI

In the UK, we're getting the idea that global warming means more rain and the increased likelihood of a ruined summer barbecue. Elsewhere in the world, it's the very survival of the ground you stand on and a whole way of life that's at stake.

Kiribati, an island nation made up of thirty-three atolls and reef islands in the centre of the Pacific Ocean, feels every moment of climate change, and it is rapidly lining up to become the new Atlantis. At the moment, the liveable land totals 800 square kilometres, about the same as the Shropshire Hills: in other words, small. The population stands at around 100,000, but already some are having to makes choices about a future governed by climate change. As the seas continue to rise, the islands are beginning to disappear. In addition to the swamping of land, there is the much bigger if more subtle threat of salt penetrating the freshwater supply and the soil. Before the seas overwhelm the land, they may kill it by stealth, seeping into the highly porous limestone (which comprises most of the rock) and forcing the fresh water out.

For Kiribati's people, once a well has become contaminated, fresh water must be sourced from another island, further increasing the demands on the limited local resources, or shipped in at a cost to the community. Neither option is sustainable. The islands themselves have *some* ability to respond to sea-level rise, in that the coral polyps that form the surrounding reefs can increase their growth rates and thereby their size. But this isn't a quick process, and it relies on perfect conditions for coral growth rather than seas experiencing increased temperatures and ocean acidification.

Although much has been put in place to try and save Kiribati and its people's way of life, the truth is that unless something drastic happens, the current trend of climate change will deliver most of those 800 square kilometres back to the Pacific Ocean.

When ice caps melt: freshwater finale?

The question if or when the ice caps melt is a matter of debate, but the potential effects of such vast amounts of fresh water are not to be sneezed at. It's a much bigger issue than the flooding of low-lying islands and coastal areas.

Certainly, rising sea levels are already posing dangers, as Kiribati well knows. You *could* argue that it's not all bad, especially if you don't live in these areas: the shallow seas that develop, especially in temperate and subtropical areas, could be extremely productive and support large carbon dioxide-munching blooms of plankton, conceivably sucking so much of the gas out of the atmosphere that global temperatures would drop and allow the ice caps to re-form. But before we get carried away, we should remember that this isn't the kind of thing that would happen overnight. And in the meantime, we'd get battered in other ways.

The flooding of the oceans with fresh water would cause some major changes, as the lighter, less dense meltwater would sit on top of the heavier seawater. The effect would be to stifle or shove off course life-giving currents such as the Gulf Stream – a death knell for any animals relying on those currents. It's bad news for us, too, given that the oceans' currents are the true masters of the world's weather and climate. Adding that much cold fresh water isn't going to do anyone any good.

When sea creatures melt: acidification

Threats to ocean life come in many shapes and sizes, including changes in the water itself. Salt water is not acidic by nature – it should have a decent pH of around 8.2, depending on what part of the ocean you are in. It is, though, a critical level for all sea creatures, as it affects the chemical reactions needed for life. When the pH starts to drop and the oceans begin to acidify, the result can be carnage for fish and invertebrates.

How so? Well, with greater acidity it becomes harder to extract calcium from the surrounding seawater, and so corals, molluscs, echinoderms (such as starfish and sea urchins), crustaceans and plankton find it more difficult to create strong shells, tests and skeletons. Fish are not immune, because they begin to struggle to successfully form the ear bones (otoliths) needed to hear properly and maintain balance. Then there's the problem of maintenance, for acidic water can dissolve shells and skeletons nearly as fast as the animals can form them. In such circumstances, the animal either has to work twice as hard to keep up the calcium carbonate structures it relies on for life, or it literally melts away.

The major cause of ocean acidification is the amount of carbon dioxide currently in the atmosphere. The phytoplankton in the oceans would, in theory, readily absorb and utilize this excess CO_2, trapping it and sending it down into the depths, but there's a vicious circle: the hard tests they build as their floating homes are also being slowly degraded and dissolved by the acidic water they now float in.

Heavy metal hazard

An extra dose of fresh water in the ocean might seem a relatively harmless sort of additive compared to, say, mercury. Now, some of you may know that I'm quite a fan of heavy metal ... but not this type, for it's a serious drag.

Mercury enters the seas via rivers, rain and run-off. The principal culprit is human activity, notably in the form of mining and coal-fired power plants, while a minor culprit is volcanic activity, offering up a small amount of the stuff. Either way, when mercury enters the oceans, it becomes the compound methylmercury, which can be rapidly absorbed by the tissues and muscles of organisms. It is the predators of these food chains that truly suffer through a process known as bioaccumulation.

Take a small target species – such as krill, herring or sardine – and they will collect small amounts of the heavy metal in their tissues as it passes through gills and is taken in during feeding. OK, they're only small animals, so there's only a small amount they can absorb. But in the next link of the food chain, larger predators (which are also taking in methyl-mercury through their gills) want to eat a lot of krill/herring/sardine to keep themselves going, ingesting the sum total of all their prey's absorbed metals. Repeat the process, all the way up to top ocean-spanning and long-lived predators such as sharks, and these kings of the ocean can be carrying dangerous levels of heavy metals in their tissues. This not only has consequences for the health of slow-growing, slow-to-mature top preda-tors, but also results in fish entering the human food chain packed with deadly toxins. With good reason, many health authorities recommend restricting the consumption of, for example, swordfish or shark to once a month and suggest pregnant mothers and children avoid them altogether.

A plague of plastic . . .

While human beings aren't the sole generators of mercury in the oceans, they can't escape responsibility for littering the ocean with something that is never found in nature: plastic. It has only really been around since the 1960s, and yet nothing else we have created has had such an insidious impact at every possible level of the oceanic ecosystem.

At the most obvious level, plastic is ugly rubbish that litters beaches and clogs harbours. So much of it is one-use and disposable, and without proper recycling arrangements umpteen million drinking straws, coffee cups, plastic bags and takeaway food cartons find their way to the sea. It is here that the throwaway items become long-term lodgers. Something that has played just a brief part in our lives can go on to live in the oceans for up to 600 years, potentially 1,000 years, and maybe even longer – we don't really know. And once in the water, plastics can interact with all levels of aquatic life. Turtles, whales and dolphins have all been found dead with stomachs full of plastic waste, having mistaken it as jellyfish; they have literally starved to death on a diet of rubbish. As the waste breaks down, the chunks of multicoloured plastic get smaller, and seabirds and fish take great interest in these bite-sized pieces of red, pink, blue and green, easily mistaken for squid or prey fish.

It is a sobering thought that there is an area of mainly plastic waste in the Pacific Ocean the size of Texas ... and it is not the only one.

... and microplastic

When plastic particles get even smaller, around 1 millimetre across and just a few millimetres long, they acquire a new name: microplastics. The category includes nurdles, the small plastic beads that are heated and pumped into moulds to create so many of the plastic products we use in our lives. They're the king killer of the microplastic world, not just because they themselves seem so edible to larger animals, but because they readily break down into invisible but equally damaging pieces. Another form of microplastic that has recently had a lot of adverse publicity is microbeads, the tiny pieces manufacturers use in, for example, exfoliating facial scrubs and toothpaste.

No matter what their size and origin, a hell of a lot of microplastics are consumed by marine creatures, sometimes by accident, sometimes mistaking it for prey. And it is happening across the spectrum of ocean life. Worms and crabs have been found with microplastics integrated into their gills or digestive tracts. Fish find them clogging their gills or stomachs. Larger predators such as shark, tuna, swordfish and seabirds bioaccumulate the microplastics ingested by all their prey. We don't yet know the full effects of the build-up of microplastics in these animals, but what we do know is alarming. Small plastic pieces act like sponges, soaking up dangerous pollutants, which are then very likely to be released into the animal's tissues as the microplastic is ingested. Once plastic in the ocean has degraded into microscopic particles, it also gets to work on small fish fry still in the plankton. Either these juvenile fish become addicted to eating the tiny fragments, or the chemicals that are leaching out and pooling in the nearby water affect fish development and maturation.

So widespread are microplastics that, without doubt, if you enjoy eating fish ... you are also eating plastic. The realization of the dangers posed by microplastics is today's 'hole in the ozone layer' moment: just as when, in the 1980s, collective international efforts banned the CFC gases responsible for ozone depletion, we must act now to stop the sickening spread of these little plastic monsters.

A race to the bottom: deep-sea mining

While plastics and heavy metals getting into the sea represent one sort of problem, human activity to *extract* metals from deep in the ocean is another kind of hazard facing this strange, delicate and unique environment. Deep-sea mining for minerals is a fairly new field, as is deep-sea research, but right now it's mining that's ahead in this race to the bottom. Why? Today, metals such as nickel, zinc, gold and copper are much sought after, not least for their usefulness in the manufacture of the microchips and processors without which our phones and laptops would be lumps of scrap. Although a metal like copper can be found in large deposits on land, others are becoming harder and harder to source terrestrially, so mining companies have turned to the world's seas.

Drop down to the deep ocean and you can find some of these metals in abundance at hydrothermal vents, active or extinct. These vents are located about as deep as you can really sink, at around 3.5 kilometres in some places, and the ecosystems there are largely undisturbed. Mining, however, is not a subtle act, and the deep-sea variety usually consists of simply sucking the minerals to the surface for processing, or using a continuous-line bucket system – essentially a conveyor belt of teeth eating up the mineral nodes and transporting them to the surface. The problems here are threefold. First, the unique habitats targeted for mining play a critical role in the lives of the deep-ocean flora and fauna, and so removing them can be cataclysmic. Second, the messy mining of the seabed can strew plumes of fine sediment into the water column, where, at such depth, they can take years to settle again. (In addition, processing of the minerals at the surface creates more plumes of sediment as the waste is washed back into the sea. All these fine particles can affect filter-feeders, zooplankton development and light penetration in shallow waters.) Third, we are carrying on in ignorance. We genuinely *do not know* enough about the seabed to be mining such important ecosystems in this way.

Too much too soon: overfishing

To be fair, the damage caused by plastics and metals is a recent development and a sick kind of collateral damage, not a direct attack on the seas themselves. By contrast, overfishing, to satisfy our limitless appetite for fish, is one of the simplest and most dangerous human onslaughts the ocean has had to face.

Quite simply, overfishing is the constant taking of too many fish resulting in a crash of the population targeted, because it has no time to recover its loses. Overfishing has drastically reduced the numbers of well-known species such as cod and tuna, in some areas by 90 per cent. This crash means fewer fish for the fishing industry, propelling ever more ingenious and ruthless methods to meet quotas and pay bills. Overfishing breeds overfishing – it's a recipe for disaster.

Scientists around the world have monitored economically important fish stocks and have regularly produced numbers for total allowable catches for governments and the fishing industry. Where these quotas have been adhered to, there have been improvements in fish populations, such that some stocks, considered as good as dead in the 1970s, are now classed as manageable. Sadly, too many fisheries still take beyond what is deemed safe by the scientific community. The effects of overfishing are not just felt on the targeted, commercially valuable species, but also on unrelated species caught up as bycatch: that's anything you weren't targeting in the first place, and which can range from albatross to dogfish. Losing high-end predators or beautiful seabirds to bycatch is very saddening, but so is the sheer waste. Many fish caught as bycatch are perfectly edible and commercially viable, but the rules governing quotas often mean that it cannot be landed legally or sold on by the fishing vessel. The dead fish are tossed back overboard. It's total madness.

Boom and bust: dynamite fishing

As far as crude and destructive fishing practices go, this one's the ultimate blast. In dynamite fishing, you set your explosive in the water and *boom* – kill any and all creatures within the concussive range of the explosion. Fish, molluscs, coral, sharks, crustaceans – nothing is safe. Dynamite fishing, or blast fishing as it is sometimes known, occurs mainly in poorly developed coastal areas around the tropical regions of the world. It is most notoriously adopted in the Philippines, where close to 15 per cent of all fishermen use the method. Often it involves homemade explosives, and, needless to say, deaths and injuries to fishermen are common.

For sea creatures, the underwater blast causes such a huge change in pressure that shoaling fish can be stunned and their swim-bladders damaged or ruptured; then their prone bodies float to the surface for easy collection. But many more fish are lost under the water and left to die or rot on the reef. Moreover, the long-term damage to corals blasted by the explosion means that the environments in which the fish prosper are also obliterated – so no more fish stocks. It's like farming cattle with a flame-thrower: you get your beef, but you've torched your field in the process.

Dynamite fishing is illegal, but policing miles and miles of remote coastline of developing countries is extremely difficult. At least there's been some success when the local communities unite to protect their reefs and other delicate marine habitats.

A catch-all catastrophe: bottom-trawling

Dragging your net through the water and seeing what ends up in it – trawling – is an ancient method of fishing. However, as boats have got bigger and engines have got stronger, and as machines have replaced manpower, trawling has got way too big, and no method demonstrates this more than what is known as bottom-trawling. It's a killer.

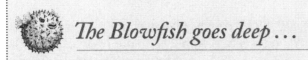

The Blowfish goes deep ...

A DEADLY COCKTAIL: CYANIDE AND SEAWATER

Cyanide fishing sounds just as bad as dynamite fishing, and frankly it is. It involves mixing a solution of sodium cyanide with seawater in a bottle, and then using it to flush out fish from complex reef environments. The fishermen easily collect the fish, now completely stunned and dazed from the asphyxiating effects of the cyanide. The practice is then repeated over and over until the catch is done.

Some of the fish caught in this way are destined for the plate, but mainly cyanide fishing feeds the aquarium industry. It is, as with dynamite fishing, particularly prevalent in the Philippines, where somewhere between 70 and 90 per cent of all aquarium fish are captured using this poisonous method. The economic drivers for the poor fishing communities are the increased interest in fish-keeping and aquariums in the Western world and the high prices that certain desirable species can command. Aside from the obvious dangers for the human divers who fish in this way, constantly risking a terrible death from cyanide, it is estimated that the combined stress of poisoning, capturing, bagging and handling the targeted fish kills around three-quarters of them within forty-eight hours. Knowing this, the fishermen catch extra fish in a twisted attempt to improve the odds. The cyanide is devastating to the reef, too, as it works on the tissues of the coral, causing increased mortality and bleaching.

Cyanide fishing is often combined with dynamite fishing, meaning that the reefs of South-East Asia are currently in the middle of an all-out underwater war!

There are a few variations, but the basic principle is simple. A large net, held open in various ways, is towed behind a boat either on the seabed (benthic trawling) or just above the bottom (demersal trawling), scooping up marine life. At the end of the net is a collection end, or cod end, where the catch accumulates. The most basic and most damaging form of bottom-trawl is called the beam trawl, in which a large and heavy beam holds the net wide open while two metal shoes on each end drag it over or across the seabed, kicking up the sediment, which scares out the fish or other targeted species. The next stage up is the otter trawl, which gets its name from the two large otter boards at either end of the opened net. These also kick up the sediment on either side of the net, creating turbid water conditions that scare fish away from the edges and into the clear middle, right in front of the net's hungry mouth. Floats combine with the otter boards to help keep the mouth open, and rubber discs known as rockhopper gear allow the bottom of the net to roll and bounce over the seabed without getting snagged.

The effects of all this? Dragging anything along the seabed causes huge damage to the delicate structures that reside there. Soft corals, kelps, sponges and the red algae of maerl beds are all Essential Fish Habitats – those areas critical for the health of fish stocks, often acting as nursery areas or feeding grounds. Smashing them to pieces with each pull of a bottom-trawling net is a monstrously bad idea – and it's not even sustainable for the trawlermen's future livelihoods.

Long lines, short lives

Longline fishing, or longlining, is a fishing method as brutal as it is effective, with few redeeming features. It's a simple practice, but one used to exploit miles and miles of open ocean. A long line of baited hooks is paid out into the ocean, sinking just below the surface in an attempt to target large oceanic fish such as tuna and swordfish. A demersal longline is one that is set very deep near the ocean floor, used to hook black cod or Patagonian toothfish.

The length and number of hooks on a longliner is controlled by quotas, but there can often be many thousands of hooks set along several nautical miles of line. When you consider that whole fishing fleets are adopting the same gear, the result is that vast swathes of the ocean become littered with baited hooks. Bycatch is a serious problem with industrial longline fishing, for while the hook may have been set for tuna, any wandering oceanic predator can get attracted by the bait and caught. Sharks are a major bycatch species, along with predatory whales, sea turtles and seabirds. Albatrosses are extremely vulnerable, attracted as they are from many miles away by the sight and smell of the longline's bait. They dive onto the hooks as they are being set and quickly drown. At least something is now being done to prevent this, as the more progressive longline fishing vessels are adapted to use bird-scarers on the boat itself, as well as a large metal cowl covering the baited hooks as the lines are set, stopping the albatrosses getting at them.

Escapology for turtles: the TED

Time for some good news, although it begins with some bad. When trawling a large net under the water, you have no idea what you are going to catch. You can use all your knowledge and experience to try and catch, say, cod or haddock, but until you pull the net in, you won't really know, and for some animals in that net it will be too late – as is the case for sea turtles caught up in trawling shrimp nets. This is a big problem. The turtles need air to breathe, so if they are caught early in the trawl they are likely to be trapped in the cod end and drown.

However, a very simple device has been developed to combat this issue: the turtle-excluding device (TED). Essentially, it's a kind of escape chute. A large metal grid is placed across the neck of the trawl net, before the cod end. The grid is angled and leads up to a fixed hole in the side of the mesh. Anything too large for the cod end will come into contact with the grid and be forced towards the escape flap in the side of the net. This super-simple but effective method doesn't just work with turtles, but with any other large species, such as stingrays.

There are a few drawbacks. Unfortunately, the application of TED technology is hard to enforce, and the devices can prove less effective when clogged with debris or when the animal is simply too big to escape from the hole. But fishing regulators are looking to tighten controls and further implement rules on the use of TEDs. This effort, combined with continuing technical improvement of TEDs, holds much promise that fishing industries will be able to continue to haul in their legitimate catches without bringing up anything they shouldn't.

When ghosts go fishing . . .

There's fishing when you're fishing, and then there's fishing when you're not. Confused? Let's put it another way. Which fisherman or -woman hasn't ever lost a bit of kit? It can be your lucky fly, that new spinner you just bought, or if you're a fishing vessel . . . it can be a whole net, the length of a football pitch. The problem is that the gear doesn't know it's been lost and it doesn't shut down – it carries on, in a kind of fishing afterlife, catching fish and other marine animals that no human will ever haul in or see. This is ghost fishing, and it's a real horror show, familiar from media footage of divers cutting entangled lines from the flukes and flippers of whales.

Marine mammals and reptiles run a much higher risk than fish when it comes to ghost fishing, because they need to breathe air. Left alone, over time nets will break down in the ocean, at least giving larger fish a chance to break out, after suitable exertion. For the air-breathers, though, the challenge is so much greater, for if they can't get to the surface relatively quickly, they're done for. Grimly, this problem ripples outwards, for the huge wealth of death hanging in an old net attracts scavengers such as sharks, where the lucky ones get a free meal and the unlucky ones find themselves trapped too, to become tomorrow's main course. There have even been recorded incidents of nets, buoyed by surface floats, ghost fishing until so loaded with death that they sink

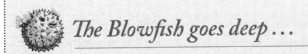

The Blowfish goes deep …

IN THE SOUP: THE SHARK'S TRAGEDY

What's the problem with fewer large predators? You might think that it would ease the pressure on the fish species they consume and which humankind loves to catch. Well, yes and no. As large predators are removed, fish populations can grow out of control: disease spreads, while their food sources are whittled down. Top predators are absolutely essential, and the presence of large predators really demonstrates the *health* of any ocean environment.

Of all the seas' inhabitants, it is the sharks that are the true masters of the planet's waters. First evolving around 420–450 million years ago, sharks are as critical to life as water itself, and if we lose the sharks, we lose the seas. It's as simple as that. The problem is that although shark fishing has occurred throughout time and in many cultures, sharks are not capable of withstanding unchecked commercial fishing methods. The vast majority of shark species grow slowly and breed late, often having just a handful of pups. This means they are extremely vulnerable to overfishing, for their populations crash very quickly once the breeding adults are removed. The years since the 1970s have witnessed a staggering 90 per cent decline in shark populations in the North-East Atlantic. That is a truly terrifying drop, and it has been fuelled by the boom in sharkfin soup – traditionally a food only of the wealthy, but increasingly popular because of rising standards of living in China. Moreover, the practice of fishing for the fins is barbaric, shameful and wasteful. Sharks are caught using long lines set for many days, and when the lines are collected, the sharks, whether dead or alive, are shorn of their dorsal, pectoral and caudal fins, and their carcasses are tossed back overboard.

Sustainable shark, skate and ray fishing is possible when there are rules like having to land the entire animal – which has the effect of limiting the numbers that can be caught at any one time. My personal opinion is that only traditional fisheries should be allowed to fish for sharks, as here the take is low and 100 per cent of the animal is used for something. At least conservation movements are starting to take hold in places like China. Fins crossed, the demand for soup will start to fall – we just have to hope that the shark populations of the world can hang on until then.

to the deep ocean ... but not forever: as their macabre catch rots away underwater, the nets regain buoyancy, rising from the grave to begin the whole grim process at the surface all over again.

What's the solution? The good news is that more and more fishing nets are being made out of digestible materials, ensuring that if they are lost at sea, the ocean's own biochemistry will soon break them down and banish those ghosts forever.

From Moby Dick to mobile abattoir

Speaking of large ocean animals, there isn't much I can say about whaling that hasn't been said before. It's a very sensitive issue, evoking a lot of emotion. In the past, whaling was sustainable. Small rowing boats would take men out into dangerous waters and chase a single whale for a day or more. Depending on the culture, different methods would have been used to dispatch the whale, for a quick death was the prime objective of these whalers. The animal would never be too big or too small, and one whale would satisfy the need of the community for an extremely long time. It was a highly dangerous activity, and many men would die from their duels with the whales and the sea, so whalers – and the whales they hunted – earned tremendous respect and reverence. It is hard therefore to decry these traditional methods and cultures.

That is a world away from the whaling of today. Large diesel-powered vessels, explosive harpoons and onboard abattoirs mean that the animals can be hunted and butchered at an astonishing rate. Industrial whaling really kicked off in the nineteenth century, and many countries with rich coastlines, such as Norway, Iceland and Greenland, had large whaling fleets. By the early 1900s, it was estimated that at least 50,000 whales were being killed annually, and the worldwide populations were starting to crash. In 1946, the International Whaling Commission (IWC) was established as a way of monitoring and conserving stocks, and in 1982 it imposed a worldwide moratorium on commercial whaling in an attempt to allow populations to recover.

So why does commercial whaling still take place? Well, some countries openly oppose the ban and issue their own whaling quotas: Japan, for example, hunts whales for 'scientific purposes', while other countries, including Norway, Russia and Iceland, openly flaunt the ban. It's a hot and angry topic, though from my point of view, while commercial whaling grabs the headlines, it's the damage done by collisions with ships, pollution, plastics, ghost-fishing nets and global warming that will really decide the future of our planet's whales.

Free-range or battery? Selecting your salmon

Salmon – once an expensive delicacy, now an affordable and common fish on every supermarket shelf. It's a transformation brought about by farming.

The farming of water wasn't far behind the farming of land in the history of modern humankind. Its name is aquaculture – the practice of farming fish, crabs, shrimps, plants, algae, anything that lives in the seas or rivers. Ancient Egyptians were fish-keepers, their speciality being freshwater tilapia, farmed in large irrigation channels. Hawaiians used to build large saltwater ponds out of lava rock and coralline algae: grates made of wood or fern allowed small fish, food and clean water in from the sea, but stopped the mature large fish from being able to get out. Nowadays, aquaculture is an intensive big business, though the practice can be much the same as those of millennia past. Salmon, for example, can be farmed in large sea pens or huge concrete ponds. Indeed, as long as you have the right pumps, filters, foods and water, you can farm anything pretty much anywhere.

All this might seem like the perfect answer to the problem of overfishing. After all, with farming we are not taking fish from the ocean . . . except that we are. Aquacultured fish still need to be fed, and the vast majority of their feed comes from fish caught at sea and processed into fish food. Furthermore, when fish are kept intensively, problems of disease, parasites and growth rates all come into play. More fish together means more chance of something nasty spreading through the population. More hormones and fish waste are produced and concentrated in the water, contributing to growth deformity and limiting the immune systems of the fish, making them even more susceptible to infection and parasites. Aquaculture done properly can be extremely successful, and there are a lot of inspiring stories when farmers have got it right. But if you're thinking about choosing your dinnertime fillet, perhaps consider a sustainable wild-caught salmon before you opt for the battery-farmed steak.

The sea's outer space: dead zones

We've spoken a lot about jellyfish's unreal abilities to rapidly increase their numbers over mere days, so let's look in a bit more detail at just what this can mean: dead zones.

You need a few preconditions to start off a decent jellyfish bloom: plenty of food, especially if it comes from agricultural run-off, few predators, some swirling currents – but just one jellyfish! Once jellyfish get budding and cloning, potentially doubling their numbers daily, and if the prevailing winds and ocean currents keep them lodged in the same area, they start to strip *everything* out of the water. First, fish eggs, phytoplankton, crustacean larvae, salps, copepods, literally anything floating in the plankton is consumed; then, as the jellies start to starve under their own feeding pressure, the water starts to die too. As their

soaps. When you remember that the Deepwater Horizon leak covered more than 800 kilometres of coastline, you can imagine just how many animals were affected. Plus, once you have caught and cleaned the affected animals, what do you do? You cannot release them while the slick is still washing up on their beaches and covering their feeding grounds.

To clean up the oil requires a huge investment of time and money. Freshly spilled oil can be set aflame to burn off. Larger slicks can be contained using booms – floating barriers that contain the spread – and then the oil removed using skimmers from barges or boats. Dispersants and surfactants are also used, the idea being to break down the clogging effects of the oil and clear the water's surface. The problem here is that as the oil breaks down, it forms small droplets, which are then far more wide-reaching. Some scientists have pointed out that the droplets can sink to the seafloor, where they are the perfect size to be ingested by filter-feeding organisms – and to kill them.

Naturally occurring oil isn't unheard of in the marine world, because seeps and leaks have occurred for millions of years, as cracks form in the seafloor and expose oil deposits. Therefore, there are bacteria and micro-organisms that feed on the oil, completely breaking it down and rendering it harmless. But, these bacteria and not designed to deal with the millions and millions of barrels the human race needs to keep its machines ticking over. However, current studies are under way into how we might be able to supercharge a strain of oil-eating bacteria to help us clear up the spills speedily.

The trees of life

What have trees got to do with the oceans? Take them away, and you'll notice soon enough. The fact is that deforestation can have a huge impact on our seas and rivers. Aside from the stabilizing effects that forests can have on local climate, trees hold soils together, their roots drawing in both fresh water and nutrients. Lose the trees and you lose this binding mechanism, so the soil and water have nowhere to go but into the rivers and down to the ocean.

The soil run-off itself can clog waterways, causing them to silt up and become narrow. This can be a major issue for any species that migrates up and down the rivers to feed or breed. As for the nutrients pouring off, they can reach levels of excess – eutrophication – and the subsequent bloom of algae can really foul the waters. Since animals such as sea lampreys can only develop and mature in rivers that are pristine, pollution caused by eutrophication can wipe out entire generations.

It's not just inland that deforestation can take its toll. At the coast, palm trees play a vital role in holding tropical beaches together, so removing them (for, say, a new hotel or car park) can lead to the sand simply slipping away into the ocean, potentially smothering any reefs or seagrass meadows that may be found there and further exacerbating island erosion.

Barnacle-busting seawater

Mining on land is a pretty straightforward business: you dig! You either dig deep tunnels under the ground to exploit seams of coal or metal, or you excavate large areas of ground for the mineral content they contain. In the case of large excavations, they are usually open to the elements – and that means vulnerable to rainwater, which is an expert at breaking down solids. As a result, dissolved metals will then usually find their way into local streams and rivers, before eventually flowing into the sea.

At high enough concentrations, the metallic water becomes immediately toxic to all life. On Anglesey, in North Wales, the open-cast mining of copper ore on Parys Mountain sent so much deadly water downriver into Dulas Bay that during the mine's heyday, in the nineteenth century, ships would dock there in order to defoul their hulls of barnacles and shipworm. Studies have shown that copper and other heavy metals can have a marked effect on fish behaviour even at low levels. Some species might increase or decrease in activity, making them more susceptible to predation or starvation, while others might no longer be able to complete complex behaviours such as mating or nest-building. Even a long-disused mine, such as that on Parys Mountain, can affect predators many miles away. As run-off continues, background levels of heavy metals can remain high and bioaccumulate up the food chain, as predators feed on animals which have frequented the polluted bay.

Underwater graffiti: the trouble with tourism

Among all the threats that the oceans face, there is one common factor: us. We have a habit of knackering nature in our drive to make the world accommodate the demands and desires of the human race. Mining, deforesting, overfishing, spilling oil – those are just some of the most damaging activities. Others occur when we are trying to have some fun: the unfortunate consequence of insensitive tourism.

In the marine world, the bad impacts of tourism are many, varied and completely avoidable. Many people, myself included, love scuba diving and the trick here is to look *but don't touch*! Recently there have been cases of recreational divers scratching their names onto corals as if they were scrawling graffiti on a park bench. Not smart. Furthermore, the temptations for dive operators to make a buck by getting as many people in, through and out of the water as fast as possible have led to corners being cut on safety and respect. Too many times, divers without good buoyancy control are being shepherded onto reefs where fins and hands are breaking corals as they flail about.

Careless or ignorant boat-owners can be a problem too, because something as seemingly harmless as dropping anchor can damage vital ecosystems. For example, seagrass meadows around the world provide a unique environment for some incredible creatures: seahorses, sea dragons and sea turtles all rely on them to support their way of life, and the seagrass itself is vital for holding together the fine sand beneath, stopping it from being washed away. Anchors dropped and dragged through this environment cut and damage roots and grasses, and disturb sediments and altogether screw things up! It's all entirely avoidable, with a bit of understanding and forethought.

Lastly, a particular gripe of mine is big-game fishing. I have no problem at all if you want to fish for something massive and powerful, but do the decent thing: tag and release the poor creature! I don't remember a boxing match or a cricket game where the winner says: 'Phew, that was some contest, one of the best I've had . . . and now I'll kill you.' It's particularly maddening because responsible big-game fishing has the potential to be a vital *component* of marine conservation, introducing people to some of the world's most amazing fish, and helping us understand how species are faring. We should keep enjoying the ocean, but to do that we are going to have to start respecting it too.

Big-game brutality

To be fair, I have met many recreational fishermen and -women who are all as passionate as I am when it comes to looking after the fish they pit themselves against. The problems start when it's more about size than respect. As a rule, large fish fight bloody hard, and to catch a big marlin, tuna or shark really is a test of skill and strength for the angler. But as fishing gear has got better and better, and as big-game fishing has evolved into a lucrative business, respect has diminished. Large fish are being played and caught beyond the limits of the angler's strength, and it is the fish who are suffering.

Assuming you plan to release your catch, you have to be quick. For fish like tuna and sharks, water must be pumped over the gills constantly and every care taken not to let the fish hurt itself as it is dehooked and released. Done well, it is a joy to watch; done badly, it spells death for the fish. A large tuna or shark is not meant to come out of the water at all, so hauling it out for pictures and measurements can cause the animal internal injuries that later claim its life. Recently there has been a spate of hammerheads caught near Florida that have been played on the line for too long and not handled with nearly enough care. Unable to recover from the fight with the rod and line, they have washed up on nearby beaches in subsequent days. Combining the stress of being removed from the water with the fact that tropical seas often have a lower oxygen content anyway means that mortality rates for large marine animals mishandled in such ways can be very high indeed.

Fishing on the oceans is a great thrill and a privilege, but it also needs a huge amount of knowledge and a wisdom to know when to let the animal go. That way, you get the chance to fish for it another day. Again, it is all about *respect*.

Sea armour: mangrove and coral

Who doesn't like the seaside? It is never any surprise that people flock there, walking along the beach, picking up shells and generally messing about. But it's a love affair that can cause havoc in the areas we most like to visit. Building a big hotel along the beach at Newquay may disrupt the view; but building one in the Philippines can cost lives.

In South-East Asia, much of the coastline is covered with dense mangrove forests. Anyone who knows about mangroves will appreciate they are very fecund, but not very picturesque. Stripping them back to access white sand beaches has become a very common practice, but it is one that ignores the fact that mangroves are the shock absorbers of these tropical coasts. Mangrove roots are designed to slow down and trap small particles and sediments, providing a more stable substrate for their own development. But in turn, they are also stopping the soils and sands being washed out onto any nearby coral reefs. Turbid waters spell death for corals, and one rain shower of sufficient size can smother a reef with filth without the protection of the mangroves.

Mangroves also act as a physical barrier to storm surges and tidal waves, slowing down the waters rushing through their roots and trunks and protecting the land behind them; combined with the wave-calming action of nearby coral reefs, they provide serious defences. Lose the mangroves, and you will often lose the corals too – and with it goes your armour against the unruly waters. Indeed, the dreadful tsunami of 2013 that hit the Philippines would have had some of its ferocity reduced had the coastline been covered in tightly knit mangrove forests.

When tuna goes nuclear

Nuclear power gets a bad press, which is a shame, because it provides plenty of power without the CO_2 emissions. The problem comes, of course, when it goes wrong. At one end of the scale are the real-life catastrophes such as Chernobyl and Fukushima. Less disastrous, but still damaging, are the striking effects that poorly managed nuclear plants can have on local waterways and coastal areas – not from radiation, but from hot water.

The basic idea of nuclear energy is that unstable isotopes heat water until it boils, and the steam given off runs turbines that create energy. A lot of water is needed, so power plants suck in cold water from rivers and seas, and spew back out extremely hot water, which literally cooks the affected site. The hot water is very low in oxygen, nutrients and organic life, or to put it another way, it's sterile. So where you have an area of discharge, it can be completely inhospitable to life, and only beyond a given distance, where the water has cooled sufficiently, can the local flora and fauna re-establish themselves.

Such problems are minor, though, compared to what happens when things really go boom. When radioactive materials leak into the sea, the effects can be serious and long-lasting. As soon as radiation hits the water, it starts to dilute and spread. As it becomes less concentrated, the immediate impact and damage from radiation is lessened, so life will not immediately die upon entering the affected area. The real problem is that the deadly isotopes released into the water are often radioactive versions of chemicals we see in everyday life, so something like iodine (which is rapidly absorbed by seaweeds for growth) and iodine-131 (which is bad news) are essentially indistinguishable for the animals and organisms that utilize them. In this way, radioactive materials can very quickly become incorporated into the organic life around a site of exposure. The amount of radioactive material absorbed will determine whether the organism survives or dies. But if contamination is low enough to allow survival, then there is a good chance that the affected animal will be eaten by a predator and radiation is then passed up the food chain. So iodine-131 absorbed into a kelp frond is easily eaten by a crab, which is chomped by a fish that is lunch for a marine mammal, which, it so happens, has a thyroid gland that just *loves* iodine . . . and so on, and so on.

It's not only iodine-131. Caesium is another killer: it acts like potassium and is rapidly used by all life that has muscles. Radioactive molecules and compounds not taken in through the gills or tissues have a chance to clump together and sink down to the sea bottom. But then the filter-feeders of the seabed are likely to scoop them up, and again deadly radioactive elements enter the food chain. Of course, this twisted cycle doesn't end quickly, and it doesn't end in the ocean. In Japan's 2011 Fukushima incident, the nuclear power plant was hit by an earthquake and two tsunamis. Since then, caesium from Fukushima has been detected in tuna landed in California. It's not really the kind of thing you want to be considering next time you sit down for sushi.

Hit-and-run ships

Humankind has come a long way in the design of boats and ships, from the earliest dug-out logs to today's nuclear-powered icebreakers and supertankers nearly half a kilometre in length. We can range across the oceans wherever we want to. But even the biggest ship can't always deal with Mother Nature, and while oil spills are the most notorious kinds of pollution ships have caused, there are plenty of other shipping hazards for marine life.

To start with, you can lose your cargo overboard. OK, it's true that a few loads lost can actually be a boon, as non-hazardous materials like wood can float and create oases of cover in otherwise barren open seas.

But many other loads can be polluting. There's also the issue of the seawater sucked into the ballast tanks of cargo ships. When the water is ejected from the ship in another port, many miles away from where it was first collected, the result can be the spread of invasive species such as killer shrimp, golden mussel and Sargassum weed. Once established, these species can be impossible to shift and can wreak havoc on local ecosystems, which have no defence against these new predators or are unable to match their growth rates.

Pollution and the spread of invaders aside, ships can do terrible damage to the inhabitants of the ocean by simply colliding with them. When whales, dolphins and sea turtles surface for air, as they must, busy shipping lanes do not stop for them to take a breather. In fact, ship strikes are now the *leading* cause of whale deaths globally. Doing something as simple as slowing down to 10 knots in known whale hotspots could drastically reduce deaths. In our globalized world, nothing will stop the ferrying of goods across the oceans, but small steps like these could make big differences in reducing our impact on the oceans of this planet.

Further Reading

1 The Ways of the Sea

J. S. Levinton, *Marine Biology: Function, Biodiversity, Ecology*, 2nd edition, Oxford University Press 2001

Q. Bone, N. B. Marshall and J. H. S Baxter, *Biology of Fishes*, 2nd edition, BIOS Scientific Publishers 2004

J. Balcombe, *What a Fish Knows: The Inner Lives of Our Underwater Cousins*, Oneworld Publications 2016

2 Shore

P. Hayward, T. Nelson-Smith and C. Shields, *Sea Shore of Britain and Europe*, HarperCollins 1996

D. N. Thomas, *Seaweeds*, 1st edition, Natural History Museum 2002

P. Naylor, *Great British Marine Animals*, 2nd edition, Sound Diving Publications 2005

3 Coastal Seas

K. J. Gaston and J. I. Spicer, *Biodiversity: An Introduction*, 2nd revised edition, Wiley-Blackwell 2003

J. R. Clark, *Coastal Seas: The Conservation Challenge*, Blackwell Science Ltd 1998

A. P. Klimley, *The Biology of Sharks and Rays*, University of Chicago Press 2013

4 Coral Reef

E. E. Ruppert, R. S. Fox and R. D. Barnes, *Invertebrate Zoology: A Functional Evolutionary Approach*, 7th edition, Brooks Cole – Thomson Learning 2004

E. Lieske and R. Myers, *Coral Reef Fishes: Indo-Pacific and Caribbean*, 3rd edition, HarperCollins 2001

Scubazoo, *Reef: Exploring the Underwater World*, Dorling Kindersley 2007

5 Open Ocean

S. Jennings, M. J. Kaiser and J. D. Reynolds, *Marine Fisheries Ecology*, 1st edition, Blackwell Publishing 2001

S. R. Palumbi and A. R. Palumbi, *The Extreme Life of the Sea*, Princeton University Press 2014

J. Pepperell, *Fishes of the Open Ocean: A Natural History and Illustrated Guide*, University of Chicago Press 2010

6 Deep Ocean

C. E. Bond, *Biology of Fishes*, 2nd edition, Brooks Cole – Thomson Learning 1996

D. Fenolio, *Life in the Dark: Illuminating Biodiversity in the Shadowy Haunts of Planet Earth*, Johns Hopkins University Press 2016

C. Nouvian, *The Deep: The Extraordinary Creatures of the Abyss*, University of Chicago Press 2007

7 Frozen Seas

D. N. Thomas, *Frozen Oceans: The Floating World of Pack Ice*, 1st edition, Natural History Museum 2004

A. Lansing, *Endurance: Shackleton's Incredible Voyage*, 7th edition, Phoenix Paperbacks 2003

8 Threats to the Oceans

P. J. B. Hart and J. D. Reynolds, *Handbook of Fish Biology and Fisheries: Volume 2, Fisheries*, Blackwell Publishing 2002

G. C. Ray and J. McCormick-Ray, *Coastal-Marine Conservation: Science and Policy*, Blackwell Publishing 2004

Index